IMAGES
of America

WOODBRIDGE

VOLUME II

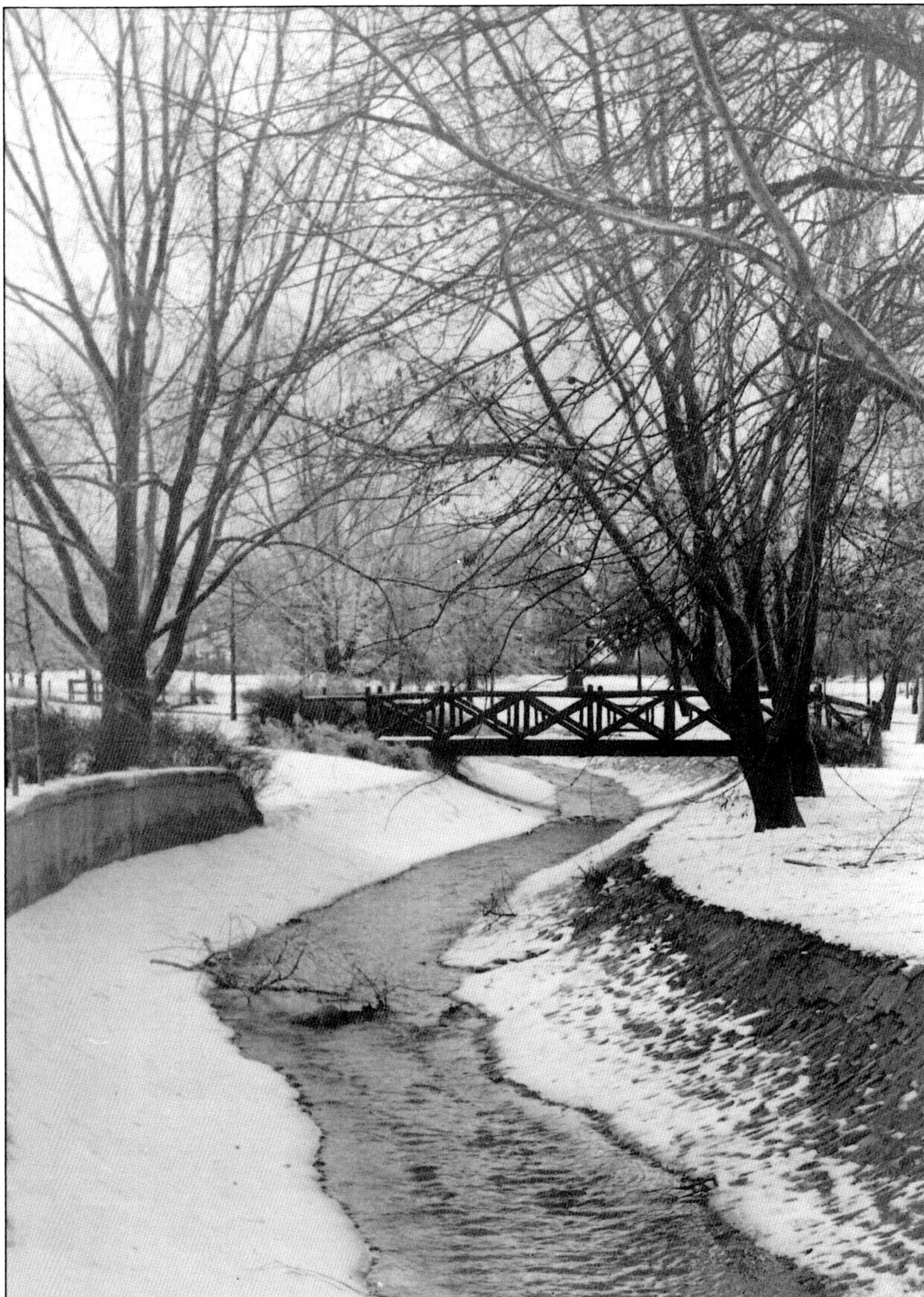

Snow Scene, c. 1950. Rustic wooden bridges cross Heard's Brook near School Street in wintry Woodbridge Park as it looked some years before the Stream Widening Project of the 1970s. At that time the Township reconstructed the brook to alleviate the flooding of local streets and replaced these picturesque bridges. Though the brook appears shallow here, it often overflowed its banks during heavy rainstorms. (George and Mary Molnar.)

IMAGES
of America

WOODBRIDGE

VOLUME II

Virginia Bergen Troeger
and Robert J. McEwen

ARCADIA
PUBLISHING

ISBN 978-0-7385-9033-2

Published by Arcadia Publishing
Charleston, South Carolina

Printed in the United States of America

Library of Congress Catalog Card Number: 99-60821

For all general information contact Arcadia Publishing at:
Telephone 843-853-2070
Fax 843-853-0044
E-mail sales@arcadiapublishing.com
For customer service and orders:
Toll-Free 1-888-313-2665

Visit us on the Internet at www.arcadiapublishing.com

To the past, present, and future members of the congregation of the First Presbyterian Church of Woodbridge, which is affectionately known as the Old White Church. "First Pres" will celebrate its 325th anniversary in May 2000 and is the sixth oldest congregation and third oldest Presbyterian church in the state of New Jersey.

R.J. McE.

To my grandchildren—Linnea Elizabeth and Julia Lorraine Gullikson and Jasmine Hope and Trevor Scott Lettieri.

V.B.T.

Authors' notes: Unless otherwise noted, all images are from the collection of Robert J. McEwen.

The authors have included many names of individuals in the captions for the photographs in this book. They have made every effort to accurately identify these persons and to correctly spell their names but realize that errors may have regrettably occurred.

Cover: **CAPTAIN CARLSEN'S HOMECOMING PARADE, 1952.** See page 36.

Contents

ACKNOWLEDGMENTS

I would especially like to thank Detective Bernie Anderson Sr., who is continually searching for interesting vintage photographs and who will then take the time to research the history behind them. Also my thanks to Frank Premako of Acme Studios, who has the expertise to copy and restore old photographs to near perfect newness. In addition, many friends and acquaintances loaned their photographs and/or patiently answered questions. They include the following: Don and Emma Aaroe, John Ambrose, Peter and Roberta Bacskay, Charles Banko, John Blair, Margaret Voorhees Booton, Philip J. Boyle, Catherine Clark Burns, Nazareth Cacciola, Bruce Christensen, Herbert Christensen, Lou Creekmur, Andrew Csepcsar, Tara Dubay, Nancy Younger Dunham, Carol Agesen Dunigan, William "Barry" Dunigan, James Elek, Sonia Carlsen Fedak, the Free Public Library of Woodbridge, Burnham Gardner, William Gerity, William Harned, the Historical Association of Woodbridge Township, Todd Howell, John Hurley, Jean Bowers Jost, Walter P. Kaczmarek, Kathy Jost Keating, Thomas Kedves Jr. and Sr., John Kuhlman, Diane Krewinkel, Frank and Audrey LaPenta, Helen Lauritsen, Emily and Margaret Lee, Mickey Manganaro, Fred McElhenny, Joseph McElroy, Ed and Debra McGuinn, Ruth Mecsics, George and Mary Molnar, Karen Carlsen Mueller, Paul Nagy, Tam Nguyen, Madeline LaPenta Peterson, Raymond and Joan Peterson, Art Quinn, Chris Quinn, Margaret Freeman Parsons Quinn, George Ryan, Robert Ringwood, the Rotary Club of Woodbridge, Wenda Rottweiler, Ray Schneider, Stella Sideris, George Stillwell, William Tolia, Nick Urban, Peter Urban, Joe Urso, Nancy Burk Vasconcellos, Clinton Township Mayor Michael Van Tassel, Robert White, Bess Wiesenfeld, and George and Barbara Wyatt.

R.J. McE.

It is only with the help of others that a book such as this takes shape and becomes a full-fledged volume of visual history. I drew upon the expertise and engineering background of my husband, Walter A. Troeger who answered technical questions and acted as a sounding board for ideas and word usages. I am grateful for his patience and support.

My list of contributors include the following: Pat McDonough Brisson, Ann and Paul Chovan, Jean Hadden Klc, Ruth Christensen Gorgas, Lynn Huber, Shirley V. Kennedy, Mary F. Macaulay, Sandy Schoonover Mezinis, Juanita Hadden Olkusz, Bertha "Chris" Christensen Peery, Pat MacManus Ritt, Otha C. Spencer, UPI Corbis/Bettmann, and Lydia Christensen Yates, who provided photographs, family stories, anecdotes, and invaluable snippets of information that have enlivened the captions which accompany the photographs. How else to express my appreciation to everyone except to say, "thank you!"

V.B.T.

INTRODUCTION

After we finished our first photo history of Woodbridge and realized how excited our readers were to delve into the intriguing past of our township, we started planning this volume. Pictures almost magically appeared from many sources, both near and far, and we again found ourselves making the inevitable choice of which photographs to use to continue the dynamic story of Woodbridge, New Jersey's oldest township.

Not only did we begin assembling images of people, places, and events that we had not included in our first book, but we also found that we were acquiring pictures that expanded on subjects that had appeared in Volume One. For readers of this book who would like to refer to photographs in Volume One on the same subject, we've prepared the following list of topics with corresponding page numbers:

VOLUME II	VOLUME I
BOYNTON BEACH p. 127.	pp. 53–68.
GREEN STREET pp. 27, 76–77, 89, 106–107.	pp. 71, 81–84, 86–89.
MAIN STREET pp. 37–60.	pp. 9–26.
POLICE AND FIREMEN pp. 44–47, 51, 60, 96.	pp. 69–78.
RAHWAY AVENUE pp. 9–26.	pp. 87, 90–95.
READING COAL COMPANY p. 105.	pp. 118–119.
SCHOOL DAYS pp.70–71, 73–75, 87, 90, 92–93.	pp. 37–52.
UNITED RAILWAY SIGNAL CO. EXPLOSION pp. 28–29.	p. 78.

Selected Bibliography

Dally, Rev. Joseph W. *Woodbridge and Vicinity: The Story of a New Jersey Township.* Lambertville, New Jersey: Hunterdon House, reprinted 1989, originally published 1873.
Lender, Mark Edward. *Middlesex Water Company: A Business History*. Metuchen, New Jersey: Upland Press, 1994.
Wolk, Ruth. *The History of Woodbridge*, 1970.

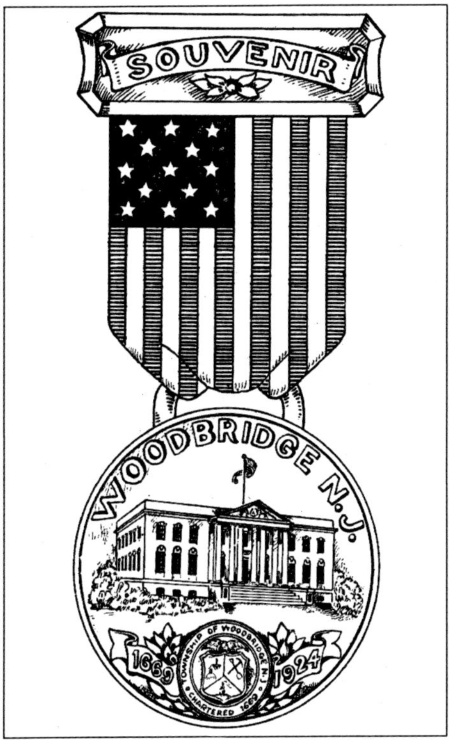

Now a collector's item, this souvenir emblem was designed by Alfred J. Geiling of Fords to commemorate the dedication of the township's Memorial Municipal Building on Flag Day, Saturday, June 14, 1924.

One

On the Avenue, Rahway Avenue

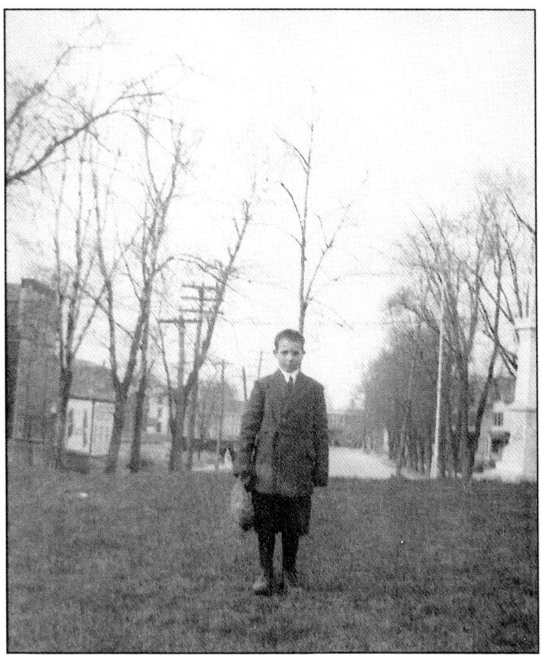

At Main Street and Rahway Avenue, 1917. It looks like Samuel LaPenta has stopped on his way to school for a snapshot at the intersection of Rahway Avenue and Main Street. Sam is standing on the property where the Memorial Municipal Building would be constructed in 1924. The Soldiers' and Sailors' Monument (1911) is visible on the right. Sam, who became a competitive bicycle racer nicknamed "Bicycle Sam," later started the LaPenta Oil Co. (Madeline LaPenta Peterson.)

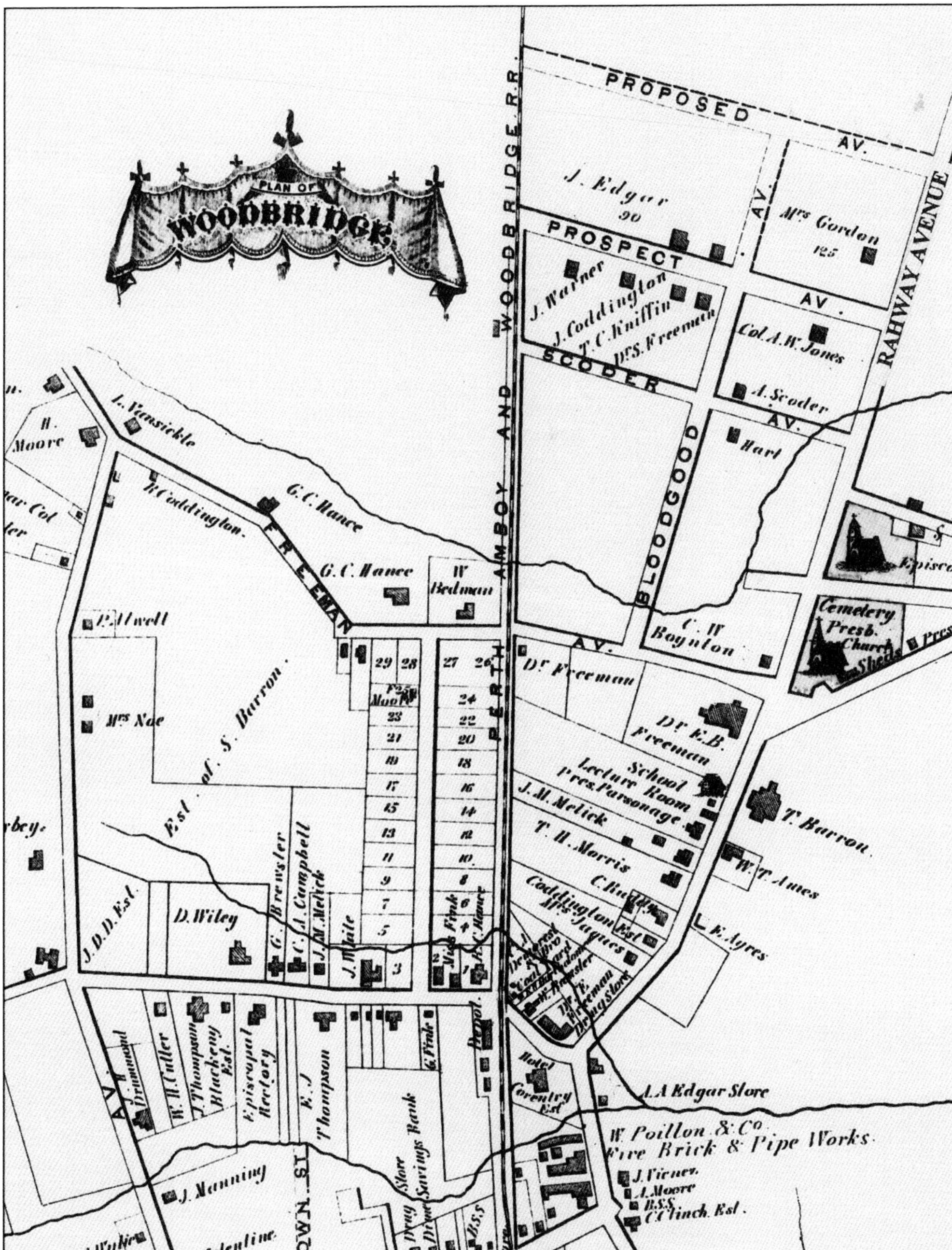

Mapping of Woodbridge, c. 1876. This segment of a larger, artistically detailed map entitled "Plan of Woodbridge" was taken from a county atlas. It provides a picture of the private and public buildings within the environs of Rahway Avenue and Freeman and Green Streets. Several of the Rahway Avenue scenes pictured in this chapter can be located on the map: the Coventry Hotel (a.k.a. the Pike House and King's Hotel), Dr. E.B. Freeman's Drug Store, Heard's Brook, J. Mattison Melick's house, the Presbyterian manse, the Barron house, and the First Presbyterian and Trinity Episcopal Churches. Bloodgood Avenue, also shown here, is now Ridgedale Avenue.

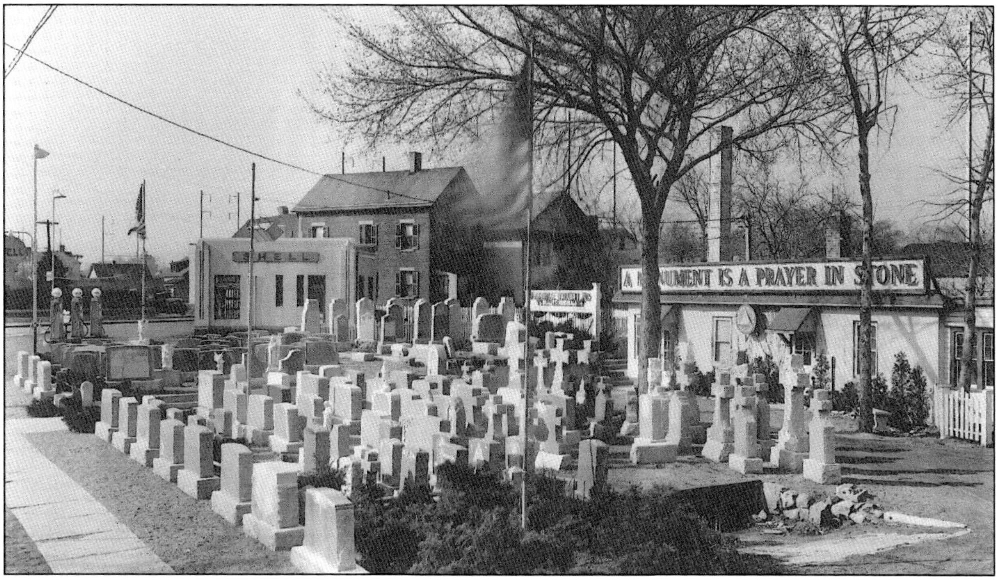

"A MONUMENT IS A PRAYER IN STONE," C. 1945. Still a thriving company, Woodbridge Monument Works, on Rahway Avenue near Main Street, was started by Charles Frank in 1936 and sold by his family in 1997. In the 1800s, the brick and clay companies, Salamander Works, and Poillon Pottery occupied the site. Until a row of shops was built near the Monument Works, residents often dug up rejected ceramic doorknobs made by Poillon, whose name is retained on a nearby street.

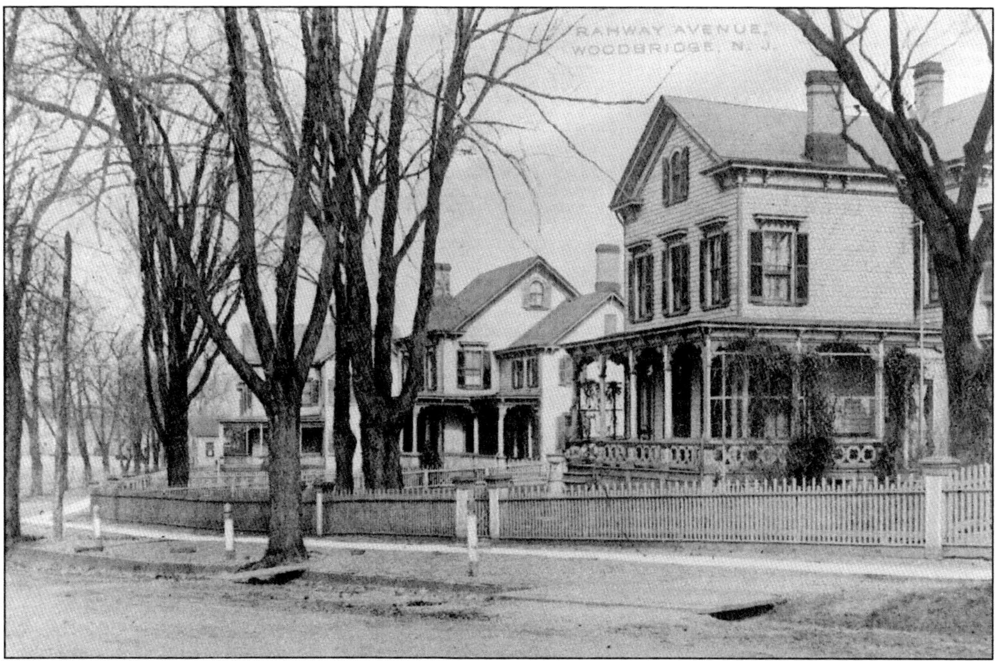

STATELY HOMES ON THE AVENUE, C. 1920. Rahway Avenue, which was paved in 1925, attracted private homes with spacious porches and curbside hitching posts as well as businesses. The Moore family occupied the house on the far right until c. 1950. Today William Harned, a descendant of the Moores, lives on High Street.

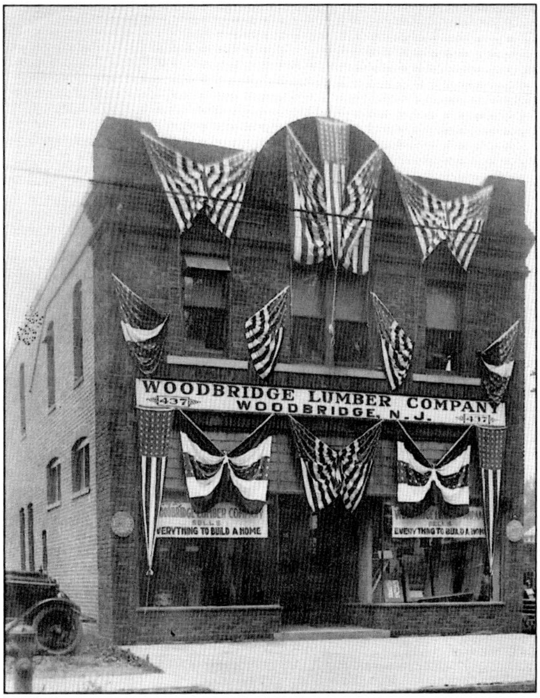

"EVERYTHING TO BUILD A HOME," C. 1930. Decorated for the annual Memorial Day parade held along Rahway Avenue in times past, the Woodbridge Lumber Company served its customers for 58 years. The company was founded by F.T. Howell in 1913. Upon his death in 1970, his son Harry took over the business. Around 1971, the Township condemned and razed the company buildings to make room for the widening of Heard's Brook to curtail area flooding. Woodbridge Lumber did not relocate.

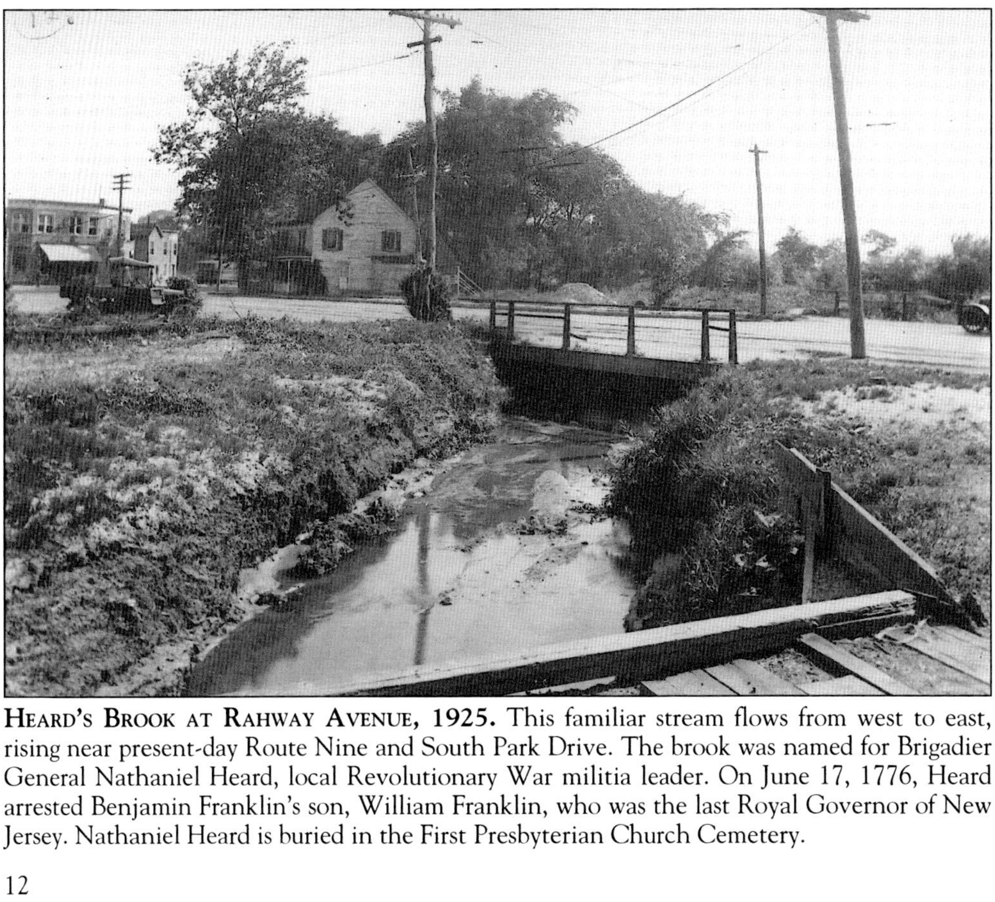

HEARD'S BROOK AT RAHWAY AVENUE, 1925. This familiar stream flows from west to east, rising near present-day Route Nine and South Park Drive. The brook was named for Brigadier General Nathaniel Heard, local Revolutionary War militia leader. On June 17, 1776, Heard arrested Benjamin Franklin's son, William Franklin, who was the last Royal Governor of New Jersey. Nathaniel Heard is buried in the First Presbyterian Church Cemetery.

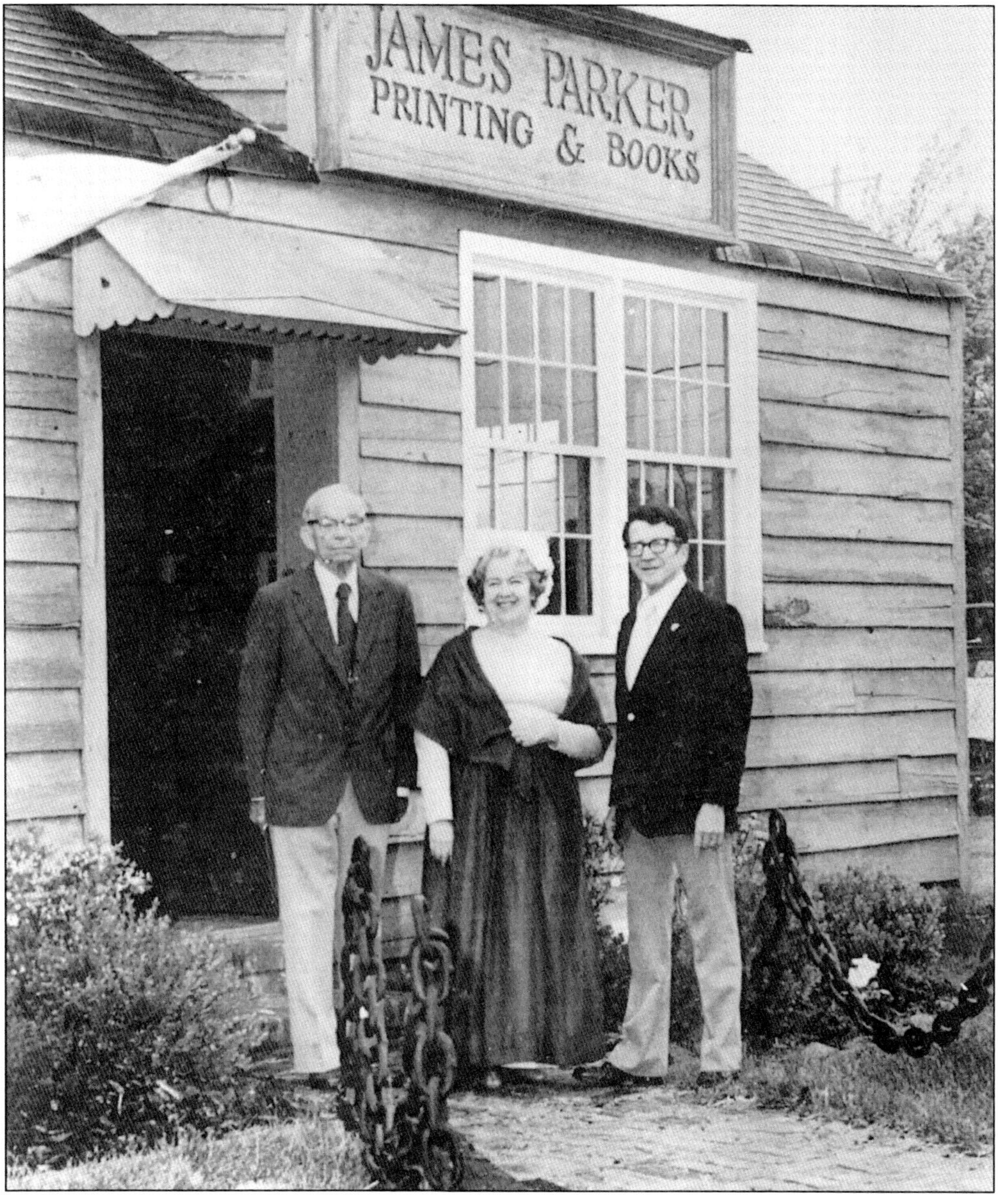

REPLICA OF PARKER'S PRINT SHOP, 1976. During the U.S. Bicentennial Celebration in town, local historian John M. Kreger (left), Woman's Club member Ruth Stoddard, and Joseph Somers, chairman of the Township Bicentennial Committee, welcome visitors to a replica of the first print shop in New Jersey, which was established in Woodbridge by James Parker. This reproduction is located on the former site of Woodbridge Lumber. Born in Woodbridge in 1714, James Parker opened his print shop in 1751 at Amboy Avenue and Grove Street. In September 1765, Mr. Parker published NJ's first newspaper, the *Constitutional Courant*. It consisted of one issue, a manifesto against the Stamp Act. Parker apprenticed with a New York newspaper and later worked in Philadelphia, probably with Benjamin Franklin. After his death in Burlington, New Jersey, in 1770, his body was brought to Woodbridge for burial in the Presbyterian Church Cemetery. During the Woodbridge Tercentenary in 1969, a commemorative monument to James Parker was erected at the Parker plot in the cemetery.

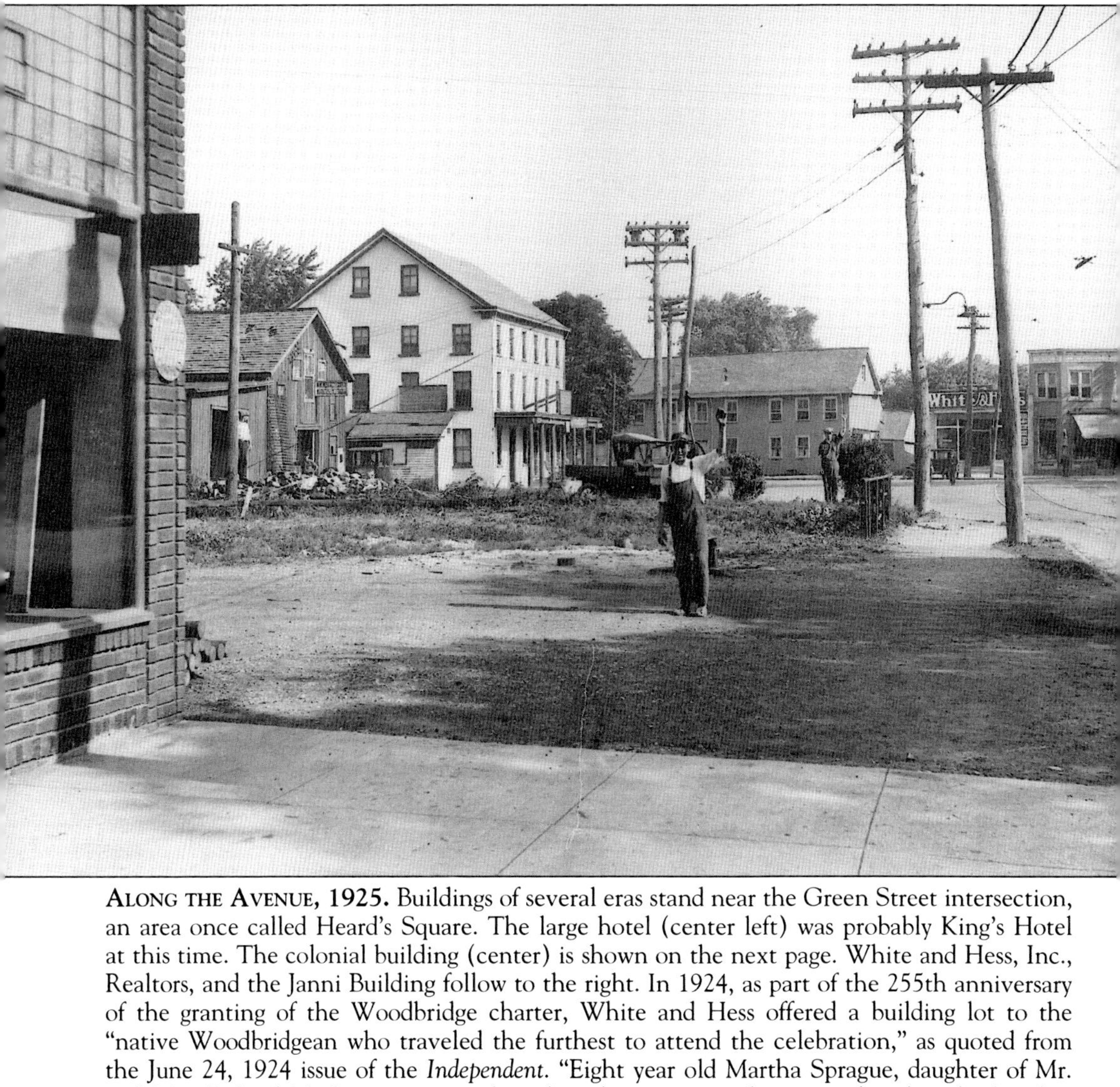

Along the Avenue, 1925. Buildings of several eras stand near the Green Street intersection, an area once called Heard's Square. The large hotel (center left) was probably King's Hotel at this time. The colonial building (center) is shown on the next page. White and Hess, Inc., Realtors, and the Janni Building follow to the right. In 1924, as part of the 255th anniversary of the granting of the Woodbridge charter, White and Hess offered a building lot to the "native Woodbridgean who traveled the furthest to attend the celebration," as quoted from the June 24, 1924 issue of the *Independent*. "Eight year old Martha Sprague, daughter of Mr. and Mrs. Roland M. Sprague, was selected as the winner and presented with a deed to her land." Martha had lived on Ridgedale Avenue until 1923 when her family moved to Leadville, CO, because of Mr. Sprague's business. Martha later married Rahway Avenue resident Stuart Schoonover, who met her at the Methodist Church. The couple lived on Wedgewood Avenue for many years. It is not known what happened to Martha's prize plot of land.

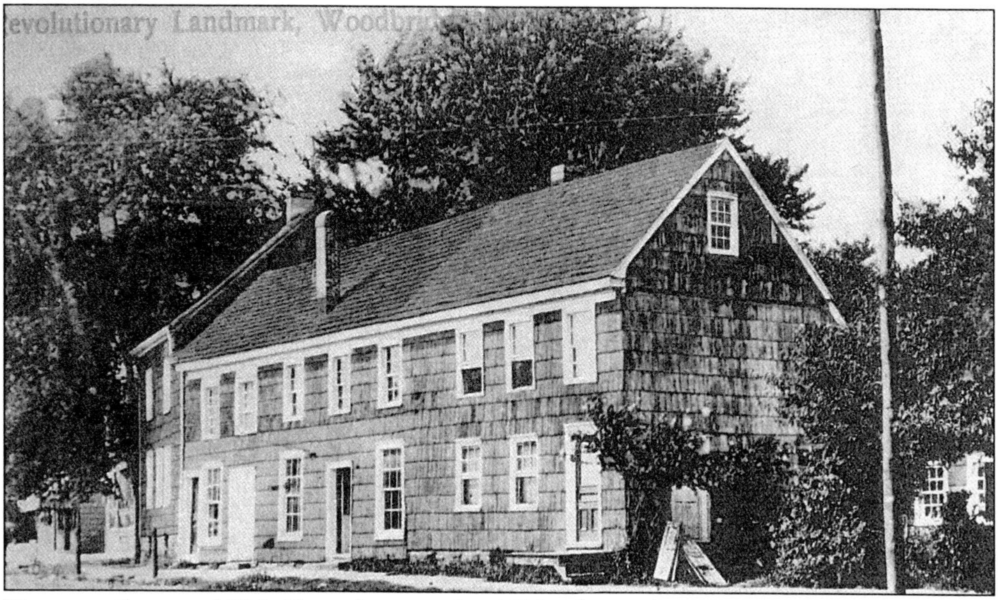

HISTORIC SITE, C. 1924. Torn down in the 1930s, this early structure served as a barracks during the Revolutionary War. The small building at right was Dr. E.B. Freeman's Drug Store. Historian Joseph W. Dally tells us that the first tea served in New Jersey was sipped here in 1730. A Mrs. Campyon, who owned the house, invited several friends to taste the tea, which came from New York. After discussing how to brew and serve it, the ladies decided to steep it and drink it from small cups. (Tara Dubay.)

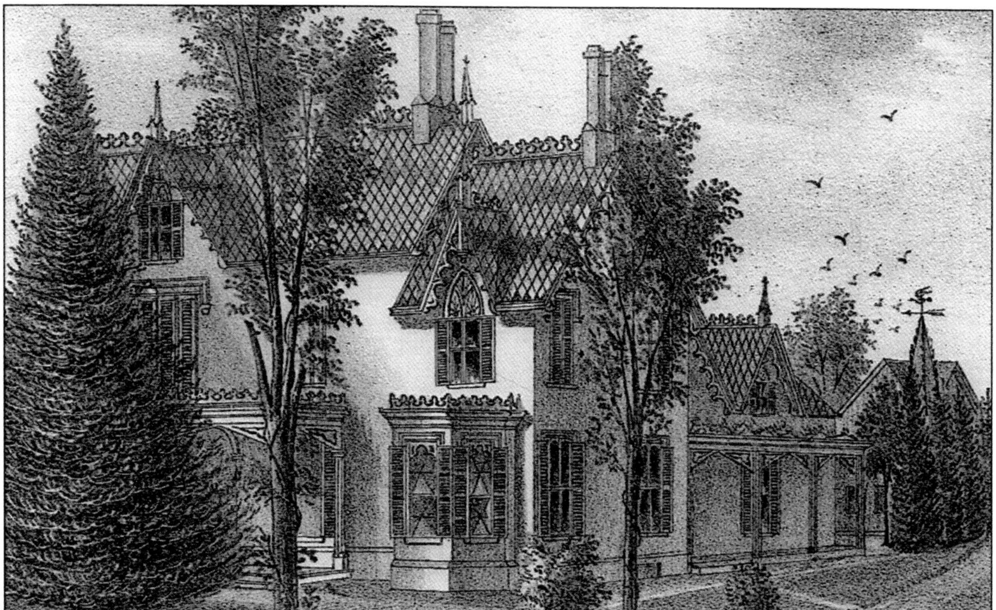

MELICK MANSION, C. 1870. According to the 1876 Woodbridge map, J. Mattison Melick's Rahway Avenue estate was comprised of three buildings. He also owned property on Green Street. Along with other enterprising local businessmen of the 19th century, Mr. Melick made his fortune in the Woodbridge clay mining business. His company, known as Melick and Bro., was located on Melick Street in the clay banks off upper Main Street.

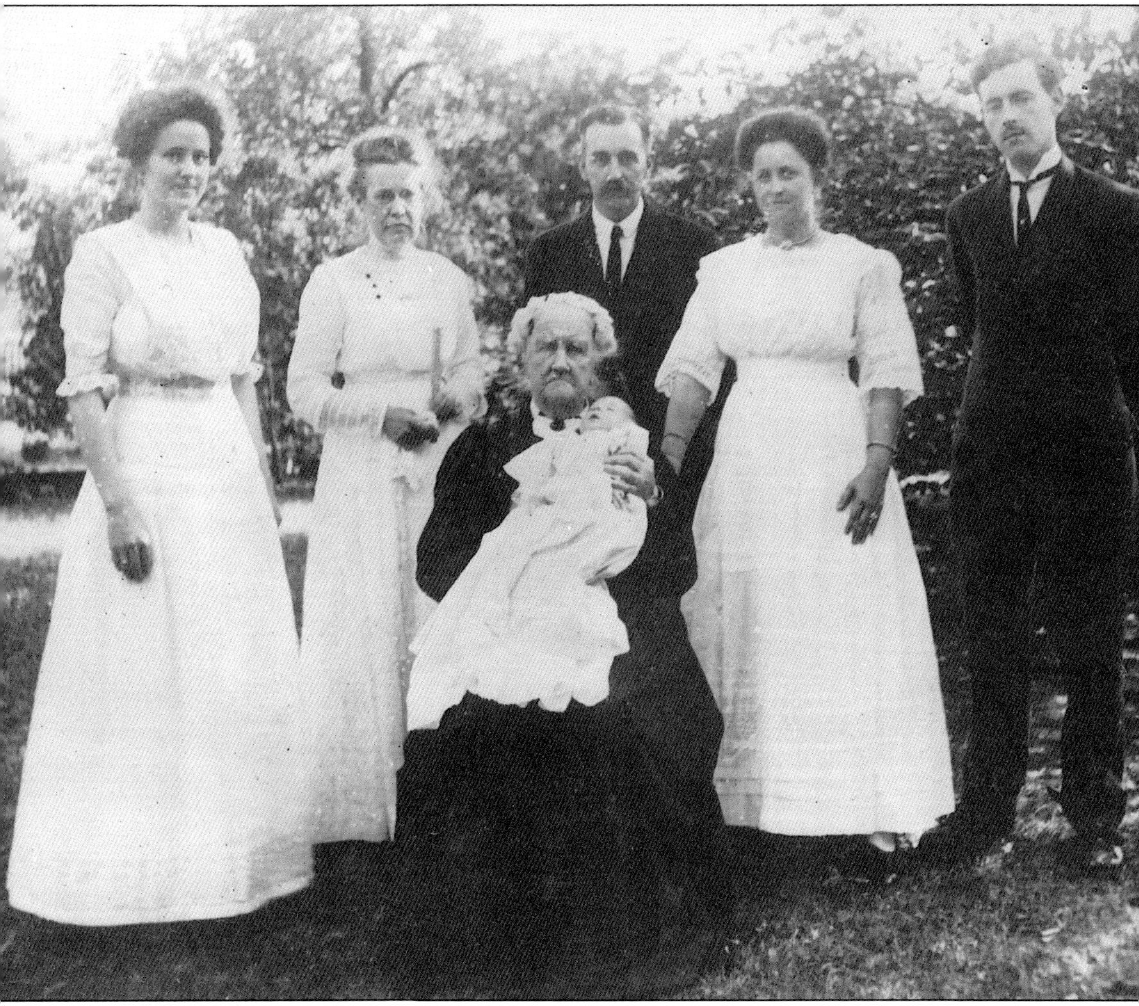

THE FREEMANS, C. 1912. From left to right family members are as follows: (seated) Mary Jane Hadden FitzRandolph (May 7, 1821–February 21, 1923) holding her great-great-grandchild, Antoinette, the daughter of Etta and William Freeman; (standing) William's wife Etta; Dr. Ellis Freeman's daughter, Susan Edgar Freeman; Ellis B. Freeman; Ellis's wife, Anna Virginia Shourds Freeman; and Ellis and Anna's son William. In a front page headline on February 23, 1923, the *Independent* reported that Mrs. FitzRandolph, the township's oldest resident, had died at her home on Edgar's Hill, shortly before her 102nd birthday. She had been "beloved by all with whom she came in contact . . ." and was buried at the First Presbyterian Church Cemetery. Her great-great-granddaughter, Margaret Parsons, who married Robert Quinn and lived on Ridgedale Avenue for many years, still resides in New Jersey. (Margaret Freeman Parsons Quinn.)

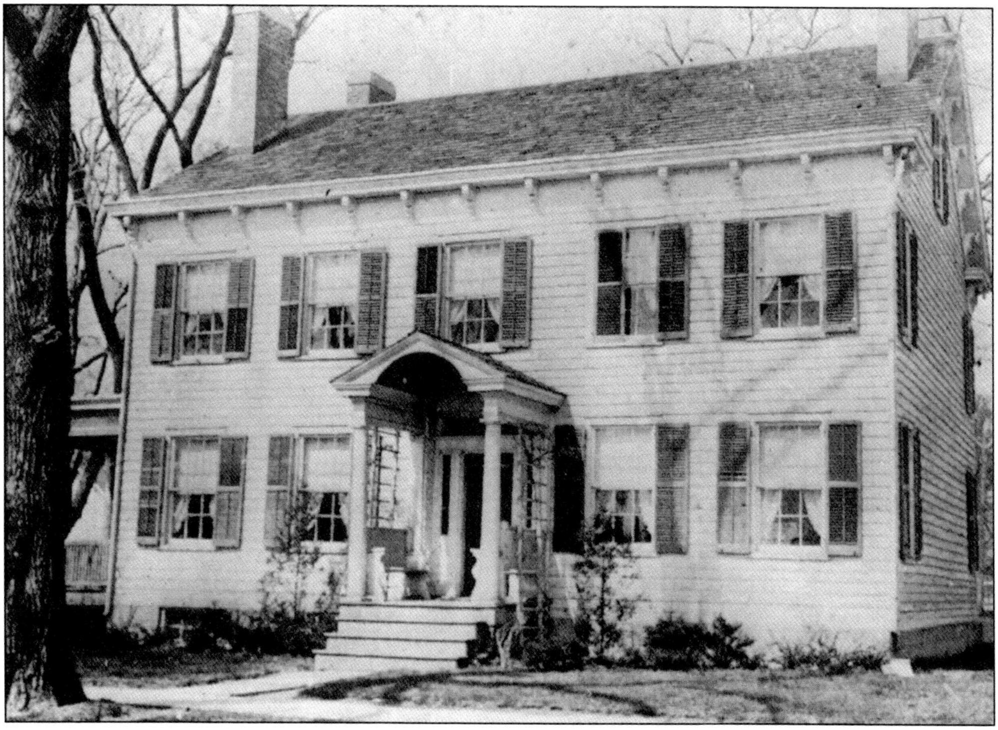

Presbyterian Manse, c. 1920. Located next door to the Melick house, this welcoming homestead, built about 1850, served for many years as the minister's residence. Federal Housing and Urban Development (HUD) purchased it from the church and demolished it in 1971 to make way for the Adams Towers, a senior citizen apartment complex. The Presbyterian Parish House that stood behind the parsonage was also torn down at that time.

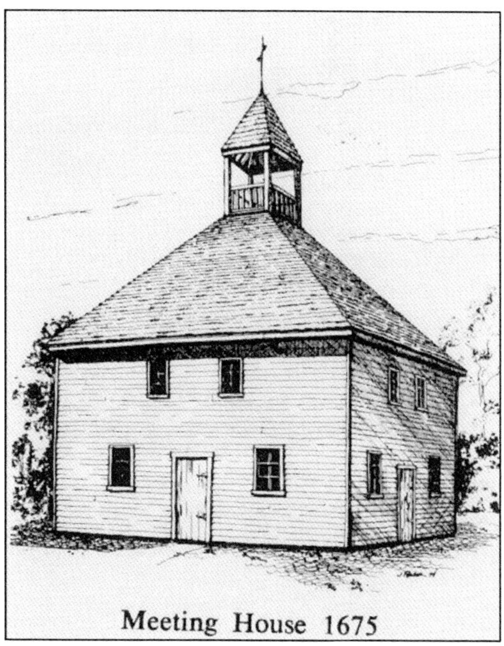

Independent Meeting House, 1675. The beginnings of Woodbridge can be traced to this modest colonial building where town meetings and non-denominational worship services were held and where the first school in town was probably located. Historian Joseph W. Dally points out that the early town fathers, mostly Puritans from New England, often joined "ecclesiastical matters with those of a political character." The meetinghouse later served as the First Presbyterian Church from 1710 to 1803, when it was torn down to make way for the construction of the present church.

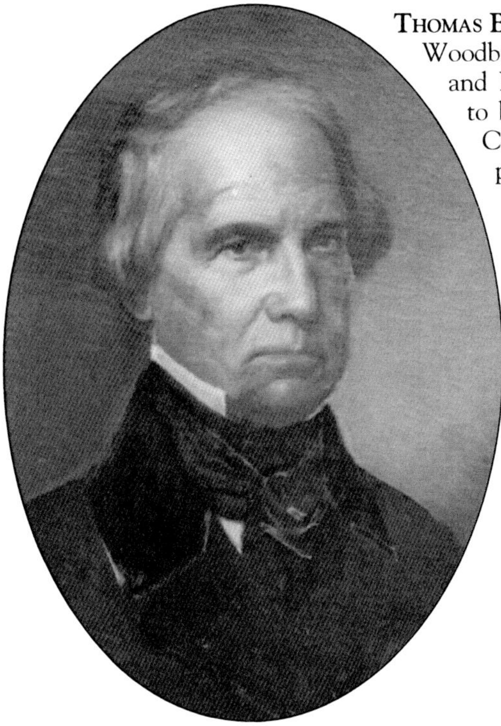

THOMAS BARRON (1790–1875). Mr. Barron was born in Woodbridge but spent most of his life in New Orleans and New York City. In his will, he left $50,000 to build a library in his birthplace. His nephew, Colonel John C. Barron, M.D., donated family property for the Barron Free Public Library. This building continues as the Barron Arts Center and is listed on the State and National Registers of Historic Places. The house below was built by Thomas's father, Joseph Barron. (Ray Schneider.)

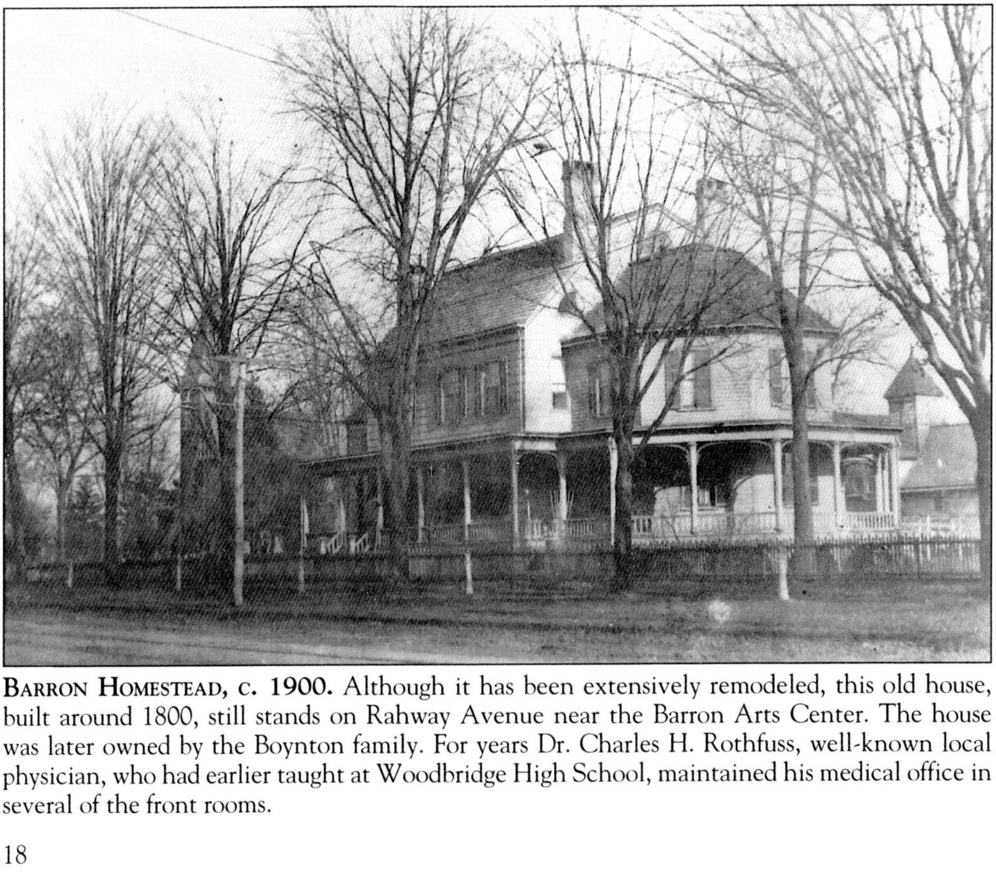

BARRON HOMESTEAD, C. 1900. Although it has been extensively remodeled, this old house, built around 1800, still stands on Rahway Avenue near the Barron Arts Center. The house was later owned by the Boynton family. For years Dr. Charles H. Rothfuss, well-known local physician, who had earlier taught at Woodbridge High School, maintained his medical office in several of the front rooms.

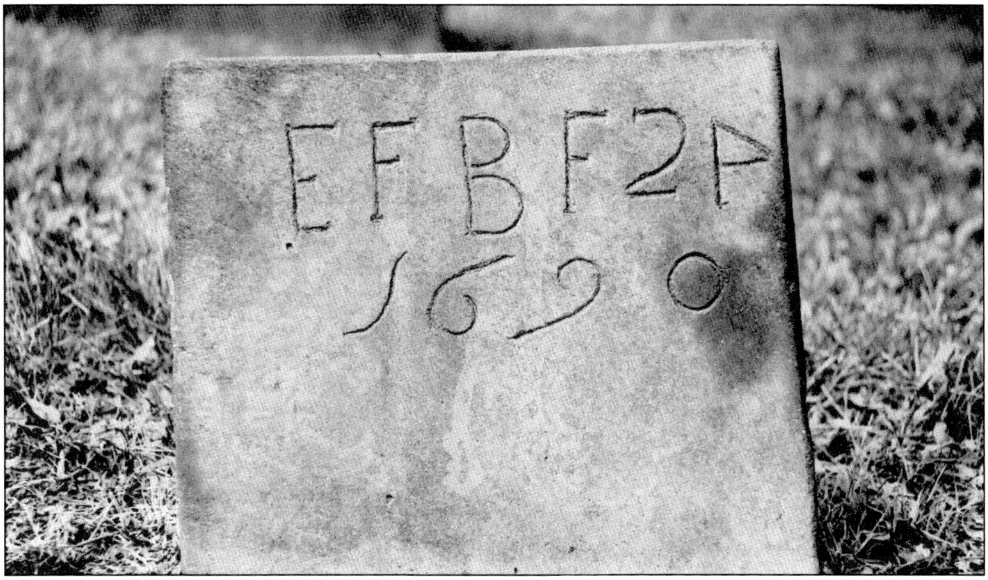

OLDEST HEADSTONE, 1690. The earliest gravestone in the First Presbyterian Church Cemetery may mark the burial place of a member of the Bloomfield family since there is an identified Bloomfield headstone next to it. It is possible, however, that an early settler named Bunn may rest here, an ancestor of the family for whom Bunn's Lane was named. (Ray Schneider.)

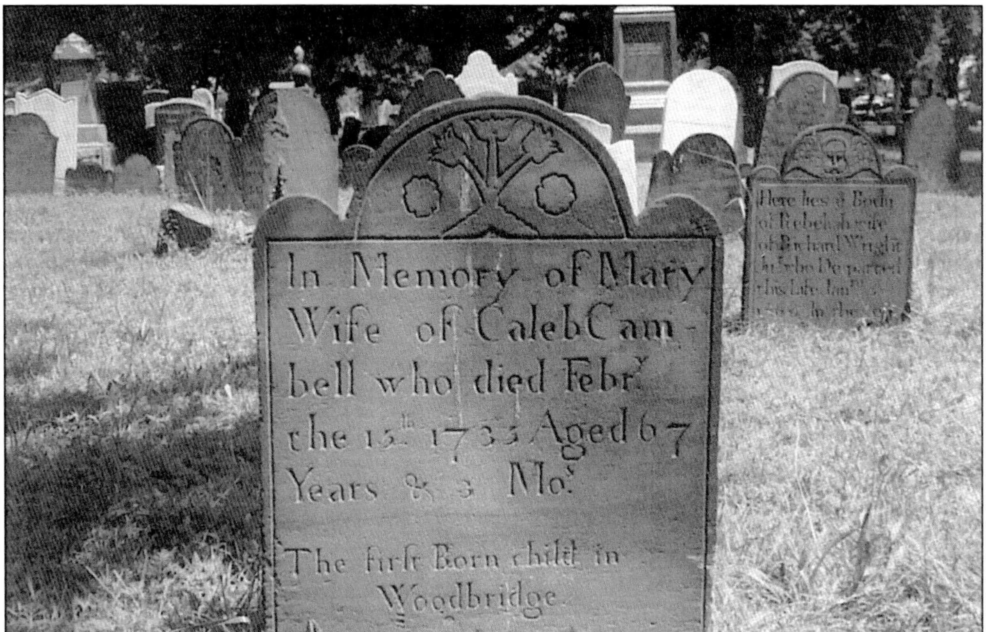

FIRST WHITE BABY BORN IN WOODBRIDGE, 1667. An ancient yet clearly readable headstone in the Presbyterian Church Cemetery marks the burial place of Mary Compton Campbell, daughter of William and Mary Compton and wife of Caleb Campbell. Mary died in 1735 at the age of 67. According to a list of "Freeholders of Woodbridge," drawn up c. 1670, Mary's father was granted a patent or title for 174 acres of land.

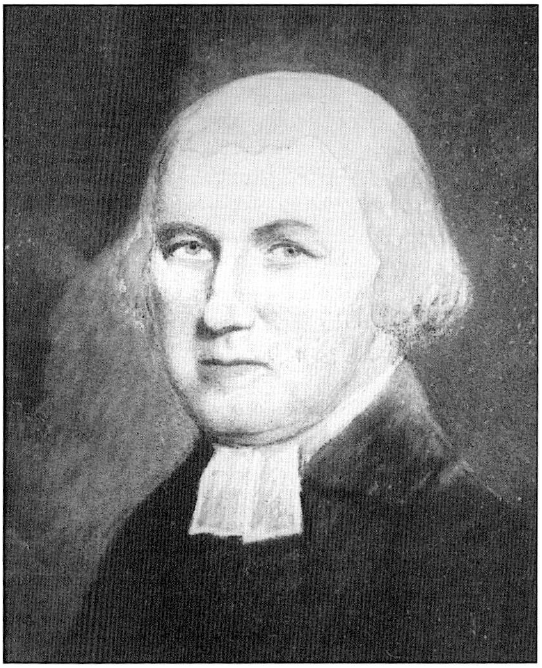

REVEREND AZEL ROE (1738–1815). Pastor Roe served as minister of the First Presbyterian Church from 1763 until his death, a total of 52 years. Historian Joseph W. Dally tells us that Rev. Roe "became prominent as a patriot . . . On one occasion he incited some of his members to assist a company of Continental troops in attacking some British soldiers near Blazing Star (now Carteret)." Rev. Roe was later taken prisoner and "compelled for a time to accept the dubious hospitality of the Sugar House prison" in New York.

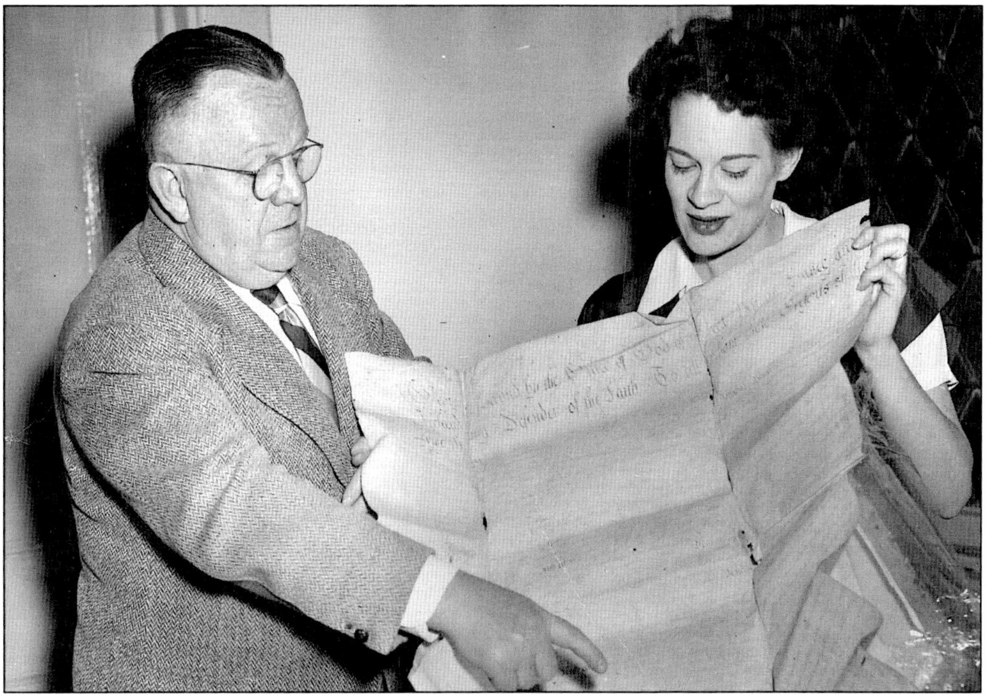

ORIGINAL PRESBYTERIAN CHARTER. During the First Presbyterian Church's 275th anniversary year, celebrated in 1950, Rev. Earl Hannum Devanny shows the original church charter inscribed on sheepskin to church secretary Mrs. R.M. Olesen. Rev. Devanny was minister of the church for 26 years, retiring in 1959. He served as a lieutenant colonel in the Army Air Force during World War II and as a pilot in World War I. He and his wife, Elsie, are interred in the church cemetery.

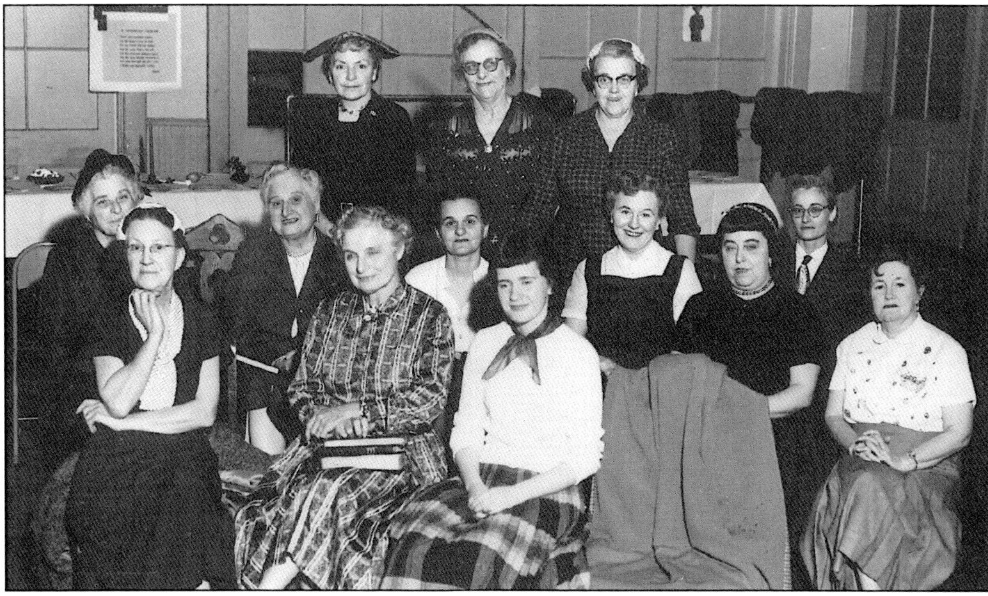

UNITED PRESBYTERIAN WOMEN, MARCH 1956. From left to right are as follows, (seated) Marguerite Doe, Emma Earley, Gertrude Brodhead, Claire Pfeiffer, Irene Eshelman, unidentified, Elsie Kravitz, Alma Wright, Billie Williams, and Susan Kruger; (standing) Mrs. William Glaucke, Mrs. Wilhelm Brown, and Gertrude Sorensen. The group was an active church organization in the 1950s.

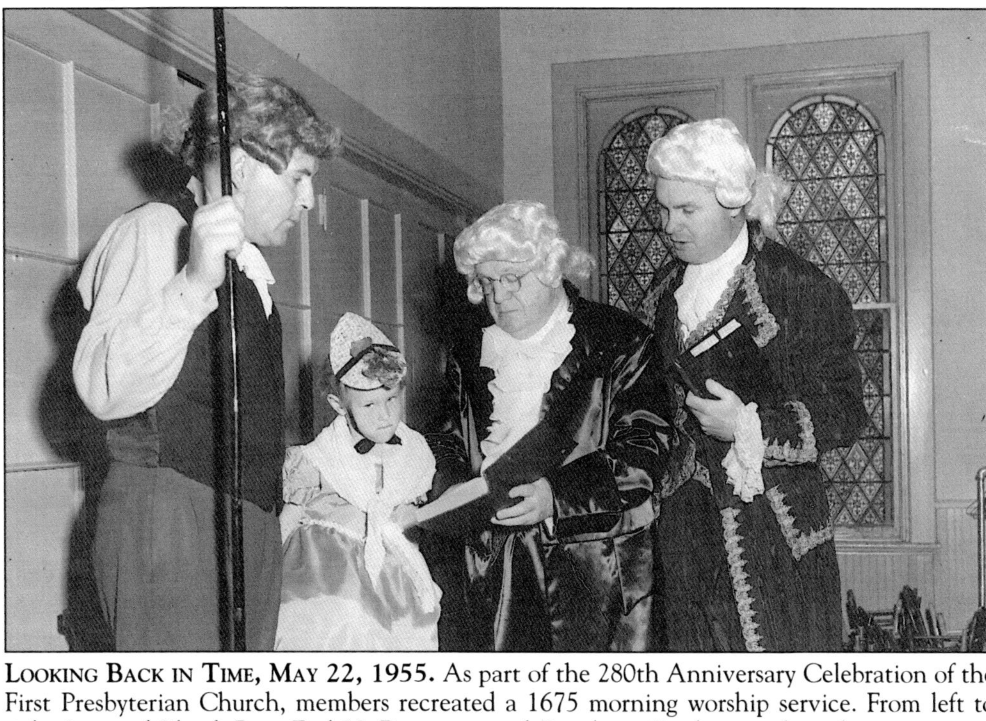

LOOKING BACK IN TIME, MAY 22, 1955. As part of the 280th Anniversary Celebration of the First Presbyterian Church, members recreated a 1675 morning worship service. From left to right Leonard Lloyd, Rev. Earl H. Devanny, and Burnham Gardner explain the scripture to Priscilla Randolph. The service even included a beadle, that fearsome colonial personage who carried a long staff and made sure that no one fell asleep.

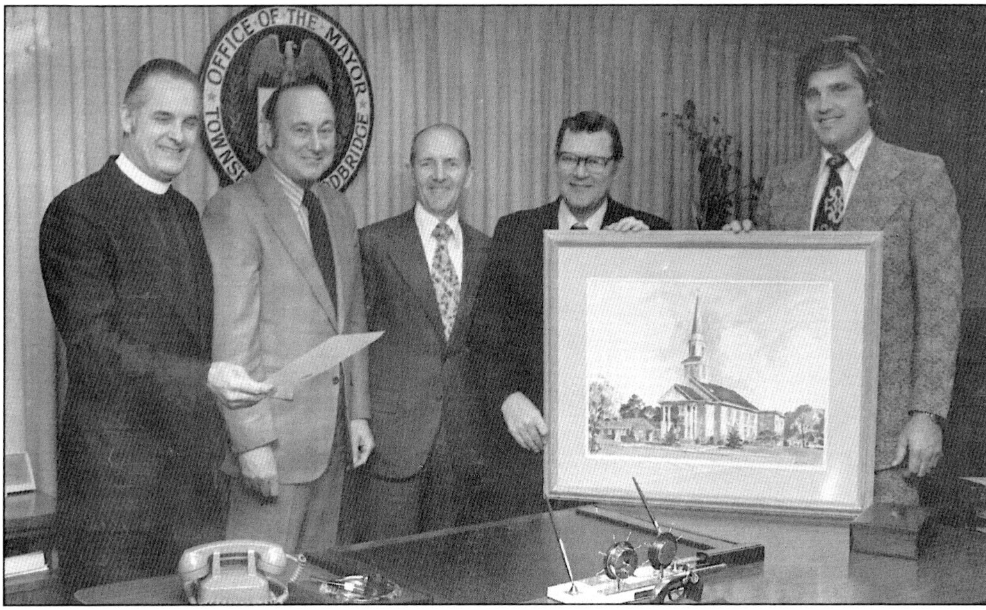

PRESBYTERIAN CHURCH 300TH ANNIVERSARY CELEBRANTS, JANUARY 28, 1975. From left to right Presbyterian Church pastor Rev. Lewis Bender, Woodbridge Mayor John J. Cassidy, church publicity chairman Stewart M. Jones, and 300th Anniversary co-chairmen Edward E. Baker and James J. Elek assemble in the mayor's office to proclaim 1975 as "The Year of the White Church," and display a picture of the 1803 church after it was restored in 1971.

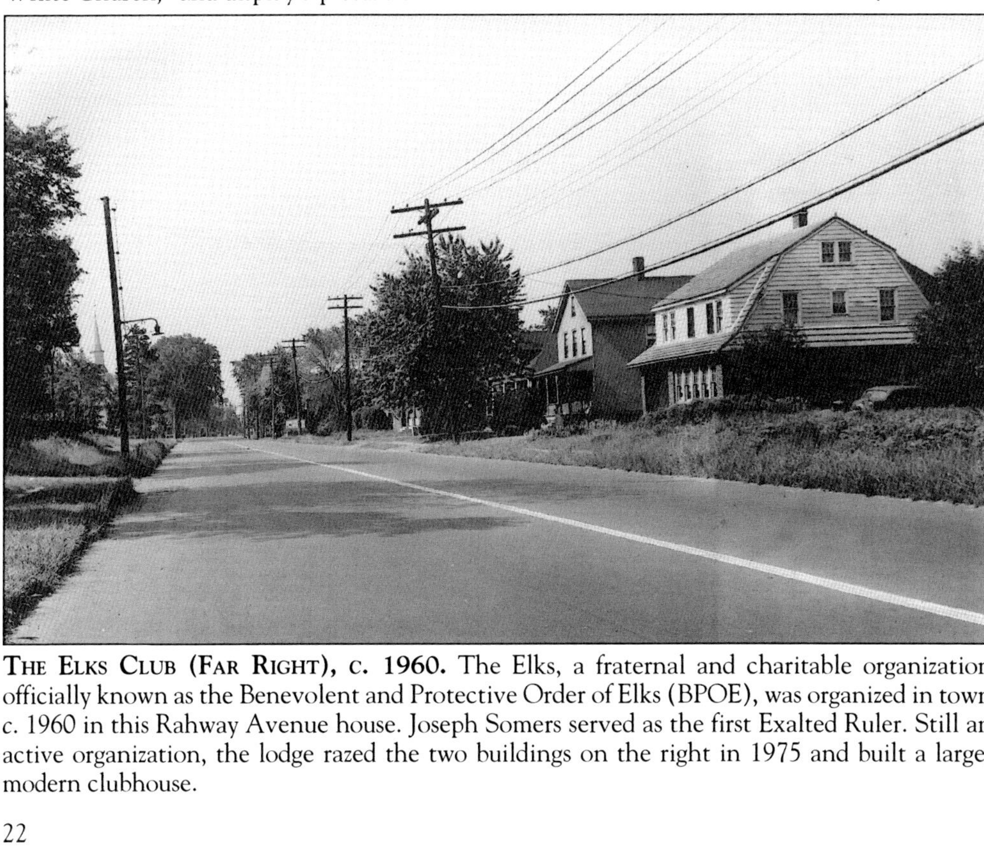

THE ELKS CLUB (FAR RIGHT), C. 1960. The Elks, a fraternal and charitable organization officially known as the Benevolent and Protective Order of Elks (BPOE), was organized in town c. 1960 in this Rahway Avenue house. Joseph Somers served as the first Exalted Ruler. Still an active organization, the lodge razed the two buildings on the right in 1975 and built a large, modern clubhouse.

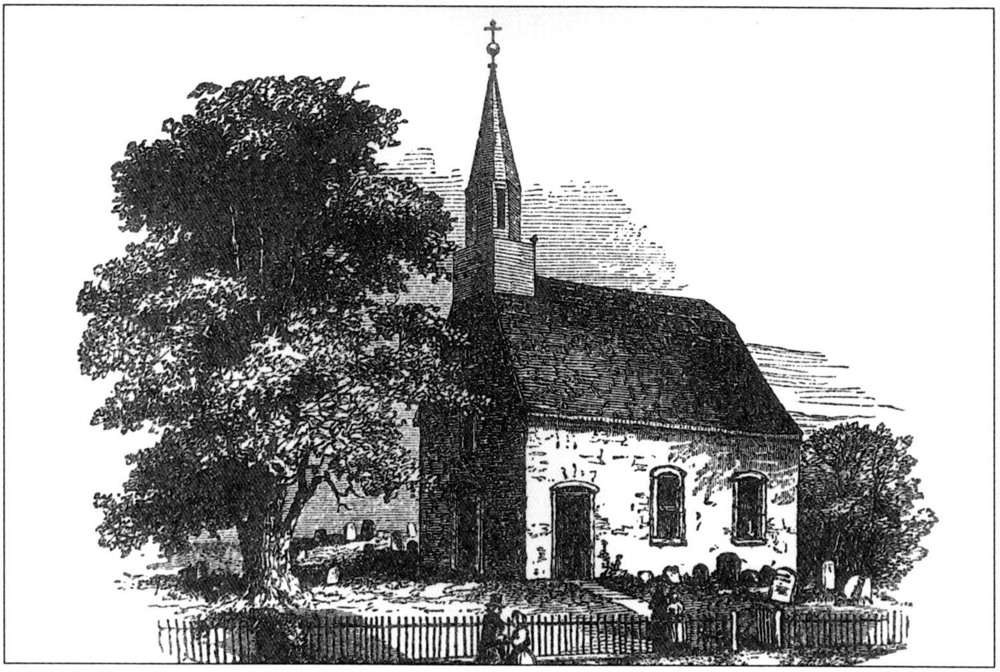

Drawing of Trinity Church's Second Building, 1838. Today's Trinity Episcopal Church stands on the location of this earlier structure built in 1756 and destroyed in 1858 by a fire in a faulty woodstove. Woodbridge Episcopalians first organized in 1698 and were granted a charter in 1769 by King George III of England. Their present church was consecrated in 1861.

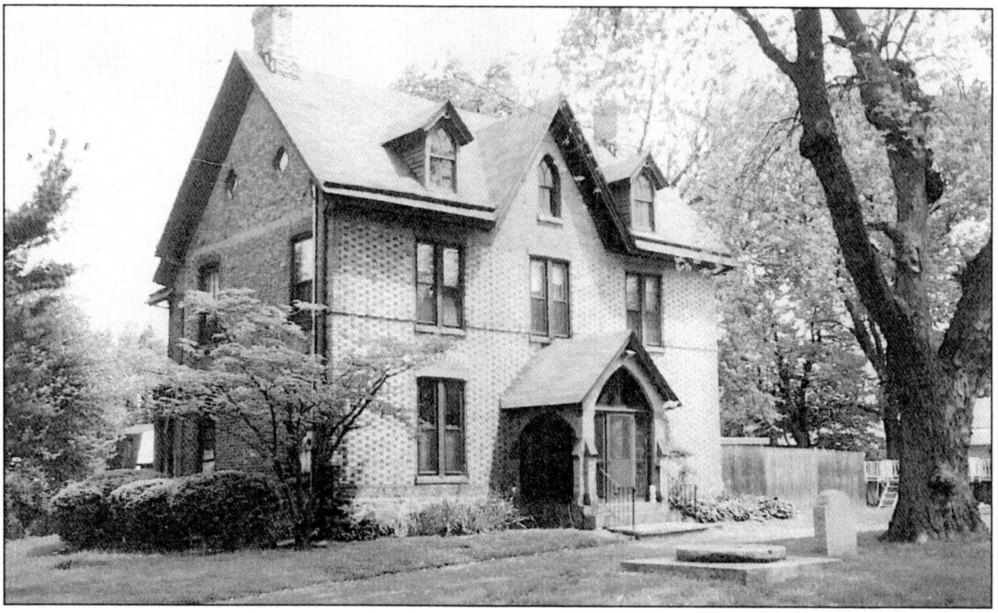

Jonathan Dunham House, c. 1920. Now the rectory for Trinity Episcopal Church, this imposing homestead was built in 1670 by the first miller of Woodbridge, Jonathan Dunham. The church purchased the house in 1872 and added Gothic Revival features. One of Dunham's original millstones remains in front of the house with the 1969 commemorative monument adjacent to it. (See next two photos.)

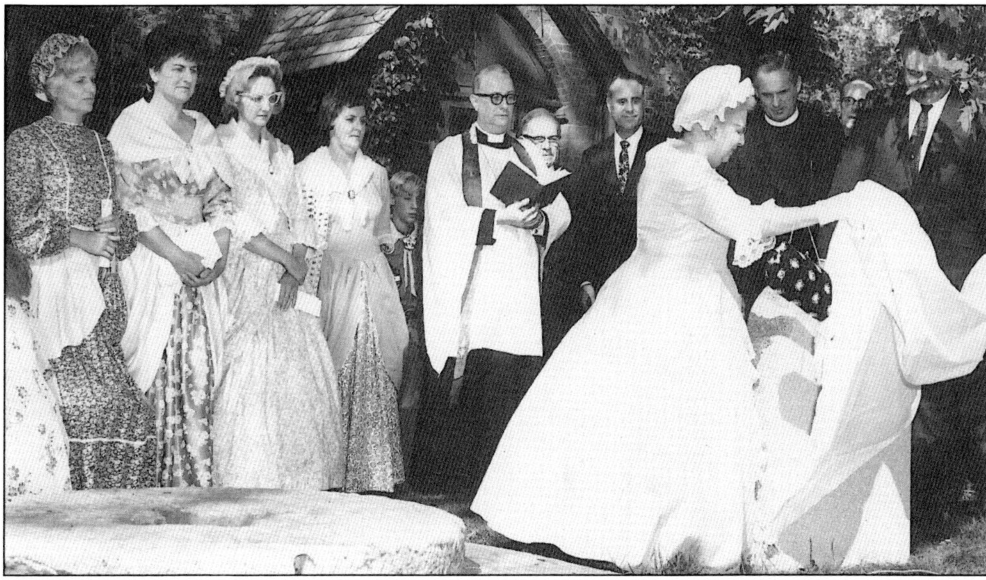

MONUMENT DEDICATION, OCTOBER 6, 1969. Chairperson of the Township's 300th Anniversary Committee Ruth Wolk (foreground) and Mayor Ralph P. Barone (far right) unveil a monument at the Episcopal rectory commemorating Jonathan Dunham. From left to right, Mary Molnar, Betty Novak, Audrey LaPenta, Mary Arway, Rev. William H. Schmaus of Trinity Episcopal, Rev. Lewis Bender of First Presbyterian, and other guests observe the ceremony.

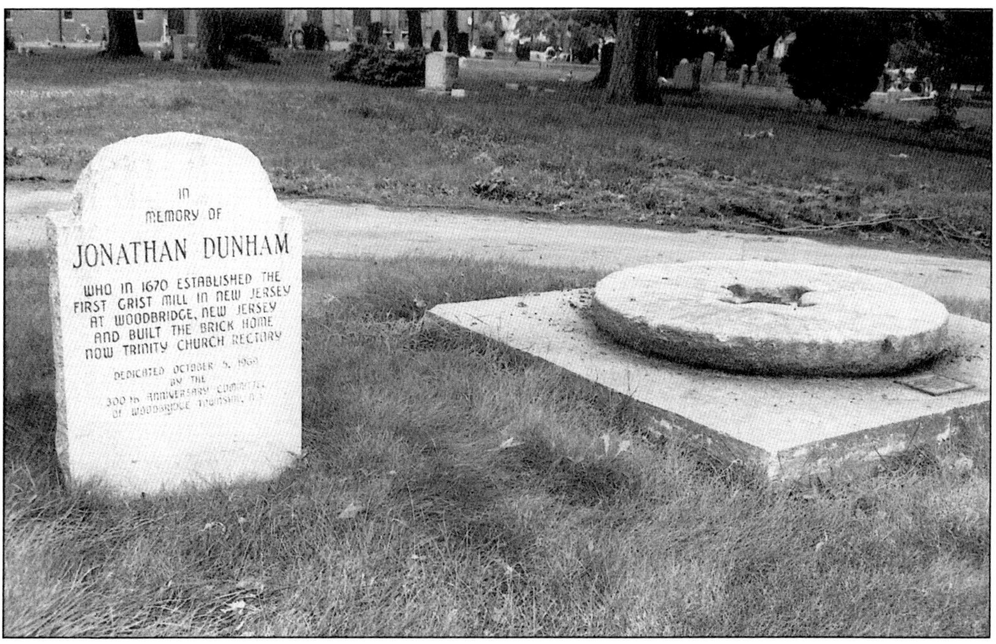

DUNHAM'S MONUMENT AND MILLSTONE. Jonathan Dunham built his gristmill over Papiack Creek (now Woodbridge Creek). Historian Joseph W. Dally tells us that the town paid Dunham for the construction of a dam. Dally also writes that, "tradition gives him (Dunham) credit for turning out the most beautiful meal; and we are assured that his toll was so light that a man who brought a bag of grain to him took back two bags of flour." (Ray Schneider.)

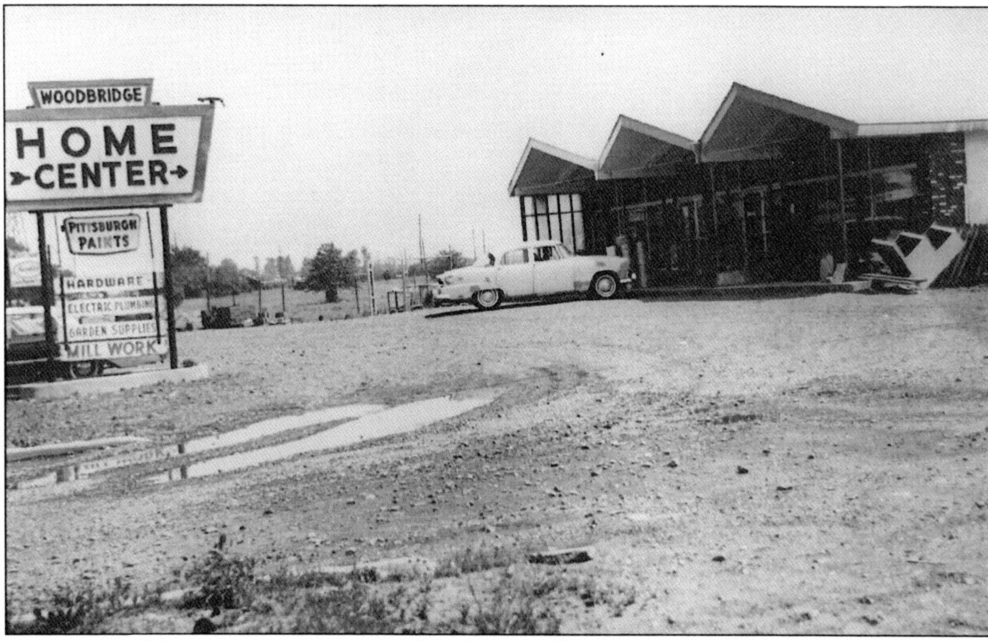

BUILDING OF MANY FACES, C. 1960. After the Woodbridge Home Center, which was built and operated by Joe Urso, closed in 1963, this building on Rahway Avenue, Woodbridge, became headquarters for the Woodbridge Free Public Library until the new library opened in 1975. The building is still in use today as the Cameo Restaurant, which is managed by Peter Toth.

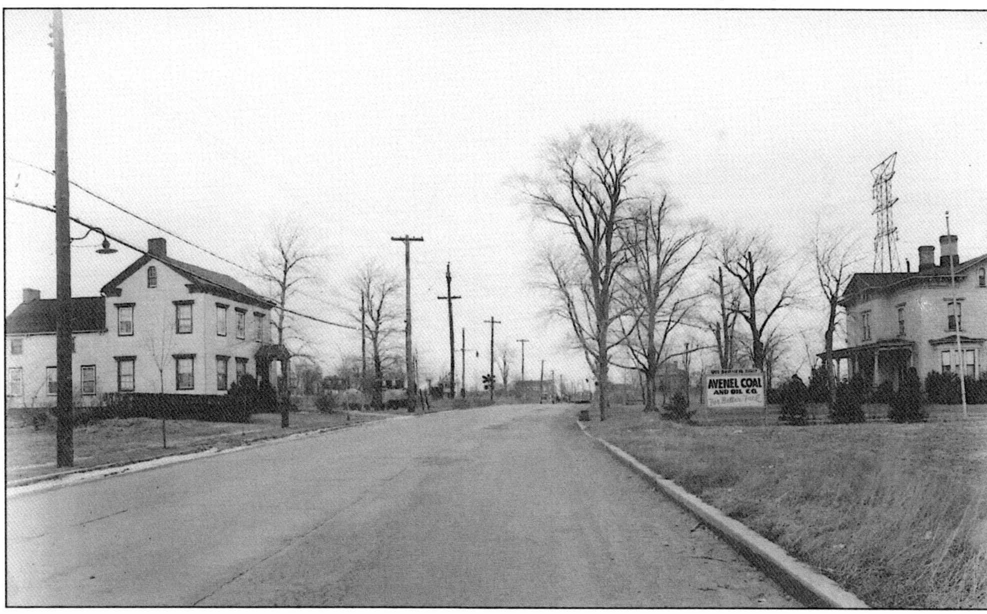

RAHWAY AVENUE APPROACHING AVENEL, C. 1945. Today's busy Rahway Avenue looks quite sparsely populated in this photo. The Obropta home (on the right) stands where the family operated a dairy from 1923 to 1941. In 1928 they sold ice, in 1930 coal, and in 1944 oil, which proved the most successful of their businesses. Mr. and Mrs. Lockie and their children, Andrew, Thomas, James, John, Margaret, Jean, Agnes, William, and Elizabeth, lived across the street until about 1940.

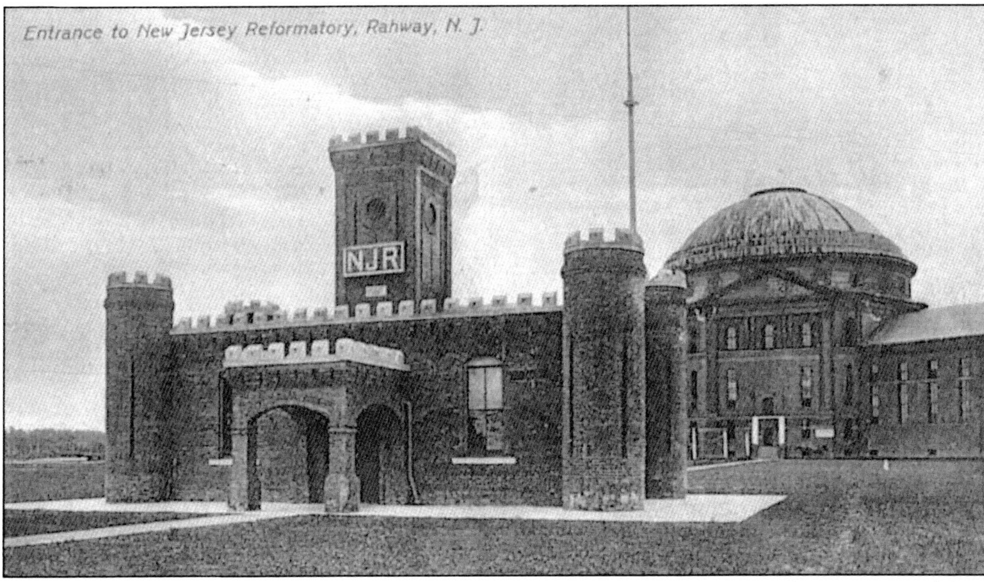

New Jersey Reformatory, c. 1930. Originally named the New Jersey Reformatory, and later called the Rahway State Prison, this domed stronghold on Rahway Avenue in Avenel is now the East Jersey State Prison, a maximum security facility. The state legislature began plans in 1895 to build the reformatory on Woodbridge land known as the Edgar Farm. The first inmates, young men guilty of a first crime, arrived on August 5, 1901. Today the prison population stands at about 2,440. (Bernie Anderson Sr.)

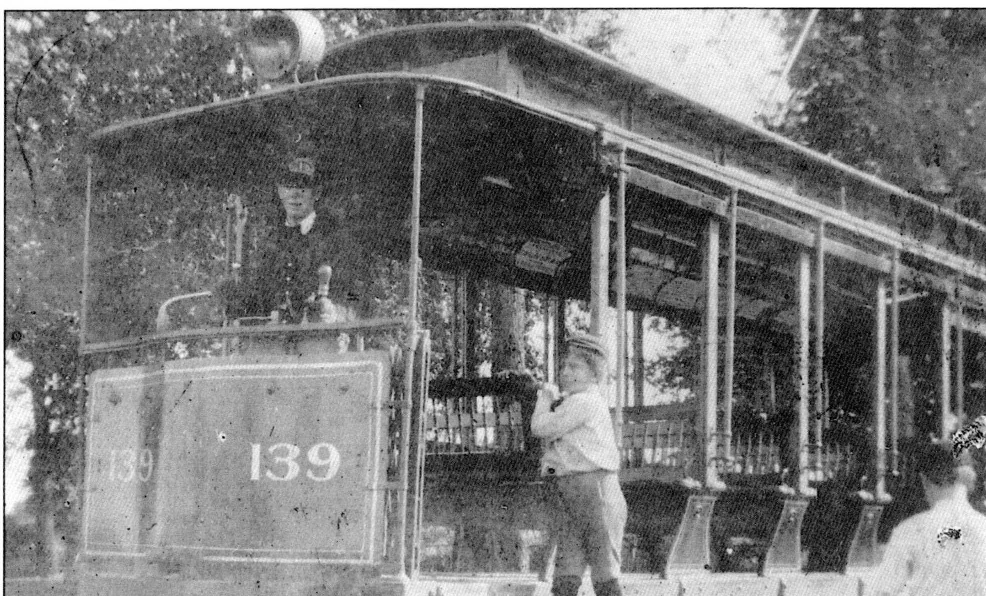

Now Boarding, c. 1895. C.W. Boynton, developer of Sewaren's Boynton Beach, foresaw the need for rapid public transportation to his resort and brought the trolley car to Woodbridge. In 1893 he petitioned the Township for a right-of-way to build a 7-mile trolley line along Rahway Avenue. Woodbridge and Rahway officials celebrated the opening of the Woodbridge and Sewaren Electric Street Railway Company on April 11, 1895, with a trolley ride, of course, and a dinner. (Margaret Freeman Parsons Quinn.)

Two

TIMES OF CRISIS

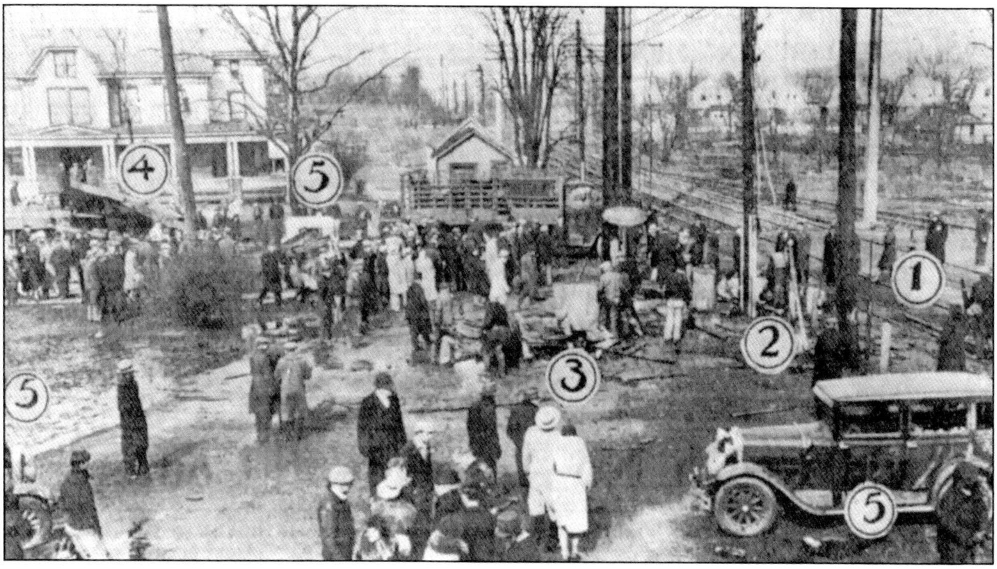

TRAGIC MORNING, FEBRUARY 21, 1935. This fatal collision at the Green Street-Pennsylvania Railroad (PRR) crossing was especially disturbing to Woodbridge residents because the Township Committee had recently petitioned the State to eliminate the town's grade crossings because of an earlier fatal accident at this same location. A year later a Shell Oil Company truck was struck by a PRR locomotive because the gates had not been lowered. Although the truck exploded, its occupants were not hurt, but the gateman and engineer were killed. Investigators believed that the gateman suffered a stroke and failed to close the gates. Finally, in 1940, all Township PRR grade crossings were elevated. The numbers in the image represent the following: 1-accident scene; 2-shed where gateman died; 3-truck trailer struck by train; 4-wreckage of truck; and 5-autos burned by flames.

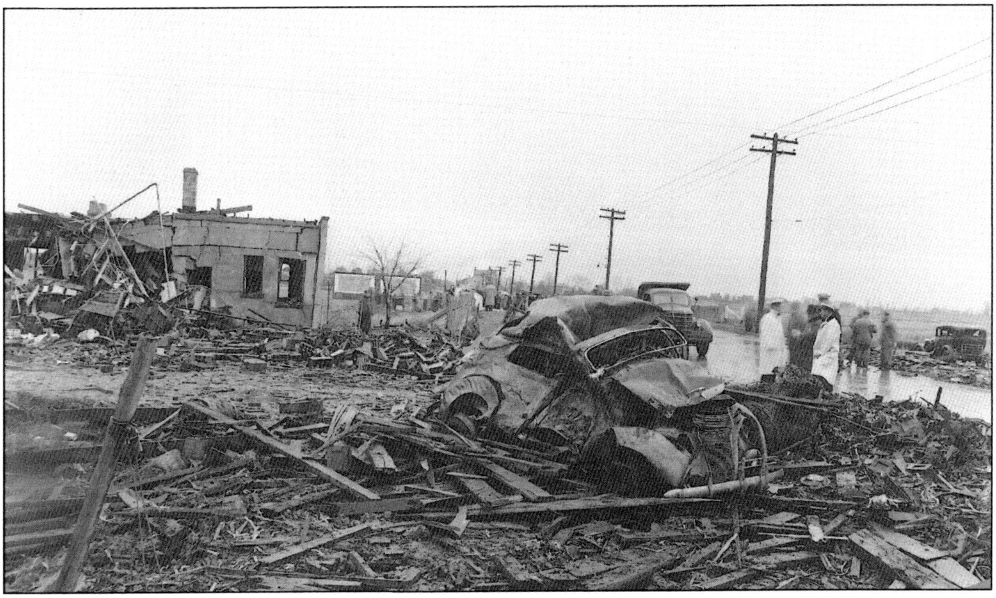

EXPLOSION, NOVEMBER 12, 1940. At 8:30 a.m. on this ordinary workday the United Railway Signal Company in Port Reading blew up. Seven of the eight fatalities were company workers—Maurice Hallahan of Fords; Violet Deak of Woodbridge; Leola Hansen of Perth Amboy; Minnie D. Beck of Metuchen; Sophie Huber of Port Reading; and two young sisters, Violet Byleckie and Rose B. Sernick, also of Port Reading. A third Byleckie sister was badly injured.

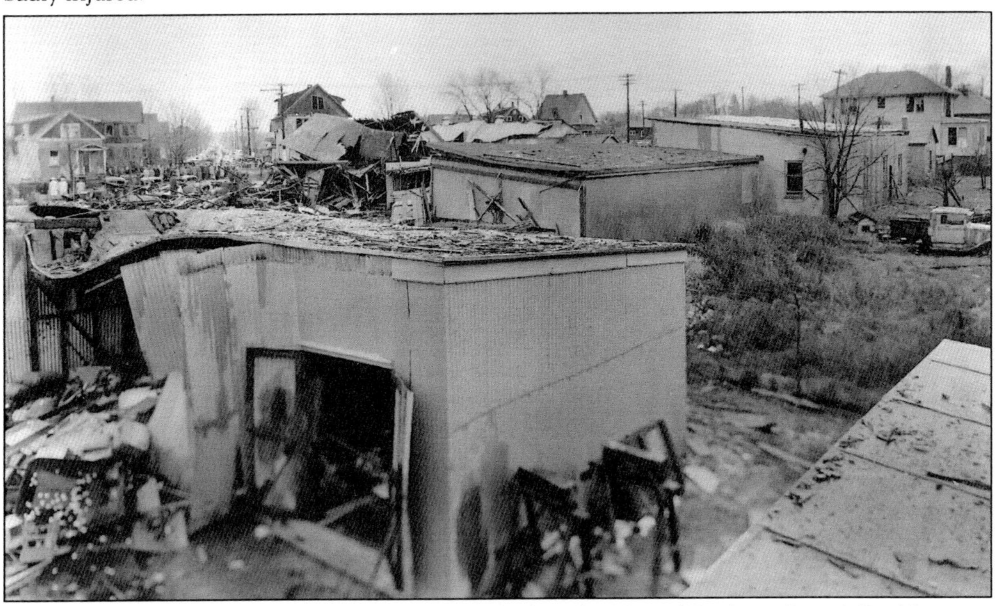

EXPLOSION, NOVEMBER 12, 1940. Also demolished in the United Railway Signal Co. blast was a Middlesex Water Co. meter repair shop located on adjacent property. Foreman Dominick LaPenta was the only water company employee killed. He left eight young children at home. National newspapers announced that this explosion was part of a plot to damage U.S. defense factories. United Railway had no defense contracts at the time, and no cause for the blast was found.

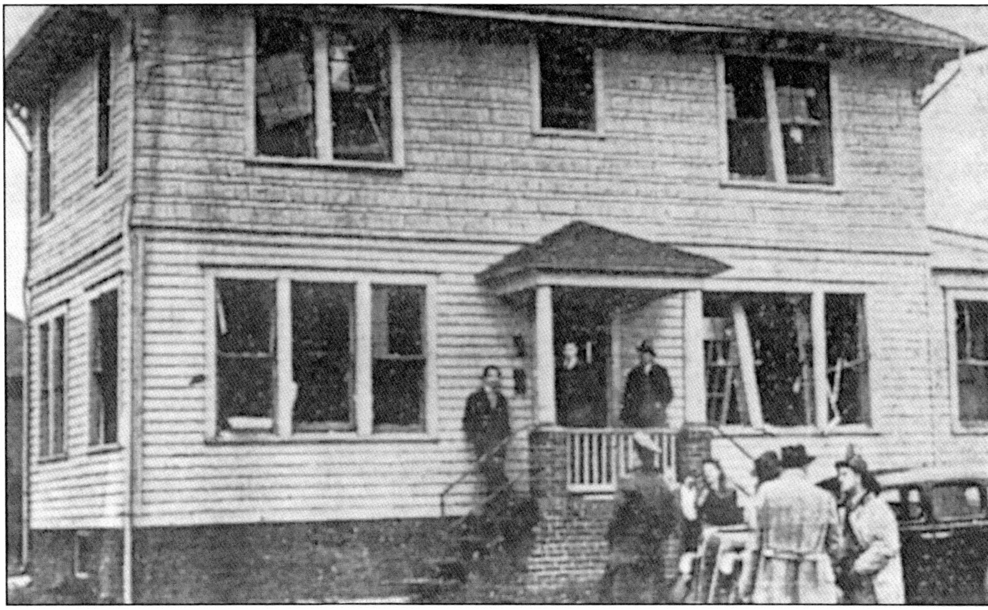

EXPLOSION, NOVEMBER 12, 1940. This Lewis Street residence, located just behind the United Railway factory, was severely gutted. The blast, which was heard for miles around, damaged nearby homes and tore down electric and telephone wires. More than 50 families were temporarily homeless. The Red Cross prepared the Craftsmen's Club on Green Street as a shelter but didn't need it because so many people opened their homes to those in need.

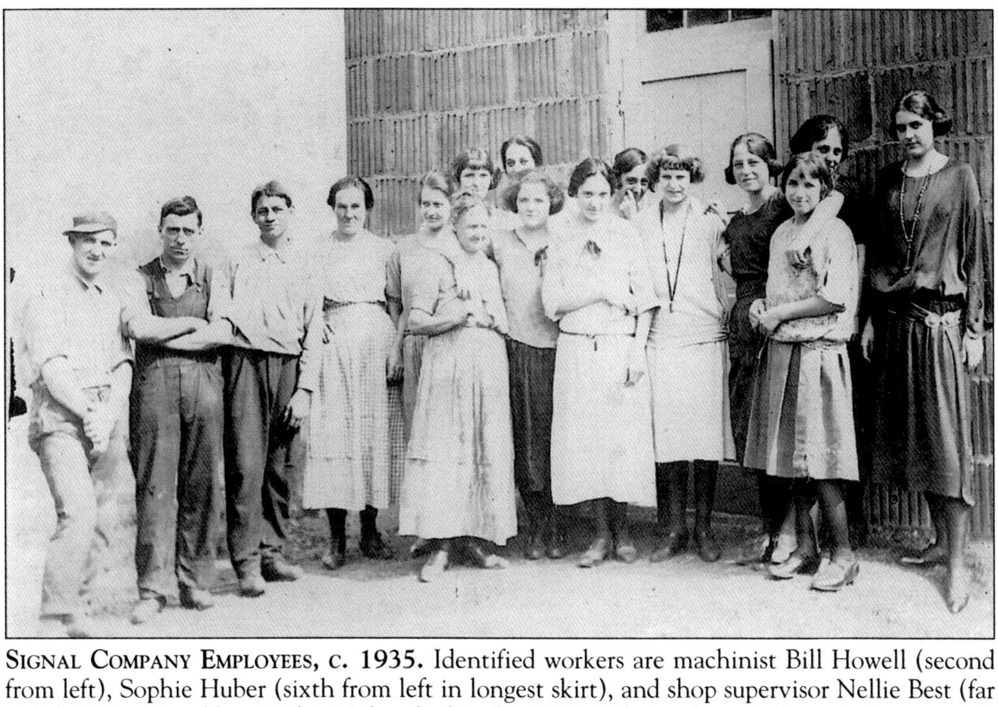

SIGNAL COMPANY EMPLOYEES, C. 1935. Identified workers are machinist Bill Howell (second from left), Sophie Huber (sixth from left in longest skirt), and shop supervisor Nellie Best (far right). By a twist of fate Sophie Huber died in the 1940 explosion because her telephone wasn't working. She had walked to work to report that she was ill and would be returning home for the day, only to be killed instantly. (Lynn Huber.)

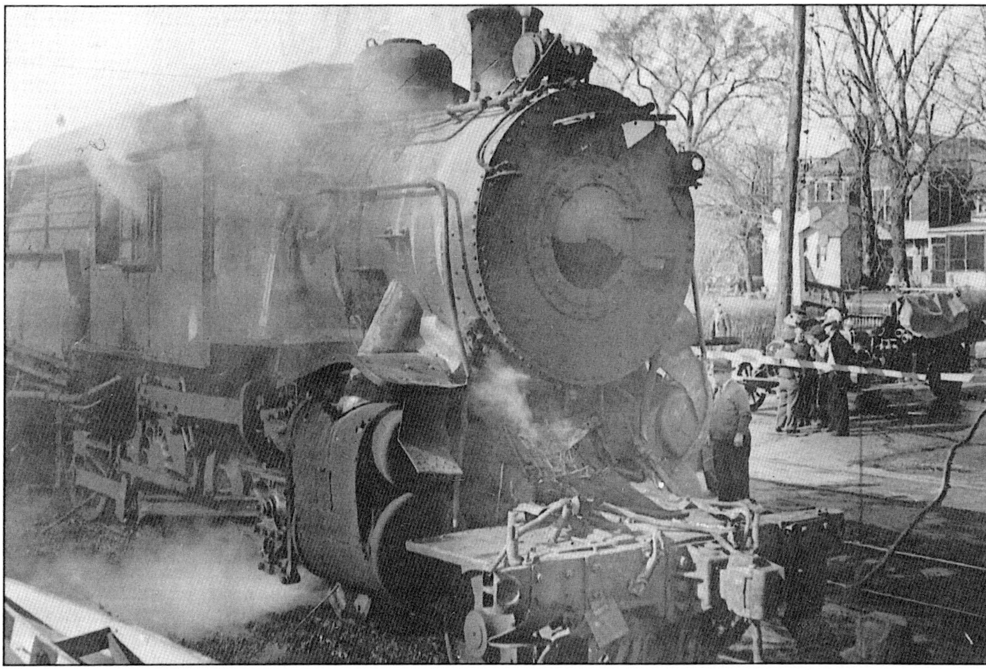

STOP, LOOK, AND LISTEN! C. 1939. An oil truck collided with a train traveling on the Jersey Central Railroad near the Sewaren Railroad Station, one of two train-truck collisions in Sewaren during the 1930s.

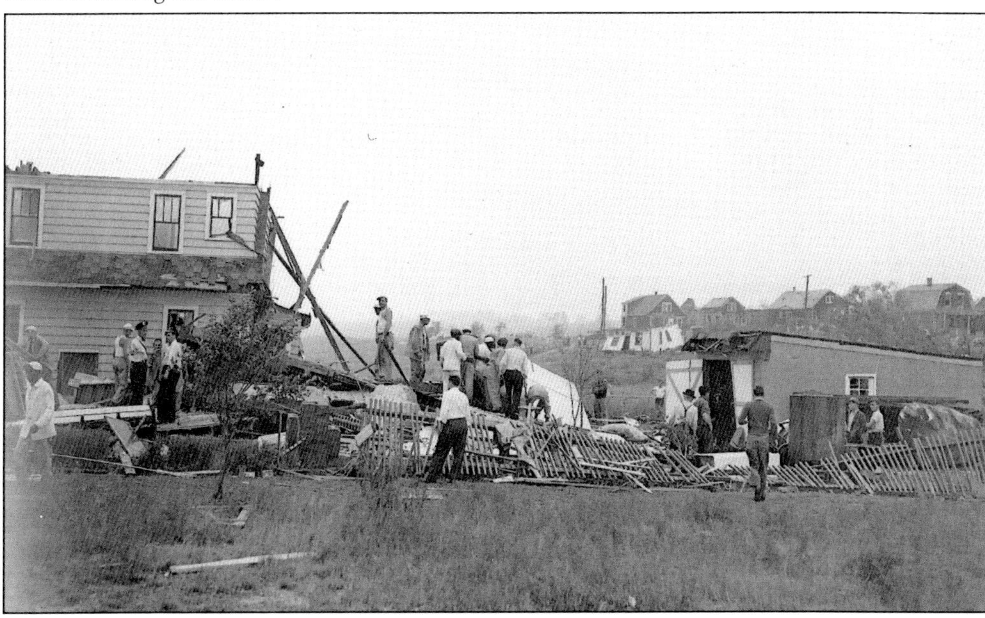

TWISTER, AUGUST 24, 1941. A tornado whipped through Woodbridge and Hopelawn on this quiet summer Sunday, ravaging an area 500 feet wide and 5 miles long. This Hopelawn home on Pennsylvania Avenue was demolished. A total of 57 houses were damaged. Many groups, including Middlesex County Workhouse prisoners, helped the police and firefighters with the rescue. Luckily, there were no deaths, though 18 people were treated at Perth Amboy Hospital. (Peter and Roberta Basckay.)

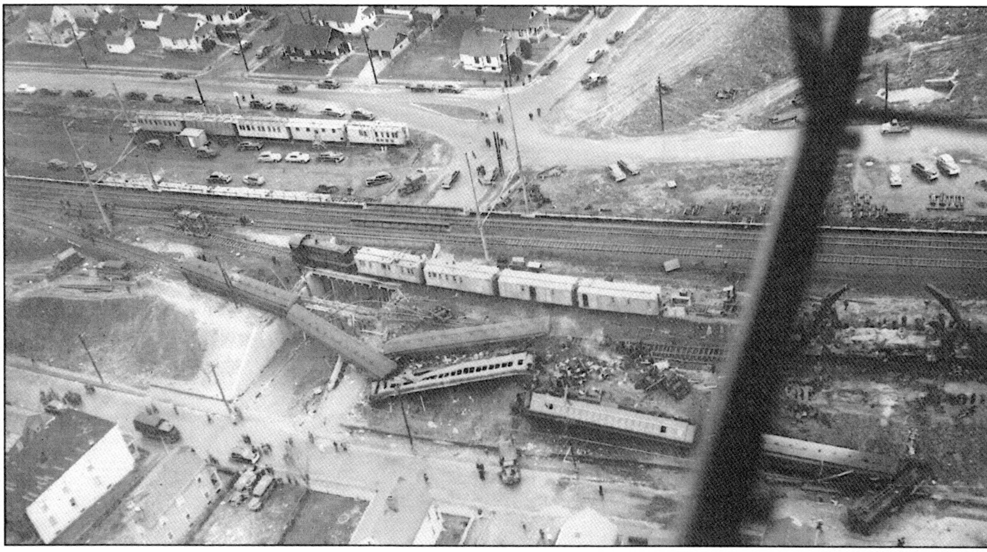

Overwhelming Tragedy, February 6, 1951. A damp, cold, and cloudy afternoon presented an ominous portent this Tuesday for one of the deadliest train accidents in U.S. history. Departing Jersey City at 5:10 p.m. for the Jersey shore, it was standing room only on the "Broker," so named for its passengers who worked on Wall Street. Striking switchmen on the Jersey Central RR forced many more commuters onto the "Broker," which crashed at 5:43 p.m. as it passed over a temporary trestle just beyond the Woodbridge station. Eighty-four people were killed and 345 were injured.

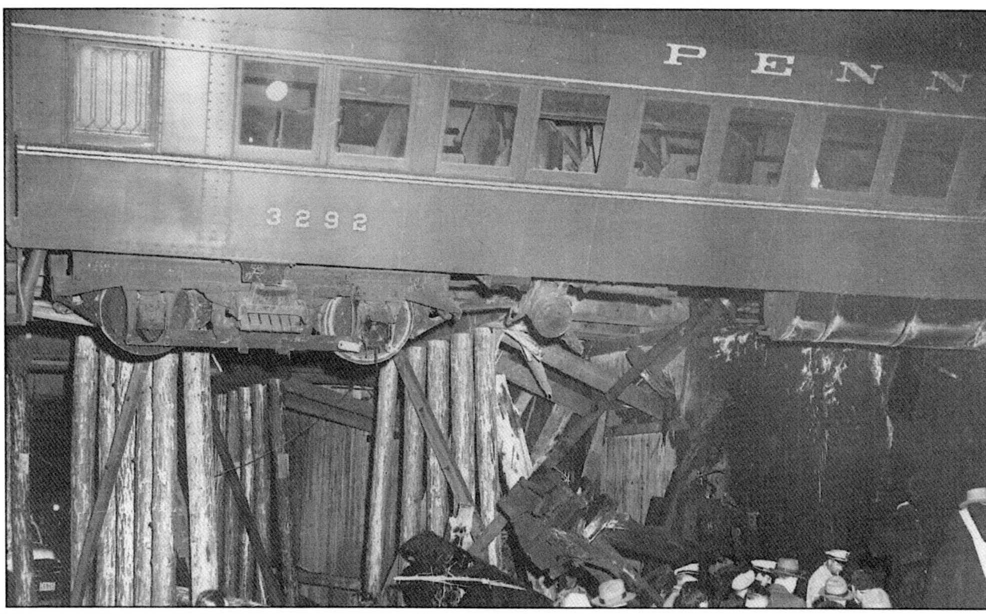

Train Wreck, February 6, 1951. The sixth passenger car on the train teeters across the Legion Street overpass. Prior to the run, the train crew reviewed the speed reduction, but the PRR did not require warning signals on the tracks when "slow orders" were published in advance. An official report cited the cause as "excessive speed on a curve of a temporary track." Although six other trains had earlier passed over the trestle successfully, this was an accident just waiting to happen.

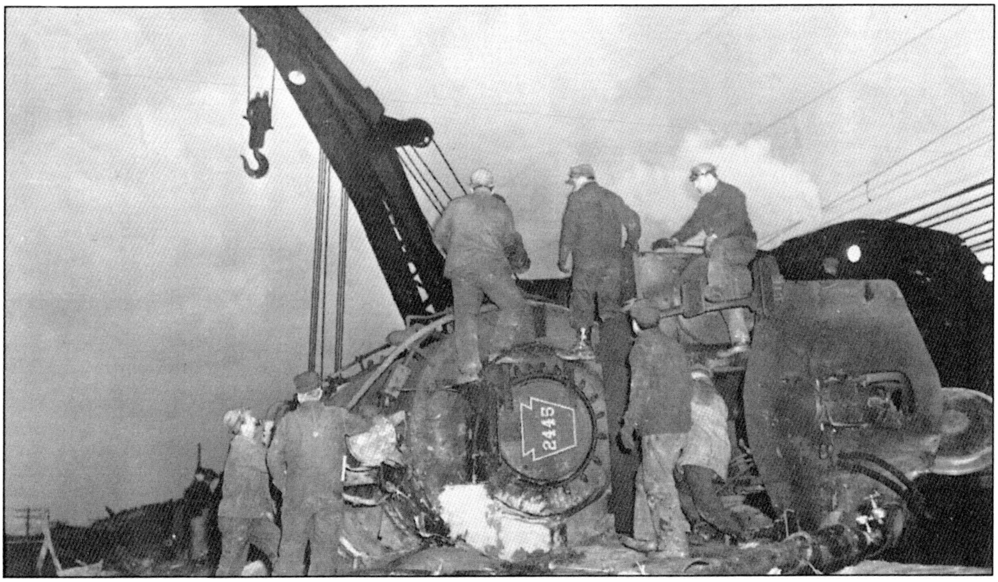

TRAIN WRECK, FEBRUARY 6, 1951. Designed for high speed passenger train service, this steam locomotive of the 4-6-2 type lies on its side with a steam-powered crane in the process of righting it. Traveling at 50 mph over a temporary wooden trestle designed for 25 mph, the weight of this 320,000-pound locomotive caused the rails to shift, which initiated derailment. The engine tender (coal car) and eight of the 11 cars went off the tracks. Damage to the engine was reported to be surprisingly light.

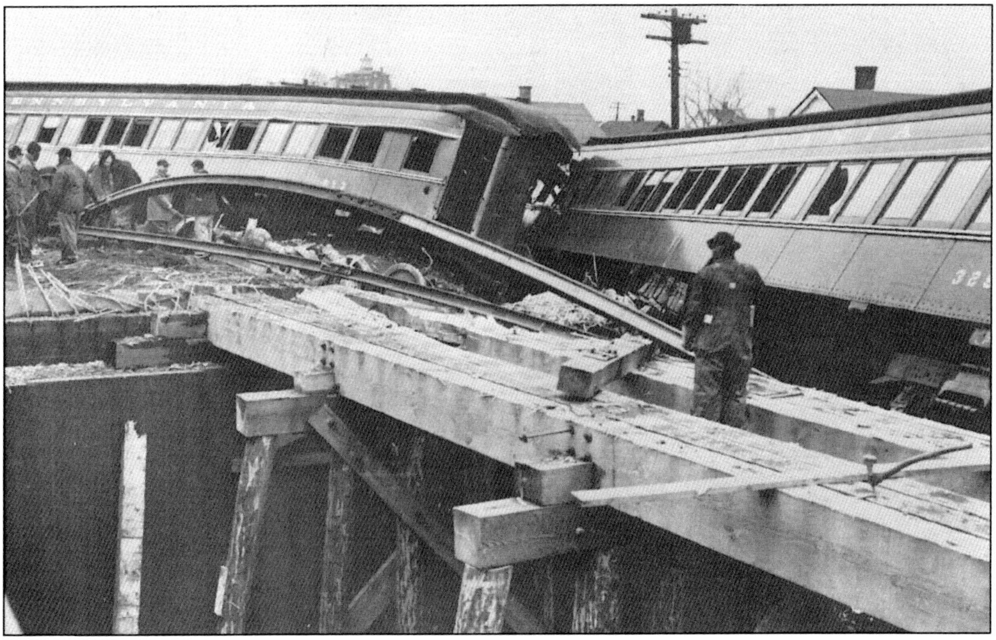

TRAIN WRECK, FEBRUARY 6, 1951. The "Broker" met disaster on a "shoofly," which is defined as "a temporary track built around some obstacle"—in this case, the construction of the new New Jersey Turnpike bridge. This "shoofly" consisted of a wooden trestle and tracks curving from the main line. Passengers in the fifth coach (left) and the sixth coach (right) were lucky since most all emerged alive. The third and fourth coaches contained most of the deaths.

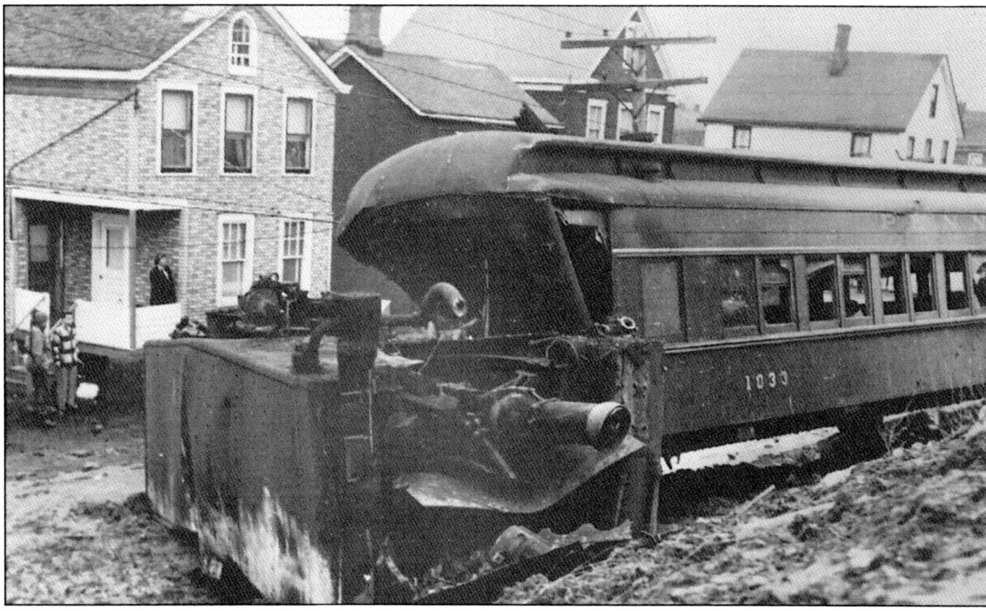

Fulton Street Train Wreck Scene, February 7, 1951. Not at all recognizable, the squarish-looking box against the passenger car is the tender for the locomotive. After breaking away from the locomotive, the tender, with its wheels sheared off, slid down an embankment upside down and was hit by the first passenger coach, No. 1033. The vestibule of this coach caved in as it was designed to do, absorbing the force of the crash.

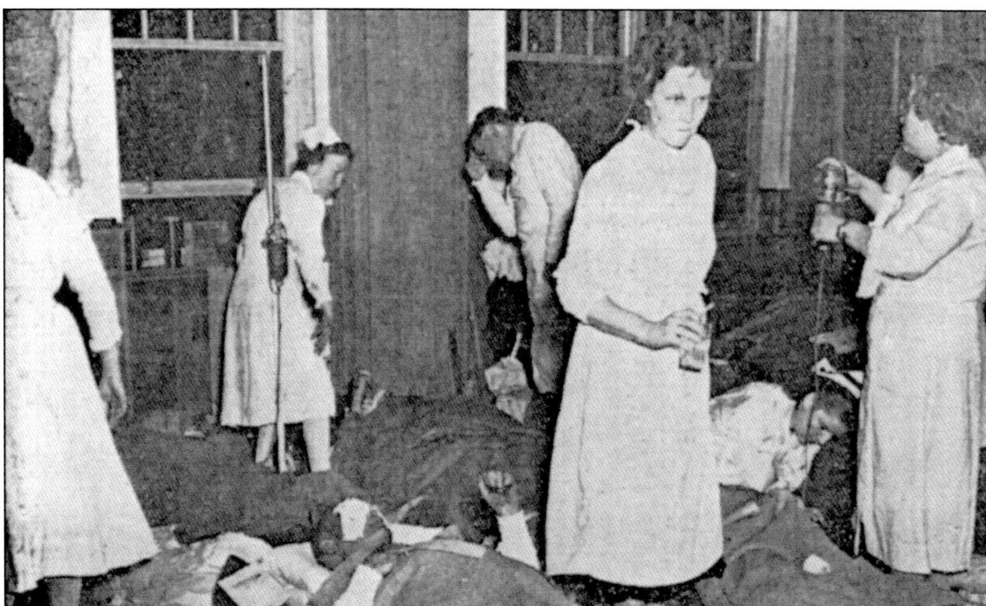

Hospital Scene, February 6, 1951. Local historian Ruth Wolk writes that, "Praise came to Woodbridge people for their valiant behavior in rescue efforts" after the train wreck. Most of the injured were treated at Perth Amboy General Hospital. Doctors, nurses, and other hospital employees worked ceaselessly to administer to the victims, many lying on stretchers in the unfinished wing of the hospital.

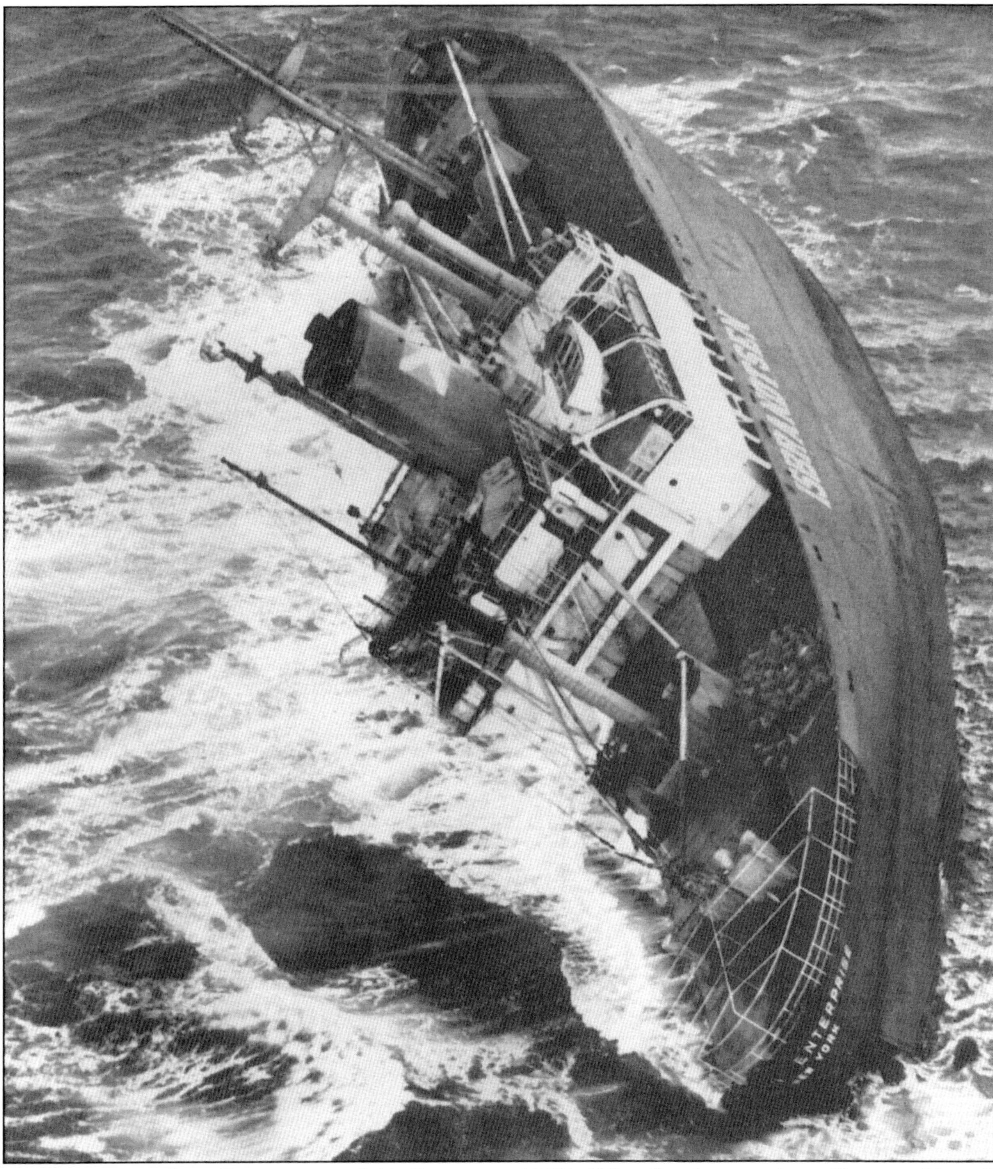

UNFORGIVING SEA, DECEMBER 1951–JANUARY 1952. Woodbridge resident Captain Henrik Kurt Carlsen remained aboard his ship, the *Flying Enterprise*, in a valiant struggle to keep her from sinking during storms in the North Atlantic Ocean. The ship barely managed to stay afloat after an "extra large wave" smashed broadside, causing the hull to crack on each side and across the deck midship. Three hundred twenty miles off the shore of England, the freighter could no longer be steered, and an urgent SOS brought help. All 40 crewmen and ten passengers were rescued on December 31, 1951. Carlsen stayed on board alone for the next five days, while a tugboat pulled the stricken ship toward Falmouth. On January 4, 1952, a mate from a rescue ship made a daring leap onto the *Flying Enterprise* to help Carlsen. Only 41 miles from shore, another violent storm severed the heavy tow line, and all hope was lost. By January 10, with the ship nearly flat on her side, both men jumped into the ocean and were quickly rescued. Within 40 minutes the ship went under. (Photograph used with permission from UPI/Corbis-Bettmann.)

Exhausted Skipper, January 1952. Captain Kurt Carlsen in unfamiliar civilian clothes rests his eyes during a press conference in Falmouth, England, shortly after being rescued from his sinking ship, the *Flying Enterprise*. By all measure he was a hero. Later Carlsen said that the worst of all "was the moment the *Enterprise* disappeared below the sea on January 21." (Photograph by Peter Anderson, used with permission from Otha C. Spencer, Campbell, Texas.)

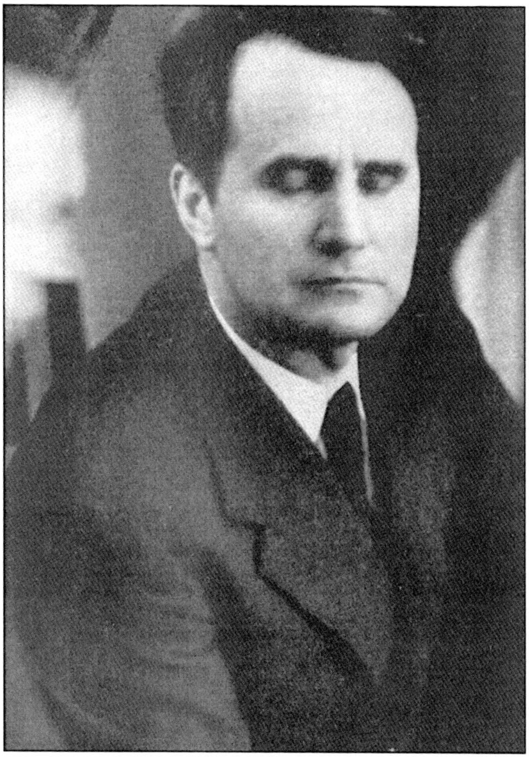

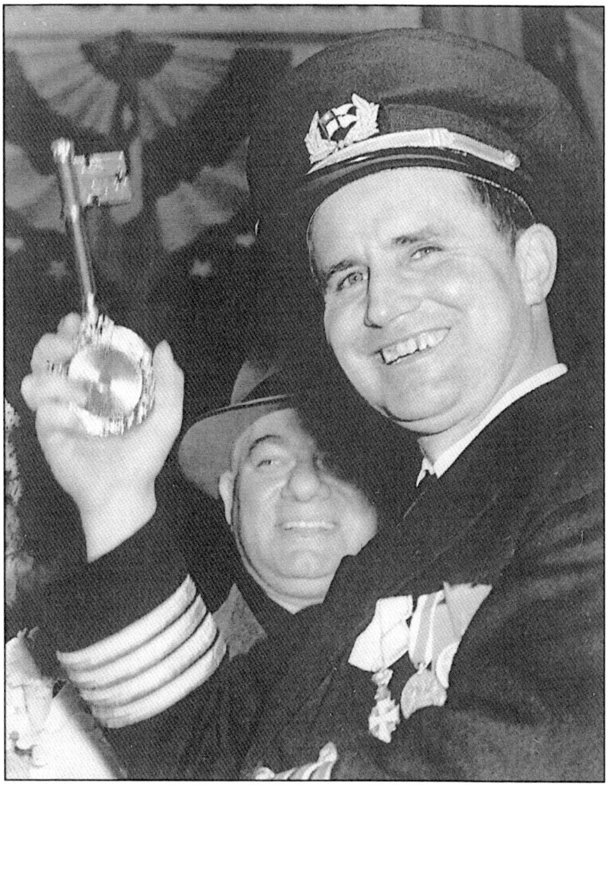

Hometown Hero, January 19, 1952. A joyous Captain Kurt Carlsen displays his key to the township, awarded to him for his exemplary efforts to save his sinking ship. Born in Denmark in 1915, Carlsen came to the U.S. in 1938 and settled in Woodbridge in 1944. Only 37 years of age when he skippered the *Flying Enterprise*, Carlsen continued to sail the seas for the American Export-Isbrandtsen Lines until he retired in 1976. (See following page.) (Karen Carlsen Mueller.)

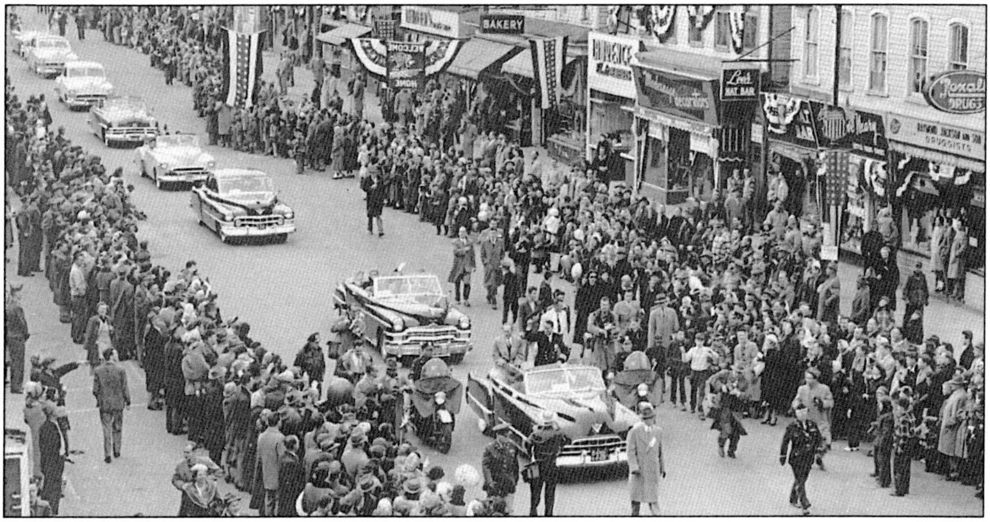

HERO HONORED, JANUARY 1952. *Above:* After a ticker-tape parade in New York City on January 17, Captain Kurt Carlsen was honored on January 19 by a homecoming parade on Main Street. A huge, cheering crowd lined local streets to pay tribute to Woodbridge's own brave sea captain. *Below:* From left to right, NJ Governor Alfred E. Driscoll, State Senator Bernard W. Vogel, Councilman Ray Albani, Mayor Hugh B. Quigley, Carlsen's daughters Sonia (wearing Girl Scout beret) and Karen, the captain's wife, Agnes Sorensen Carlsen, Carlsen, and an unidentified man enjoy the parade from the steps of the Municipal Building. When Mayor Quigley presented Carlsen with a key to the township, the mayor stated, " . . . We are proud that you, a man of courage, a man unafraid, selected Woodbridge for your home." Carlsen lived in town until his death in 1990 at the age of 75. (Karen Carlsen Mueller.)

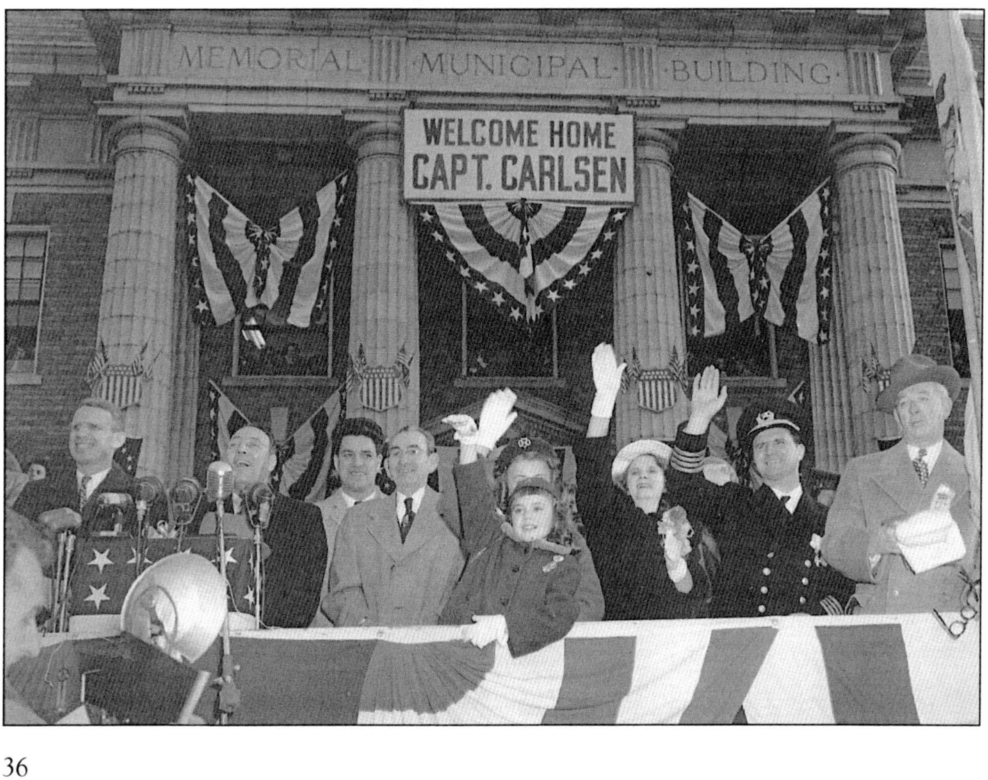

Three

MAIN STREET AND BEYOND

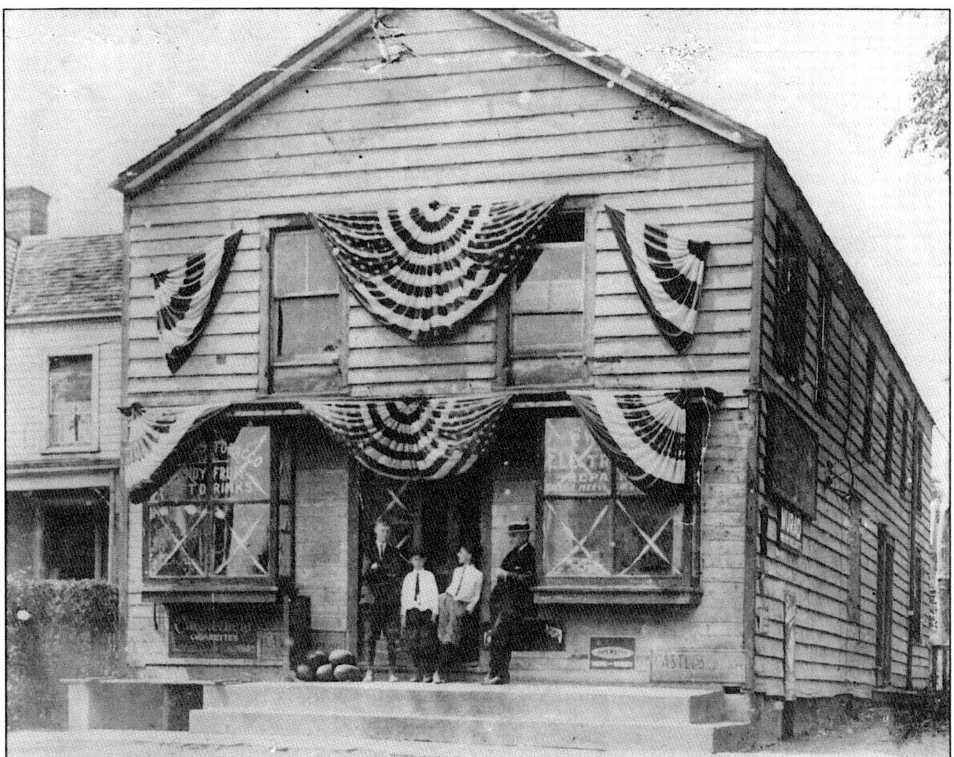

MOM AND POP SHOPS, C. 1915. This vintage building stood on Amboy Avenue at Main Street. On the right, Francesco Cacciola maintained his shoemaker shop, while his wife, Clara, operated a tobacco shop on the left. From left to right, an unidentified man, Oliver Ringwood, Harold Ringwood, and Anthony Cacciola stand in the doorway. The Ringwoods occupied the house on the left from c. 1900 to 1940. Robert Ringwood and other descendants still live in the area. (Nazareth Cacciola.)

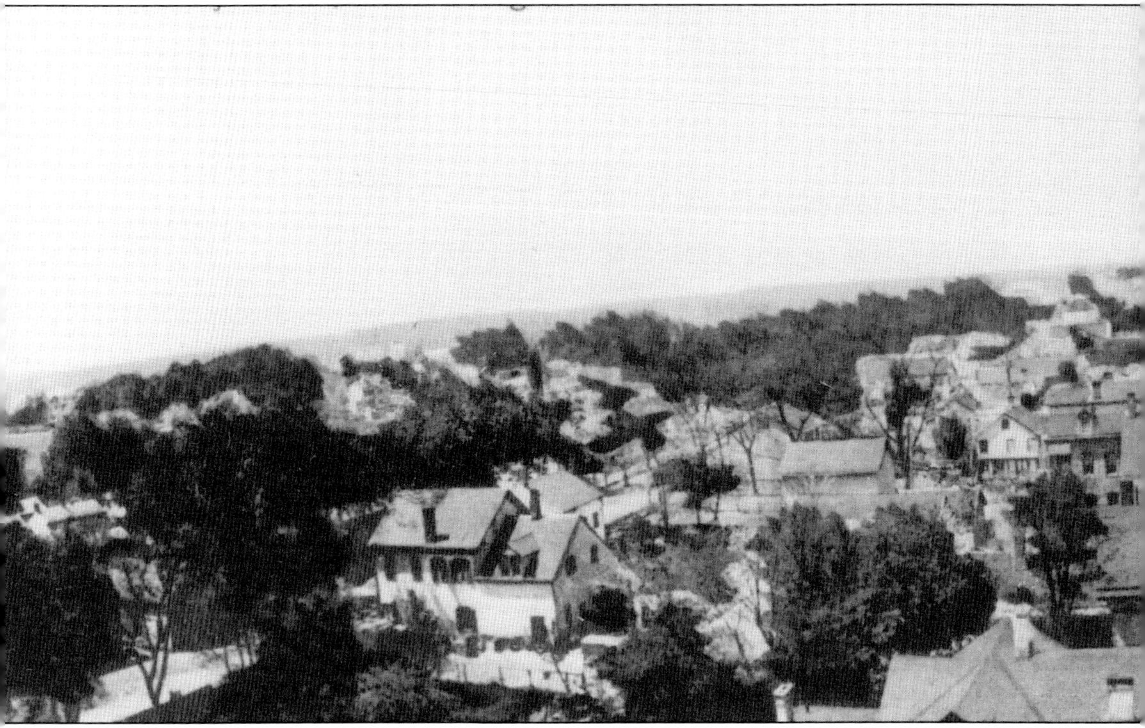

Bird's-Eye View, c. 1908. This double postcard photographed from the Methodist church steeple provides a panoramic view of the Main Street landscape at that time. The Hungarian Reformed Church steeple and the clock tower on School One are visible on the right, with the school's American flag flying high over the town.

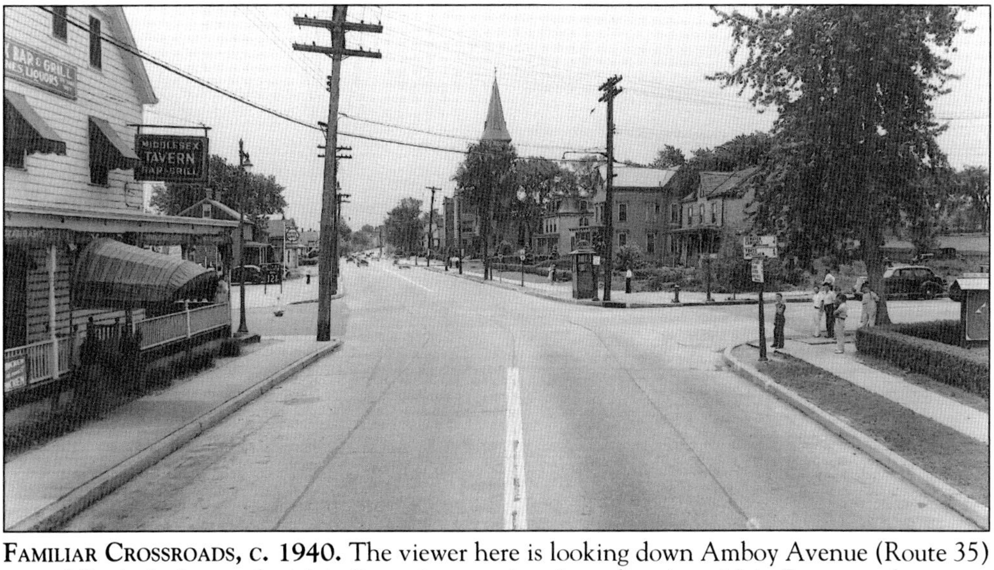

Familiar Crossroads, c. 1940. The viewer here is looking down Amboy Avenue (Route 35) toward Perth Amboy at the Main Street intersection. In earlier times Main Street was known as Philadelphia Avenue, while Amboy Avenue was listed on an 1876 map as Perth Avenue. The famous Cross Keys Tavern, now on James Street, was located where the Knights of Columbus clubhouse stands today. (The clubhouse sign is visible on the right behind the hedge.)

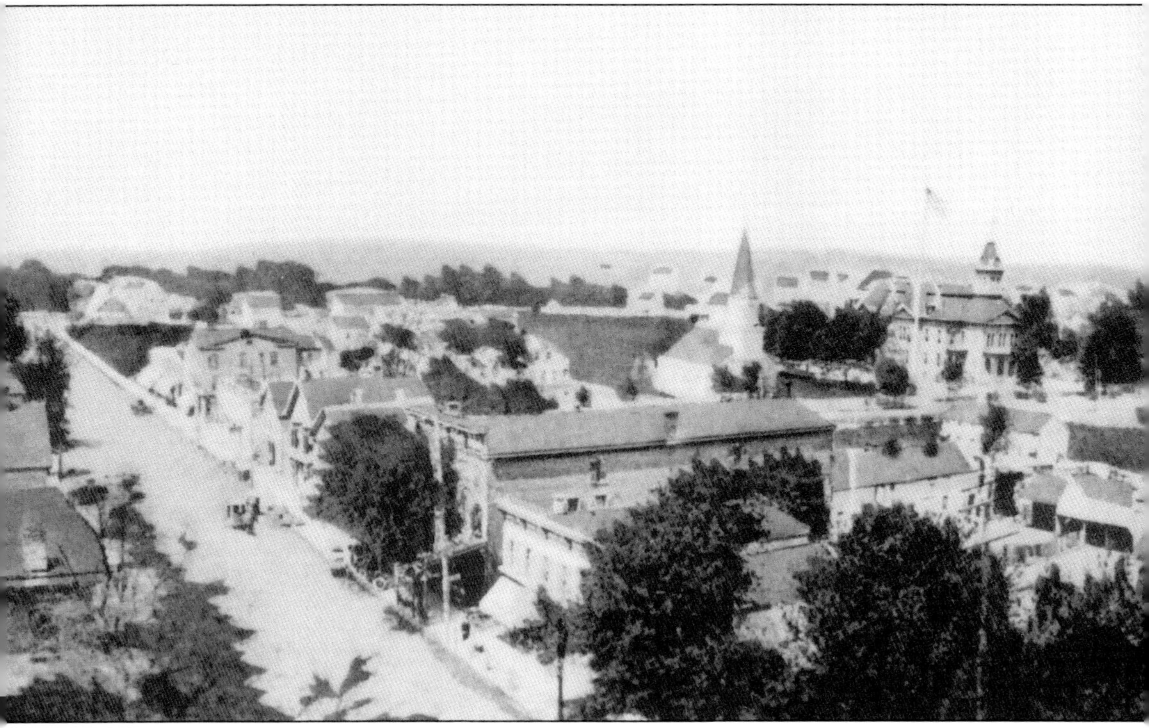

With unpaved streets, horses and wagons, and not a single "horseless carriage" in sight to stir up the dust, Woodbridge presents a tranquil, tree-lined facade in the first years of the 20th century.

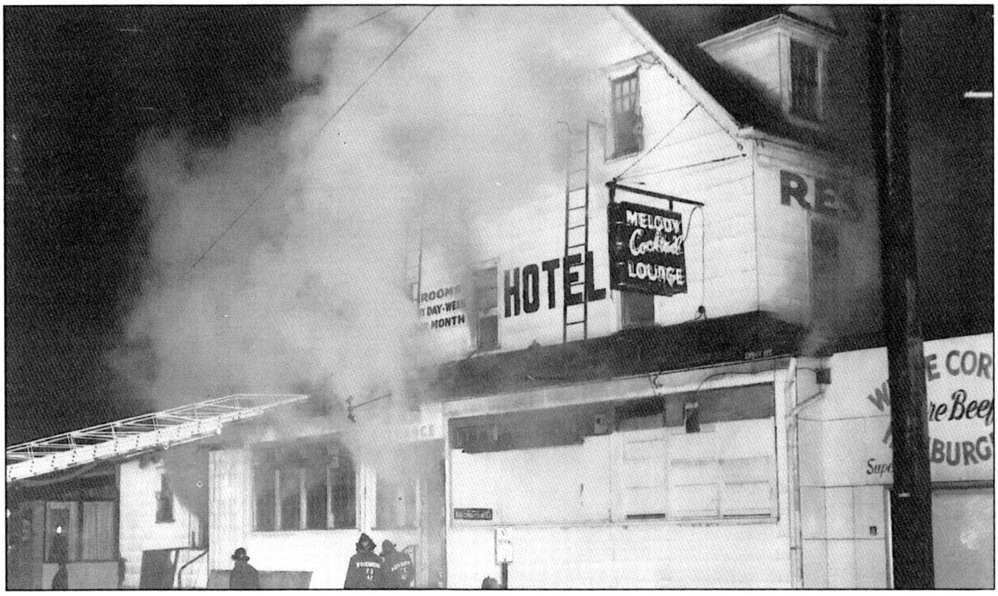

HOTEL FIRE, 1956. Although this fire didn't completely destroy the Middlesex Hotel and Restaurant building owned by the Galaida family, the hotel never reopened. An advertisement of an earlier time described the restaurant as serving "skillfully prepared dishes of farm grown vegetables and choice cuts of meat, topped off with a piece of homemade pie baked to a crisp rich brown." (Charles Banko.)

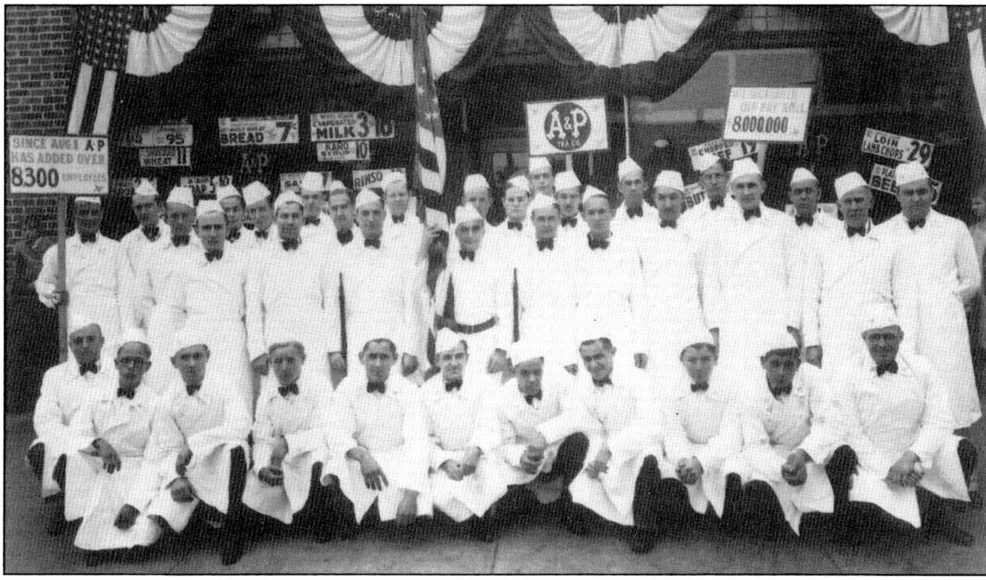

THE A&P, 1940. It looks like it was a gala opening for the Great Atlantic and Pacific Tea Company. And, yes, those were the days when shoppers could find fresh chopped beef for 19¢ a pound, five bars of Octagon Soap for 10¢, and choice loin lamb chops for a whopping 29¢ a pound! Woodbridge resident George E. Hadden Jr. (top row at right of center with hat almost touching the A&P sign) later managed the Rahway Avenue A&P. (Jean Hadden Klc.)

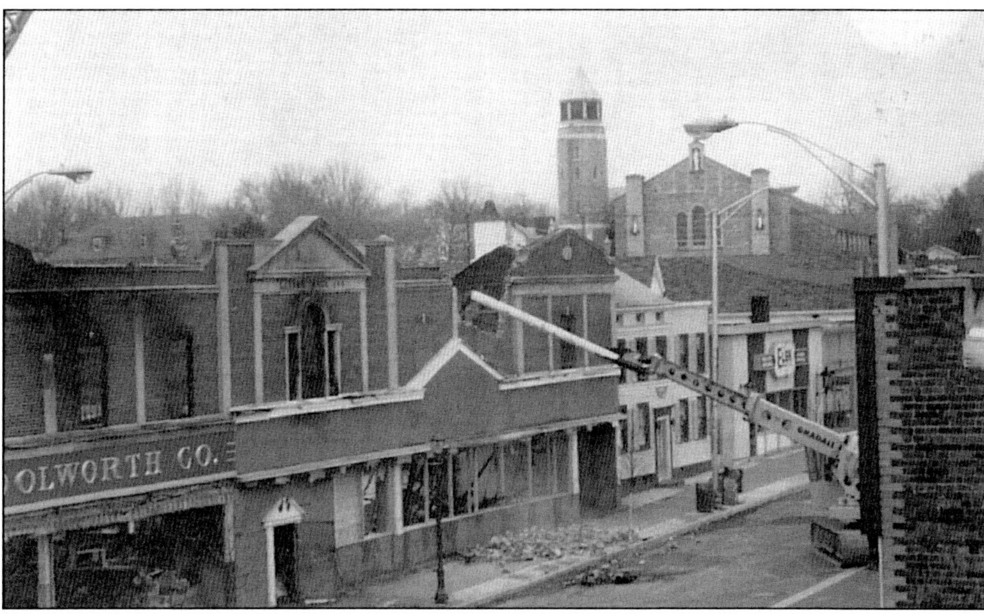

MAIN STREET FIRE, MARCH 9, 1993. After more than 50 years on Main Street, the A&P Supermarket closed its doors, and shortly thereafter a fire broke out in the building. Unfortunately the fire spread to the F.W. Woolworth store next door, which also never reopened. After the building was reconstructed, new stores replaced the A&P and Woolworth's. In the distance St. James Roman Catholic Church towers above Main Street. (Bruce Christensen.)

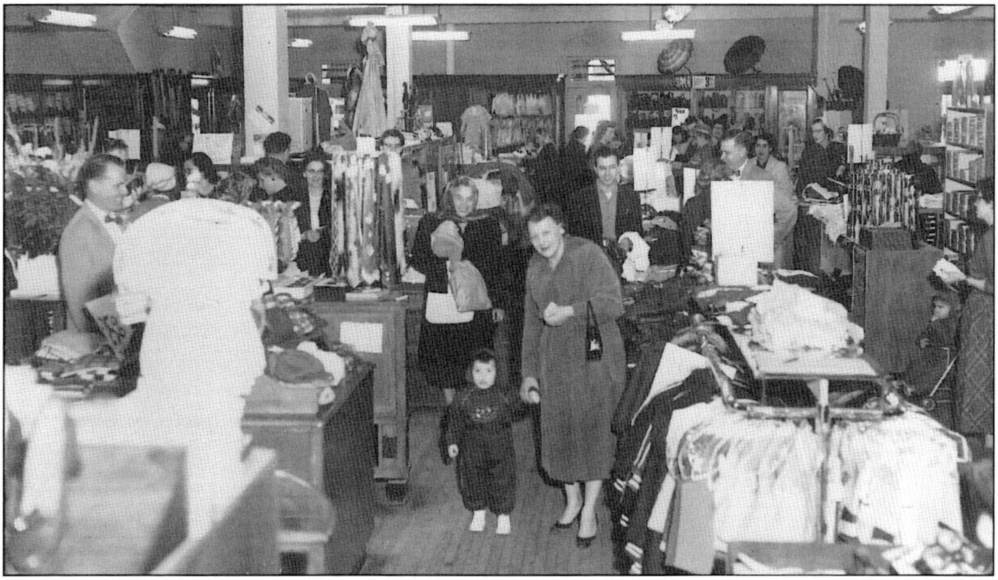

The Friendly Store, c. 1950. Christensen's Store, a retail institution on Main Street for over 100 years, was known for its variety of merchandise, which included electrical appliances for some years, and helpful employees. Brothers Chris and Peter Christensen from Denmark opened a department store in 1895 on the north side of Main Street and moved here in 1933. The Christensen family closed the business and sold their building in June 1998. (Herbert Christensen.)

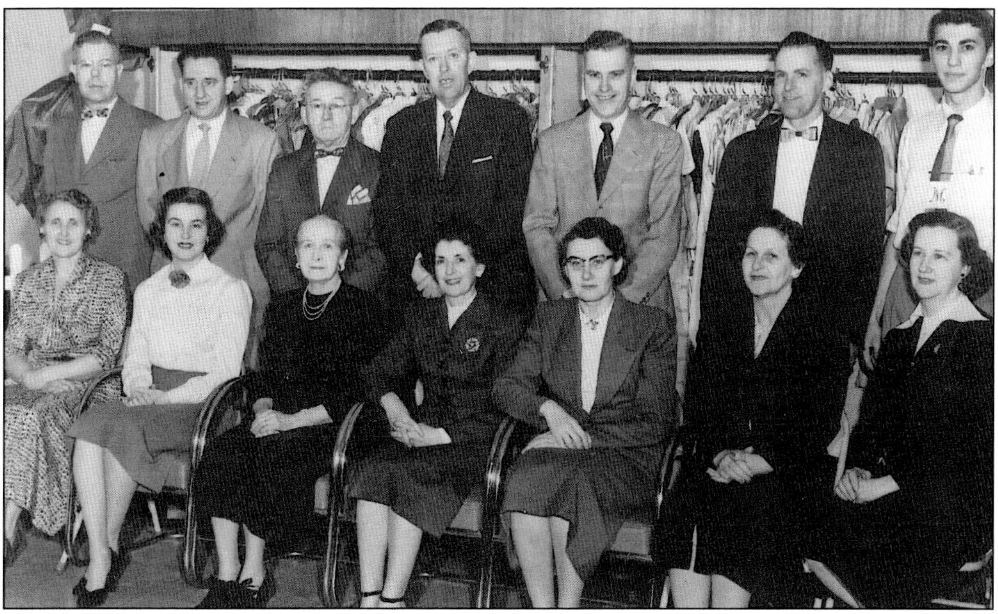

Who's Minding the Store? c. 1950. Employees of Christensen's Department Store assembled here for a photograph. From left to right are as follows: (bottom row) Helen Greiner Powers, Ruth Kuzma Dunham, Catherine Romond, Midge Keating, Mabel Rogers Shoemaker, Mabel Lloyd Scott, and Catherine "Deanie" Ascough Dunigan; (top row) Gilford Christensen, Merther Meehan, Hugo Geis, Robert Dow, Herbert Christensen, Howard Macnab, and Dennis McLellan. (Herbert Christensen.)

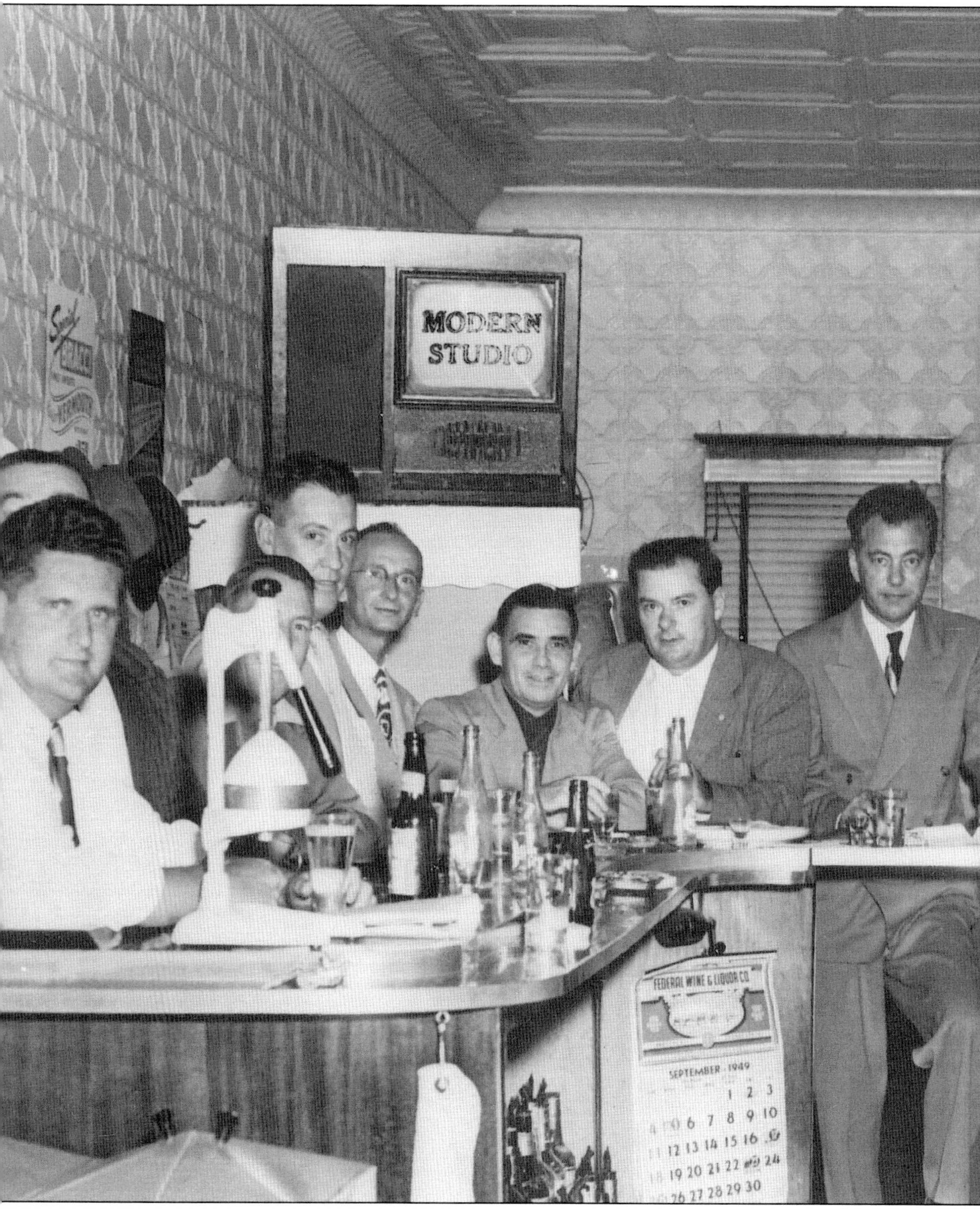

The College Inn, September 1949. Van Tassel's College Inn was a popular Main Street tavern and meeting place for many townsfolk from 1943 until 1980. It was owned by brothers George and William Van Tassel and their sister, Helen Van Tassel. Several Township politicians are among the group assembled around the bar. From left to right are John Schfranski, Steve Vereb, Bill Gerity, William "Bill" Fitzpatrick, Attorney Irv Rosenbloom, William "Billy" Warren,

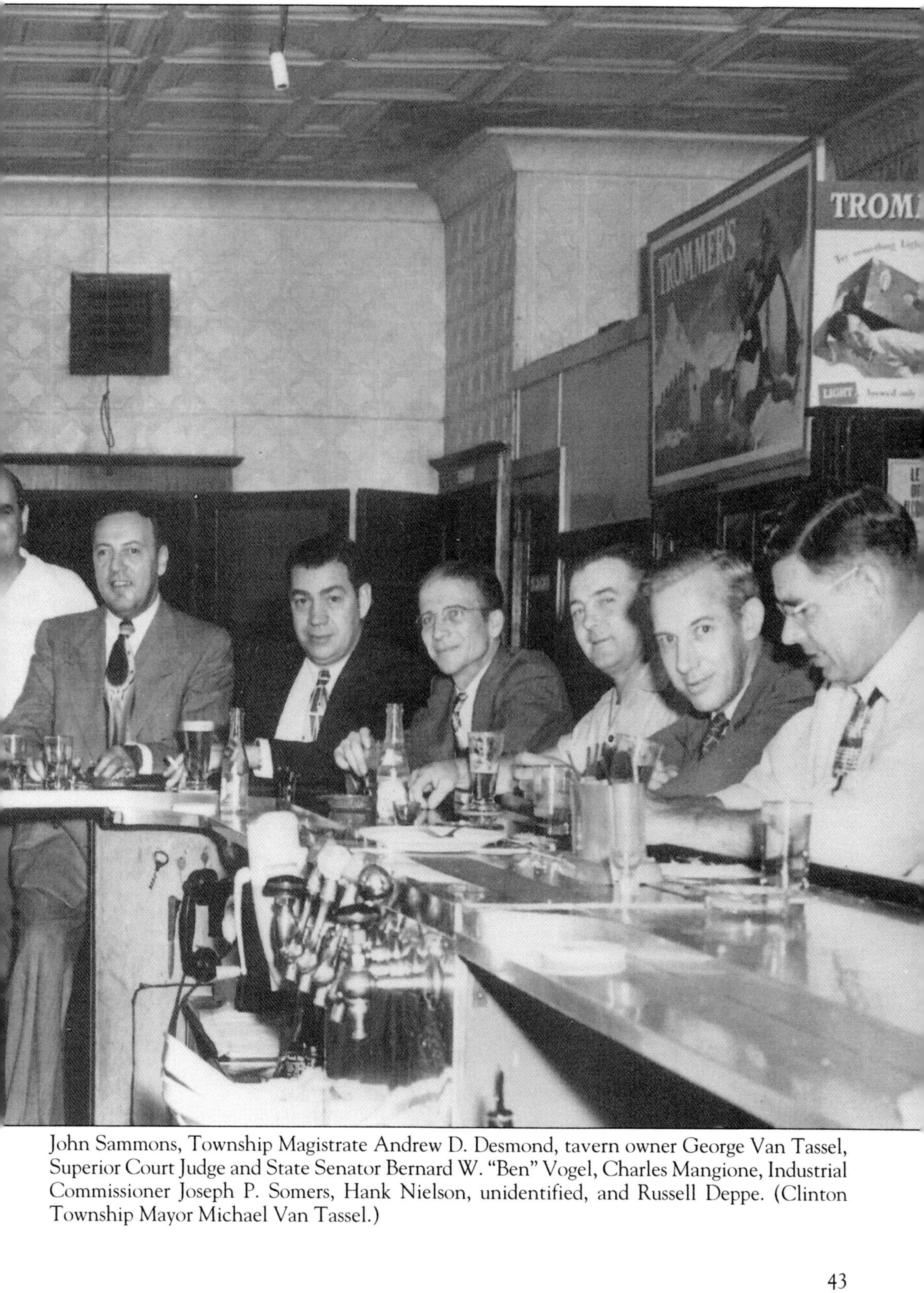

John Sammons, Township Magistrate Andrew D. Desmond, tavern owner George Van Tassel, Superior Court Judge and State Senator Bernard W. "Ben" Vogel, Charles Mangione, Industrial Commissioner Joseph P. Somers, Hank Nielson, unidentified, and Russell Deppe. (Clinton Township Mayor Michael Van Tassel.)

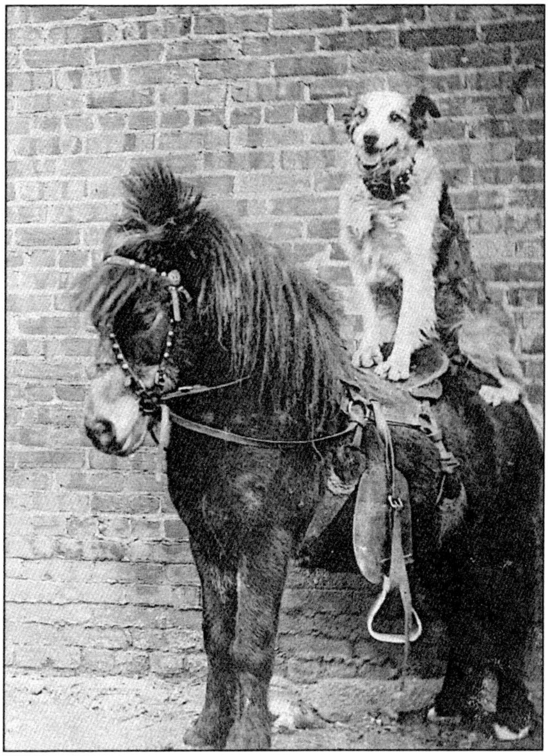

Nibsy to the Rescue! c. 1915. The firehouse mascot known as Nibs or Nibsy seems to be hitching a ride on a friendly pony, but whether they would make it to a fire ahead of the fire company's new American LaFrance pumper truck is anybody's guess! (Raymond and Joan Peterson.)

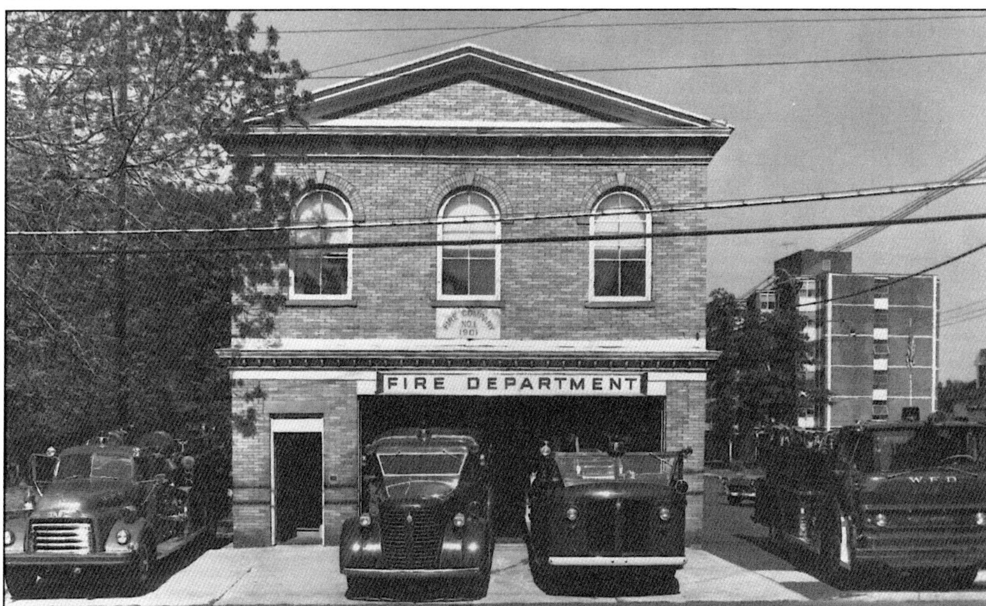

First Firehouse. Built in 1901, this original firehouse, next to Woodbridge Park on School Street, is pictured here shortly before it was torn down in 1967 to make way for an all-new facility at this location. When a firefighter dies, his name is placed on a permanent memorial plaque that is on display inside the new firehouse. The Senior Citizen Complex (at right) on Brook Street was also built in the 1960s. (Todd Howell.)

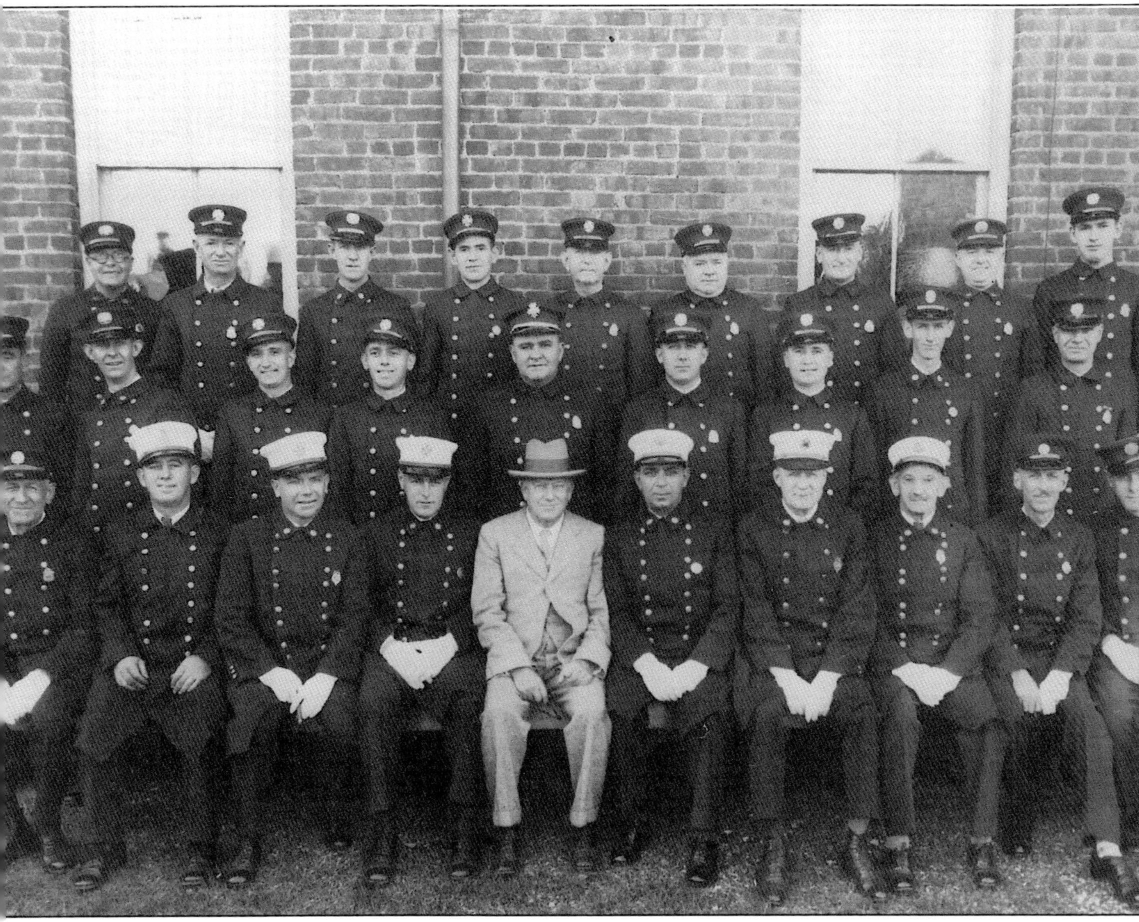

FIREMEN OF 1933. Our town's firefighters in full dress uniform assembled alongside the firehouse are from left to right as follows: (front row) Frank Bader, Charles "Monk" Messick, William Allgaier, Captain Harry Mawbey, Lem Campbell, James Catano, Edward Sattler, Ferd "Fat" Kath, Carl Hansen, and Gordon Hunt; (middle row) Ray Moore, James Zehrer, Ray Holzheimer, Peter Einhorn, William Treen, William Prion, John Prekop, "Cherry" Hunt, and Leon McElroy; (back row) Alfred Brown, Gus Demlar, Fred Zehrer, Tom Kath, Jake Jordan, Hugh McClusky, Eugene Schriner, Joe Silas, and Steve Suprak. (Todd Howell.)

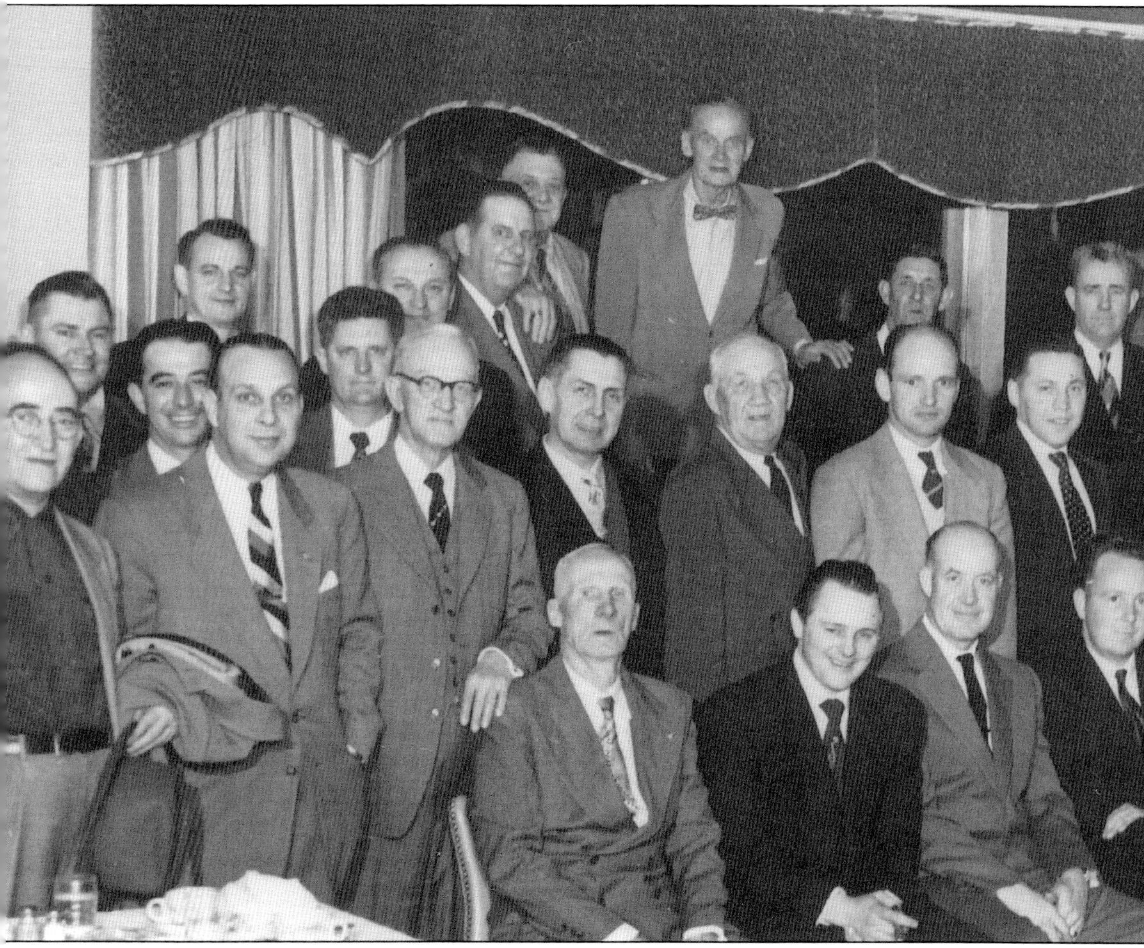

The Firemen of 1954. All active and inactive firemen of Woodbridge Fire Company Number One and friends gathered on February 25, 1954, at Howard Johnson's Restaurant for a testimonial dinner honoring two retiring paid firefighters, Art Hunt and Leo Goriss. Firemen in the front row are, from left to right, Bert Hunt, Andrew Anderson, Jesse Carrol, William Gerity, William Fitzpatrick, retired Township Mayor August Greiner, Harold Crowe, Dick Wallace, Ed Mulrenner, John Orlick, Bob Fitzpatrick, and Elbur Richards. The following firemen are pictured but their names are not in order: Chubby Andersch, Frank Bader, Julius Bernstein,

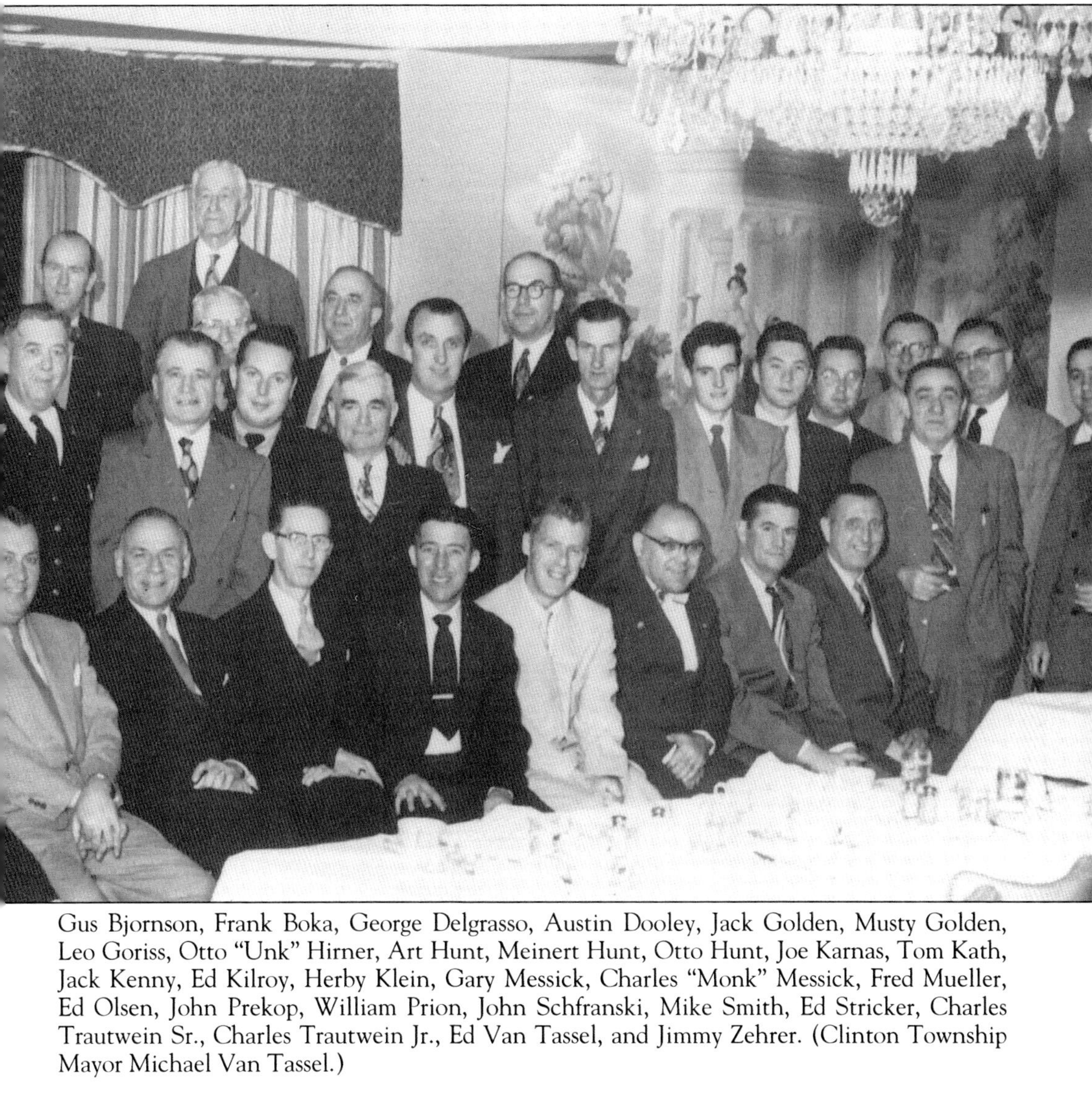

Gus Bjornson, Frank Boka, George Delgrasso, Austin Dooley, Jack Golden, Musty Golden, Leo Goriss, Otto "Unk" Hirner, Art Hunt, Meinert Hunt, Otto Hunt, Joe Karnas, Tom Kath, Jack Kenny, Ed Kilroy, Herby Klein, Gary Messick, Charles "Monk" Messick, Fred Mueller, Ed Olsen, John Prekop, William Prion, John Schfranski, Mike Smith, Ed Stricker, Charles Trautwein Sr., Charles Trautwein Jr., Ed Van Tassel, and Jimmy Zehrer. (Clinton Township Mayor Michael Van Tassel.)

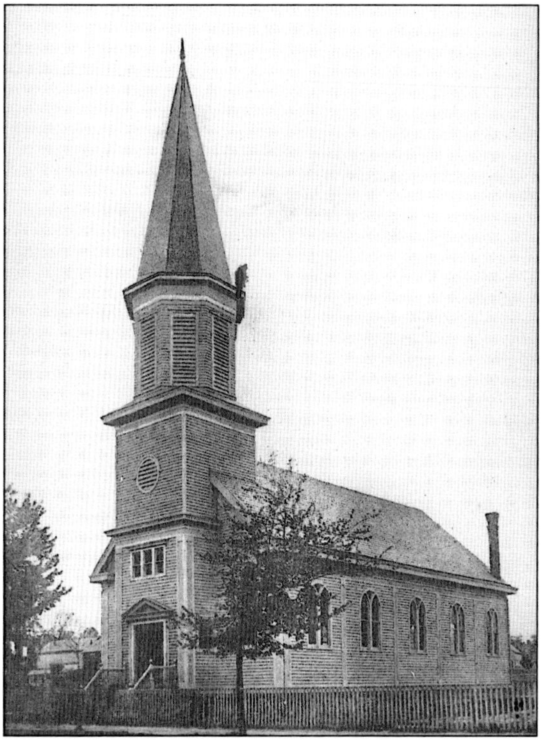

Hungarian Reformed Church, 1959. Drawn to jobs in the flourishing clay mining industry, many folks emigrated from Hungary to Woodbridge during the late 19th and early 20th centuries. Both Hungarian Catholics and Protestants founded churches in town so they could continue to worship in their native language. The Reformed Church on School Street was built in 1906 and was replaced by the present brick building in 1961.

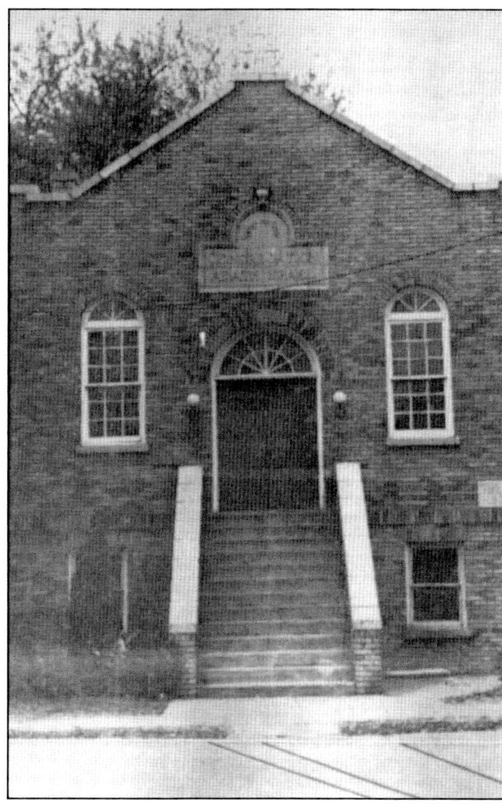

Congregation Adath Israel, c. 1930. The local Jewish congregation, which organized in 1907, built this synagogue in 1923 next to School One on School Street at South Park Drive. In 1948 the congregation replaced this small building with the Woodbridge Jewish Community Center on Amboy Avenue property donated by well-known community leader and businessman Abraham J. Neiss.

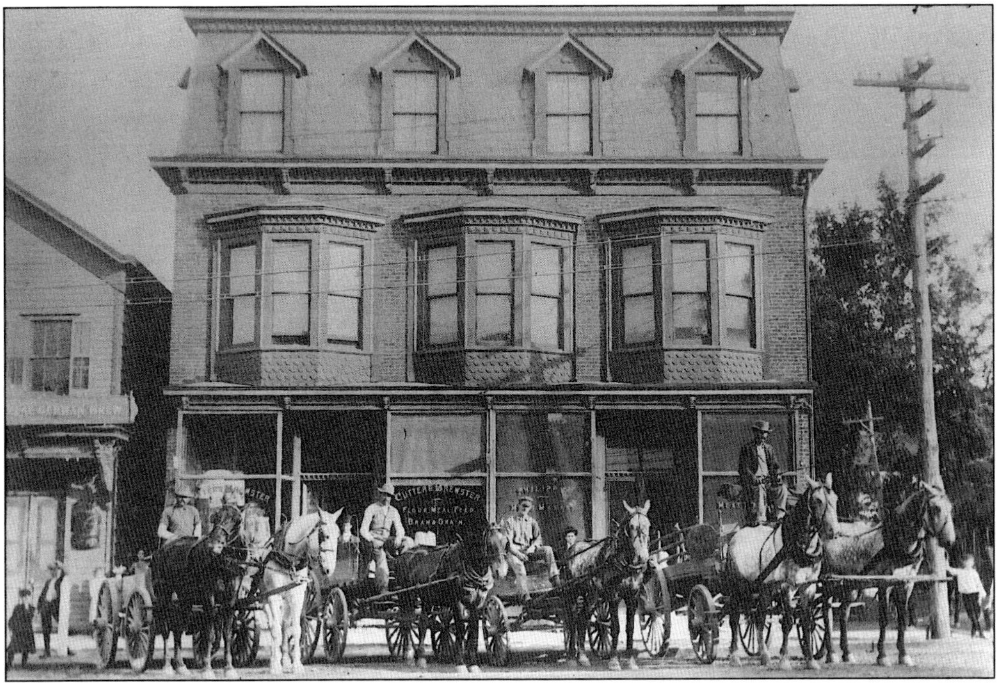

Vintage Stores, c. 1910. Four teams of horse-drawn wagons line up on Main Street at the N. William Street corner in front of Philipp's Meat Market and Cutter and Brewster's Store, which sold flour, meal, and feed. After finishing their shopping here, farmers and merchants may have dropped in at the Central Hotel next door for a mug of "Real German Brew" as advertised on its sign. (Emily and Margaret Lee.)

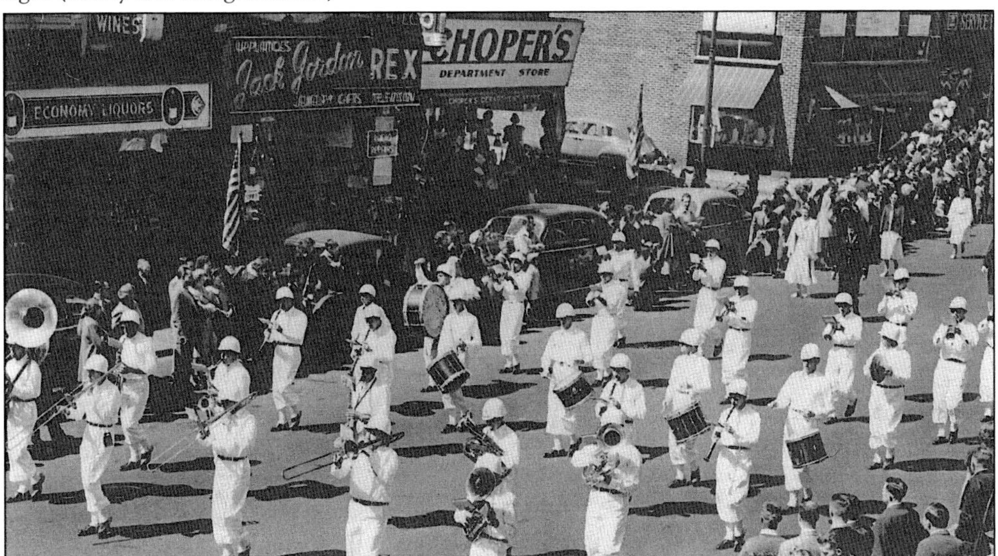

On Parade, 1948. The American Legion Post #87 band marches smartly along Main Street. The band was composed of WHS alumni of all ages and was directed by Theodore H. Hoops of the high school music department. Later the band became the Elks Club Band with Ray Holzheimer, a former WHS drum major, as director. The stores may change, but the old Cutter-Brewster building in the background remains virtually intact today. (William Harned.)

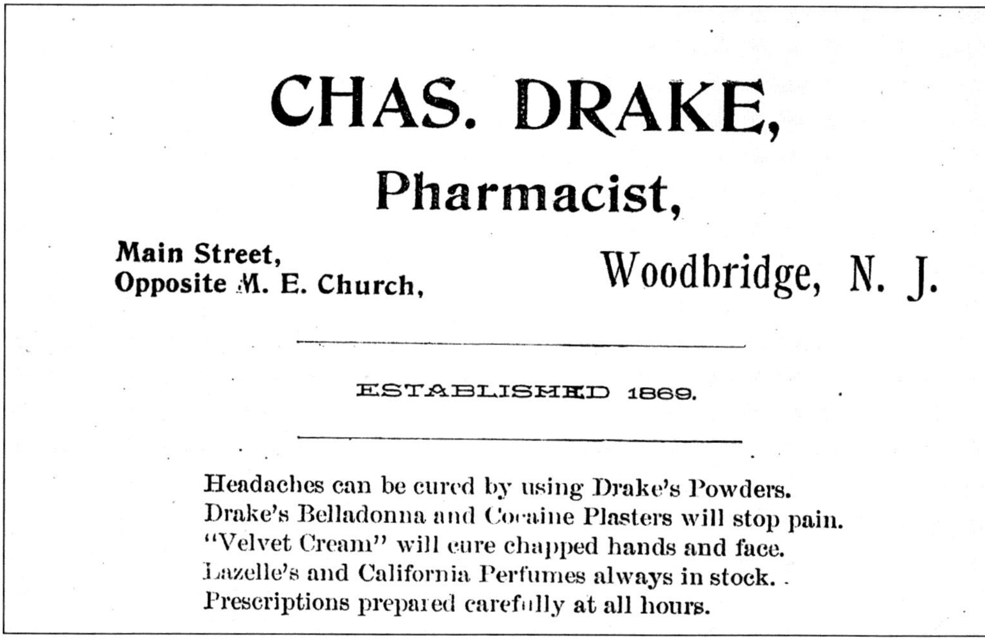

MAIN STREET ADVERTISEMENT, 1902. Pharmacist Charles Drake offers some intriguing medicines and apparently 24-hour prescription service to his customers, according to this advertisement, which appeared in a 56-page booklet entitled *History of Methodism in Woodbridge and Vicinity*. The booklet was published in 1902 to celebrate the church's 70th anniversary, and included a directory of members.

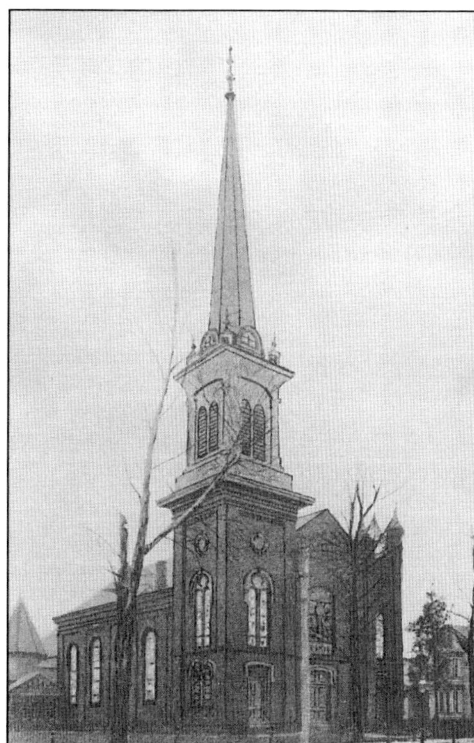

THE METHODIST EPISCOPAL CHURCH, C. 1890. During the 1700s the Methodists of Woodbridge met regularly in members' homes and heard sermons by traveling preachers such as the first American Methodist bishop, Rev. Francis Asbury, for whom Asbury Park, New Jersey, is named. In 1832 they built their first church on lower Main Street on land purchased from the Society of Friends (the Quakers). The building was later moved to adjacent land, and the cornerstone for this church was laid on June 2, 1870.

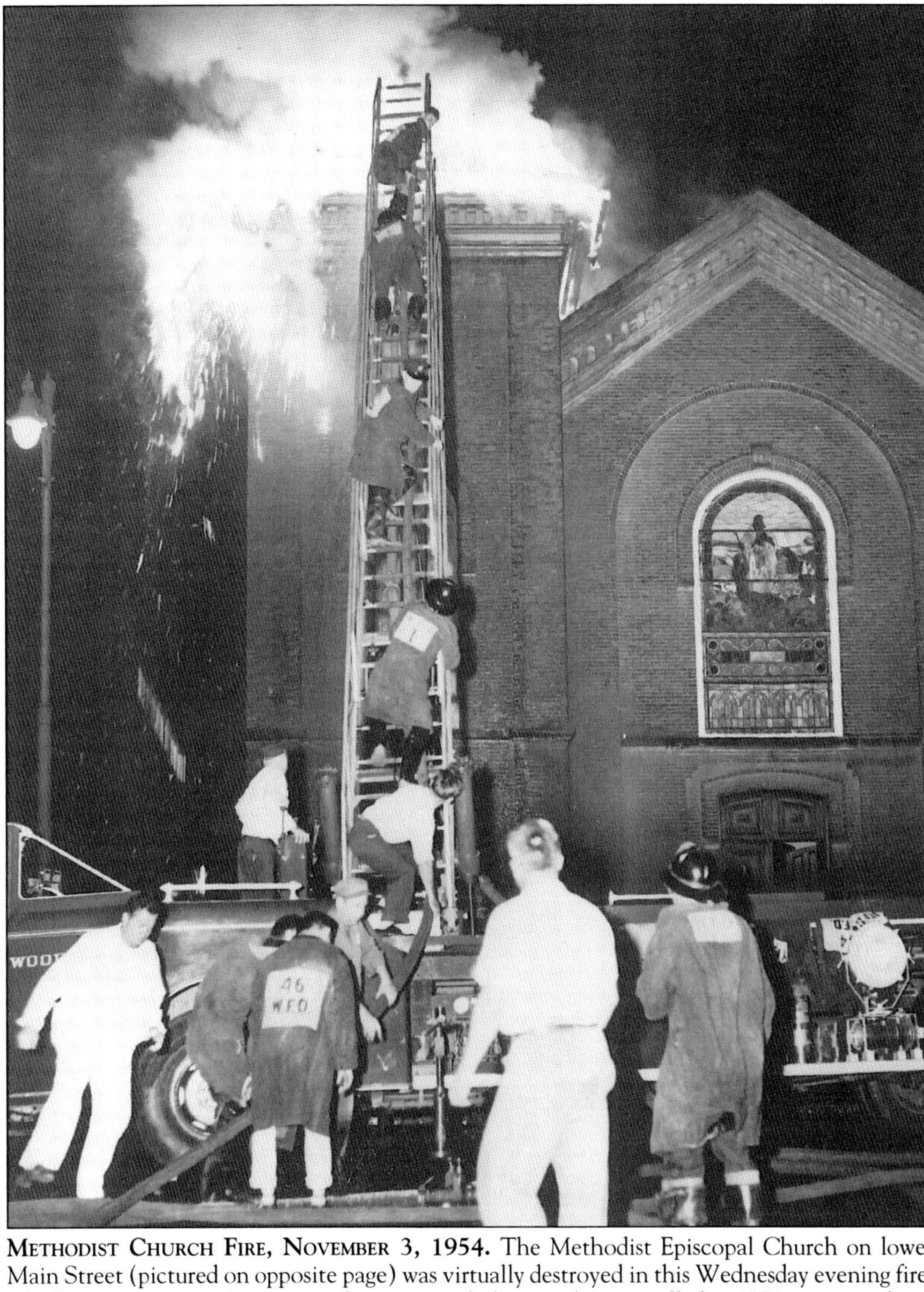

Methodist Church Fire, November 3, 1954. The Methodist Episcopal Church on lower Main Street (pictured on opposite page) was virtually destroyed in this Wednesday evening fire. The front entrance and two magnificent stained-glass windows installed in 1870 were saved and remain an integral part of the restored church. Members worshipped at the Craftsmen's Club on Green Street and shared services with Congregation Adath Israel on Amboy Avenue until their new building was ready. (Frank LaPenta.)

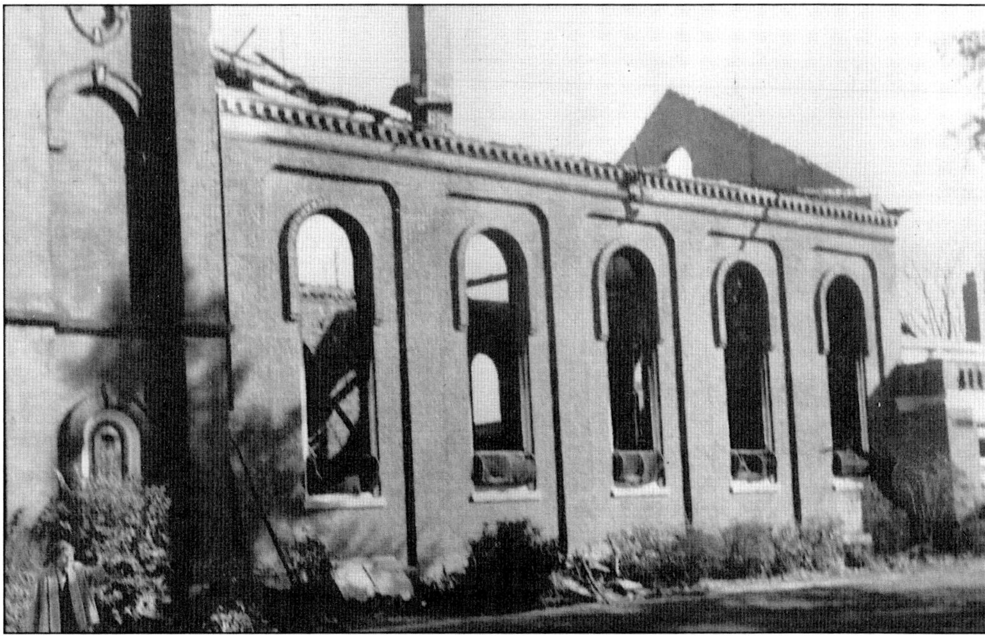

CHURCH FIRE AFTERMATH, C. 1954. This desolate, empty shell, all that was left after the Methodist church fire, was quickly transformed into a new sanctuary and educational building, which is still in use. Rebuilt by local contractors Andy Aaroe and his son Don, the new church was consecrated on November 4, 1956, during the pastorate of Rev. Clifford B. Munn. In the 1960s the church was renamed the Woodbridge United Methodist Church. (Madeline LaPenta Peterson.)

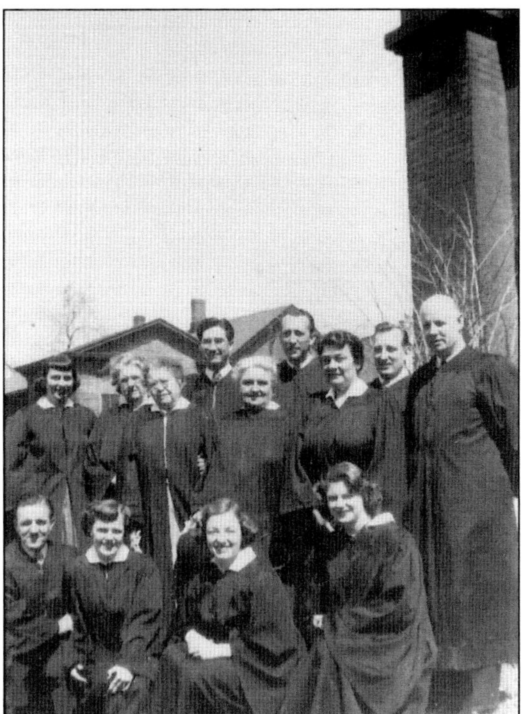

METHODIST CHURCH CHOIR, APRIL 13, 1952. The choristers look in fine voice as they gather outside the church this Easter Sunday. From left to right members are as follows: (bottom row) Michael Gutwein of Fords and his daughter Dorothy, Louise Fuge, and Dorothy M. Hendricksen; (top row) Sally Stauffer Christiansen, Sybil McGarrah, Anna McCullough, Basil Hopper, Mabel E. Treen, Chester F. Elliot, Miriam D. Bergen, assistant minister William Smith, and organist and choir director George E. Ruddy of Metuchen. (Virginia B. Troeger.)

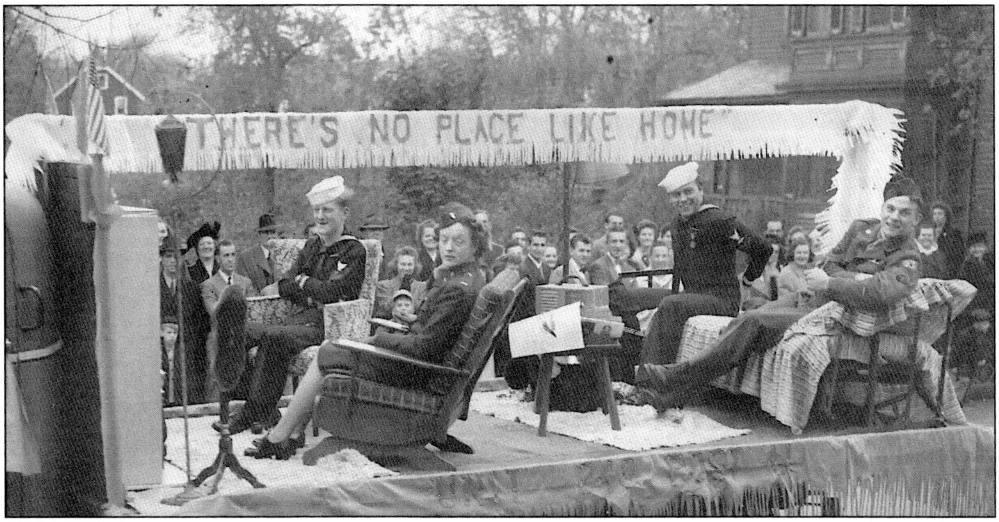

HOMECOMING PARADE, OCTOBER 29, 1946. Main Street was the locale for a grand and glorious Homecoming Parade to welcome home the veterans of World War II. Two of the many parade floats are shown here. In the top photo veterans Gerard Martyn (far left) and William O'Brien (far right) relax in a comfortable living room setting, which aptly expresses their feelings about being home again. In the lower photo, members of the Avenel Post of the Veterans of Foreign Wars send out a recruiting call for new members. Veterans' organizations such as the VFW and the American Legion and their auxiliaries remain strong community groups within the township. (William Gerity.)

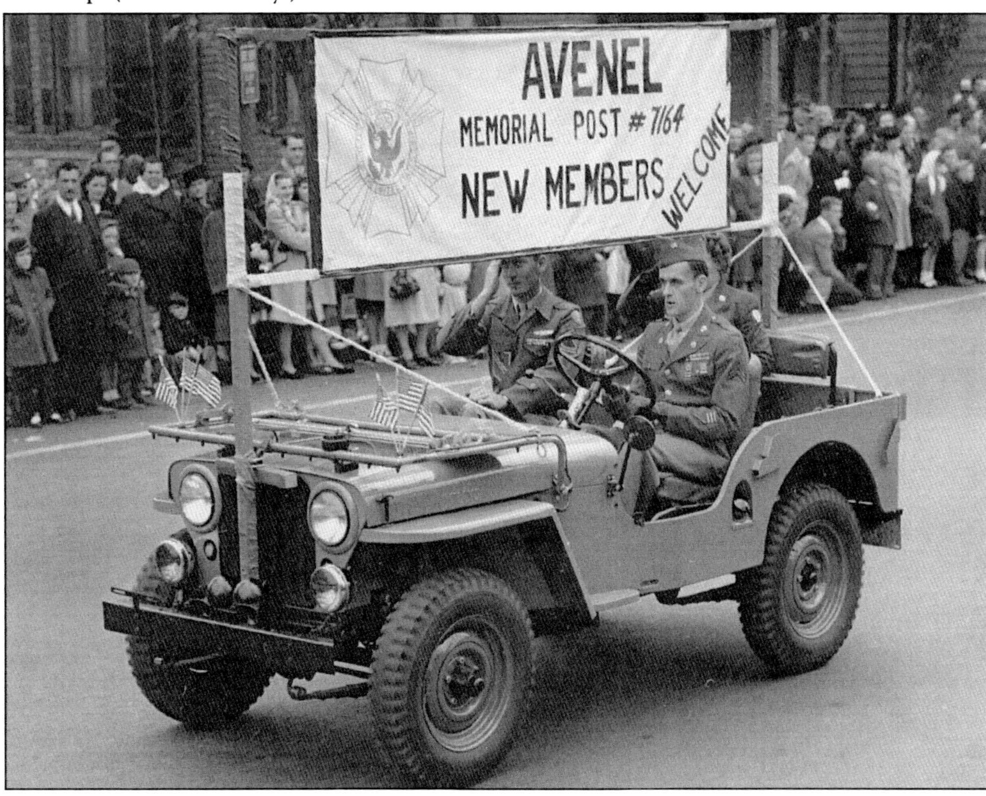

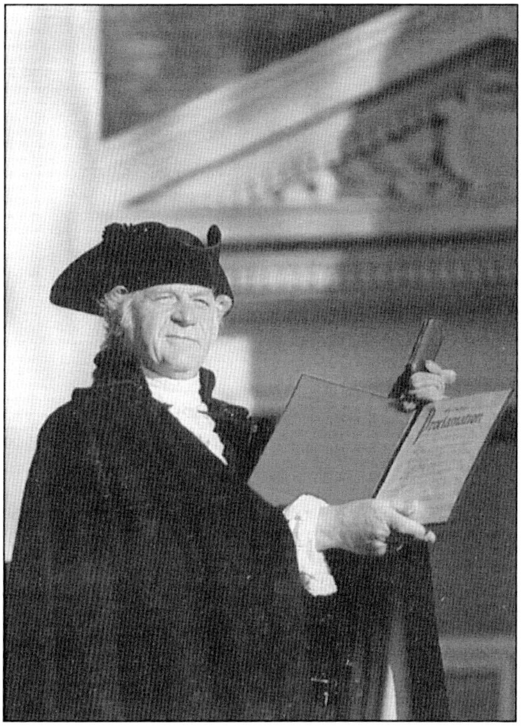

"HAIL TO THE CHIEF!" APRIL 22, 1989. "President George Washington," portrayed by actor William Summerfield, paid a visit to Woodbridge as part of the George Washington Bicentennial Inaugural Journey, a reenactment of Washington's trip from Virginia to NYC for his inauguration as first President of the United States on April 23, 1789. "Mr. Washington" stopped here at the Municipal Building and at the Cross Keys Tavern. (Photo by Tam Nguyen.)

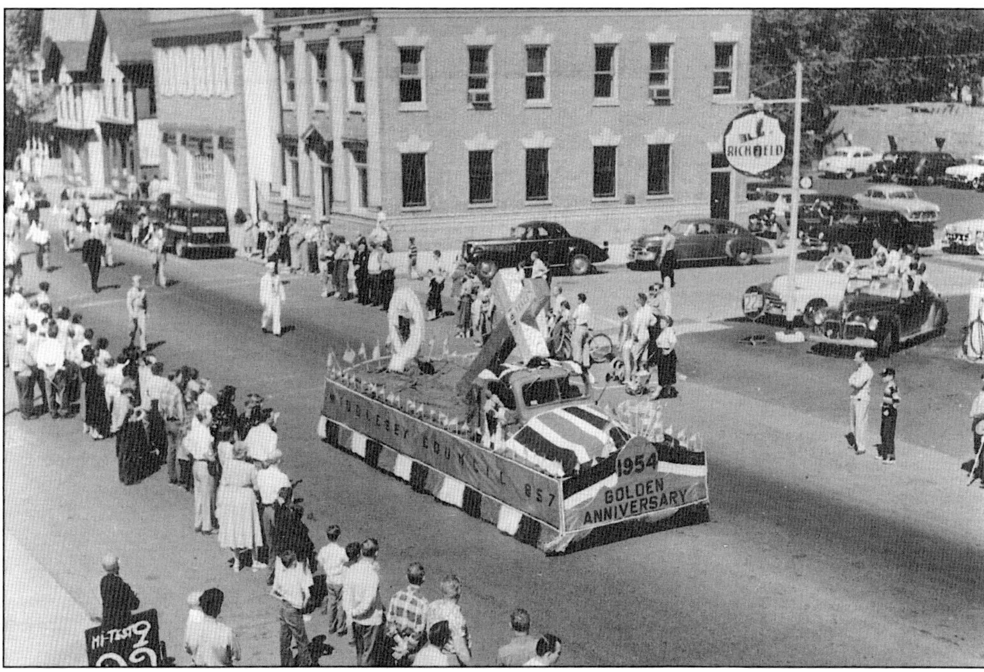

K OF C PARADE, 1954. Knights of Columbus Council (K of C) No. 857, which celebrated its golden anniversary with a parade on Main Street, is shown here marching past the Middlesex Water Company (the top center building—now the chamber of commerce headquarters), and the Pearl Street intersection. The K of C remains an active organization in town. (Nick Urban.)

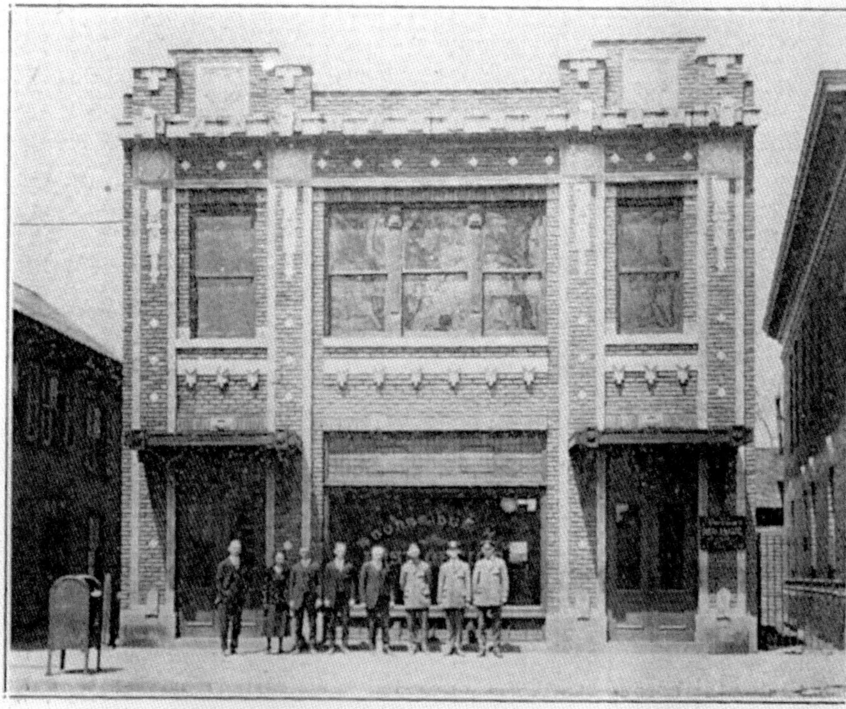

UNITED STATES POST OFFICE

Main Street

PETER A. GREINER, JR., Postmaster.

Office Hours

Executive Dept., 7 a. m. to 6:30 p. m.
Money Order Dept., 8 a. m. to 6 p. m.
General Delivery and Parcel Post, 8 a. m. to 6:30 p. m.
Registry Dept., 8 a. m. to 6:30 p. m.
Close 10 a. m. Holidays.
Delivery Service Carriers leave office
8:30 a. m. and 2:00 p. m.

No Money Orders issued on Holidays.

U.S. Post Office, 1924. This whole page advertisement, which appeared in the "Official Booklet" commemorating the dedication of the Memorial Municipal Building, provides a listing of postal services. Those were the days of two daily residential mail deliveries, brief holiday hours, a separate money order department, and postage stamps for pennies. The post office was located on lower Main Street next to the Middlesex Water Company. It later moved to Pearl Street before returning to Main Street in the 1960s. Postmaster Peter Greiner was the brother of longtime Township Mayor Augie Greiner.

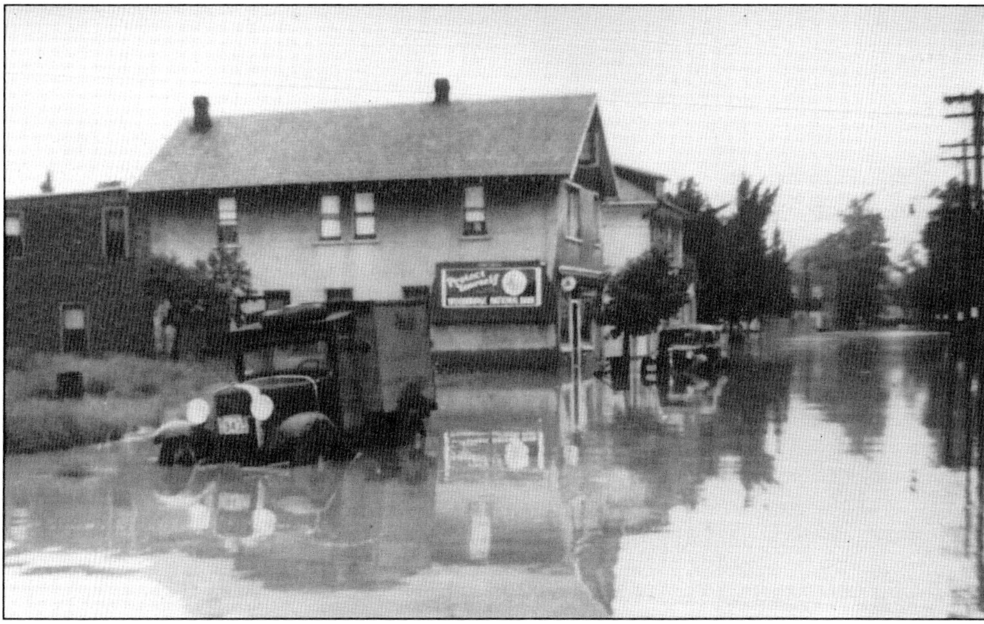

DOWNTOWN FLOODING, C. 1950. For years, Pearl Street, lower Main Street, and its vicinity became a virtual river of water when heavy rains caused Heard's Brook to overflow its banks. The Township Stream Widening Project of the 1970s brought an end to the problem of flooding and a change in the scenic appearance of the park.

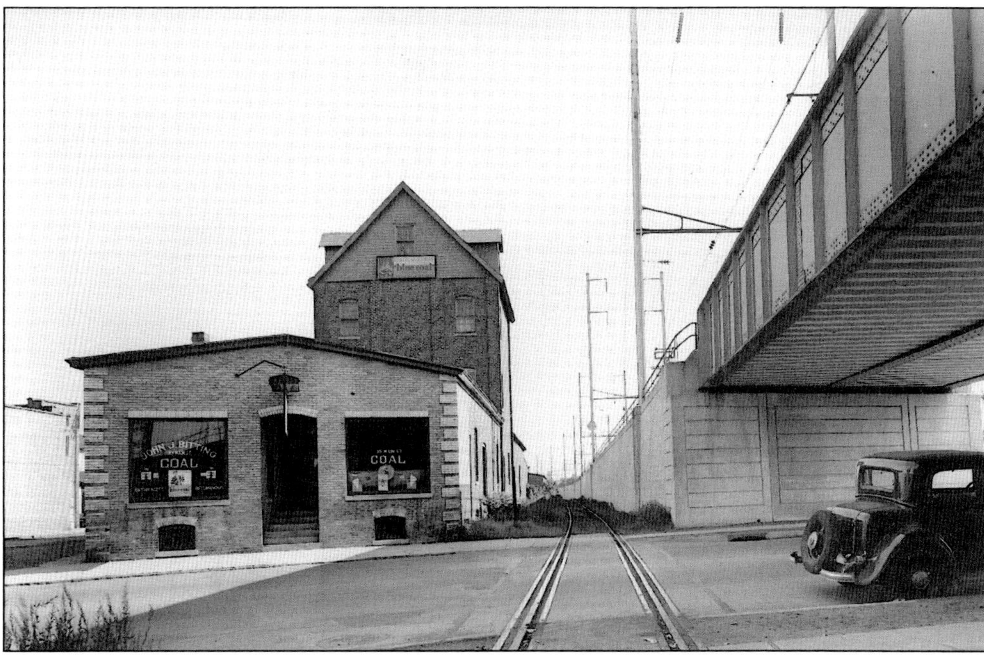

BITTING COAL CO., C. 1942. Located at 35 Main Street, John J. Bitting's coal company was one of several local coal dealers. Householders using coal faced many daily tasks to keep their home fires burning each winter. They had to shovel coal, shake down and shovel ashes, and finally carry them out for disposal. The building now houses the J.J. Bitting Brewing Co., a restaurant and bar.

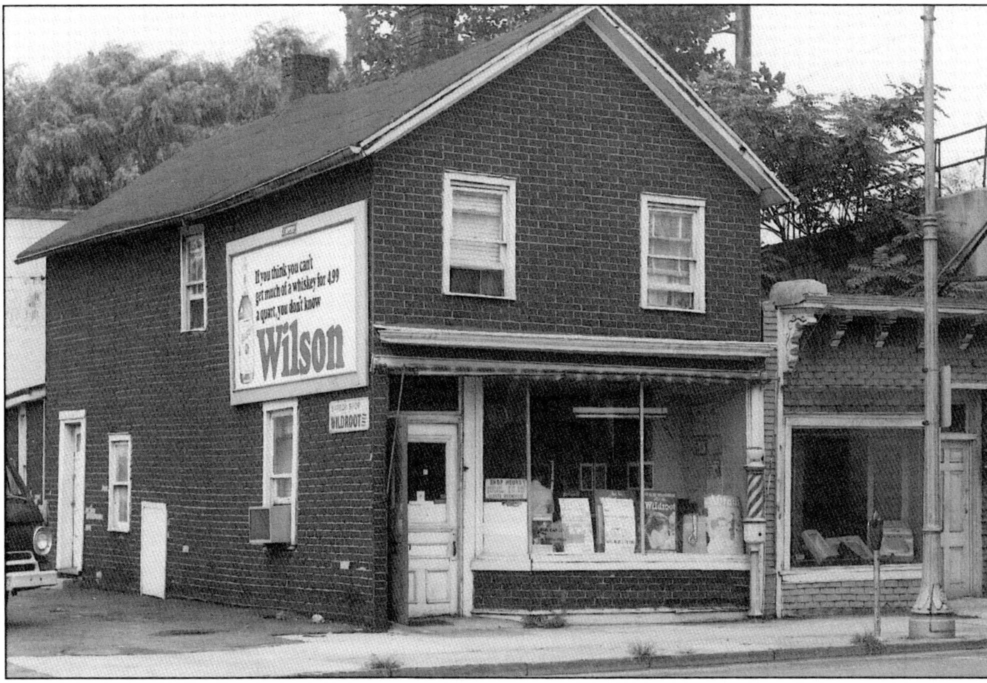

MAIN BARBER SHOP, C. 1955. A red-and-white spiraling barber's pole identifies this shop at 44 Main Street operated by Gil Sherman and Sol Dochinger. In times long past barbers also worked as surgeons, but during the reign of Henry VIII of England barber-surgeons were limited to blood-letting and tooth-pulling, practices that lasted into the early 20th century. The barber's pole is an ancient symbol representing the bandage with which a barber wrapped his patient after bloodletting (see page 59). (Bernie Anderson Sr.)

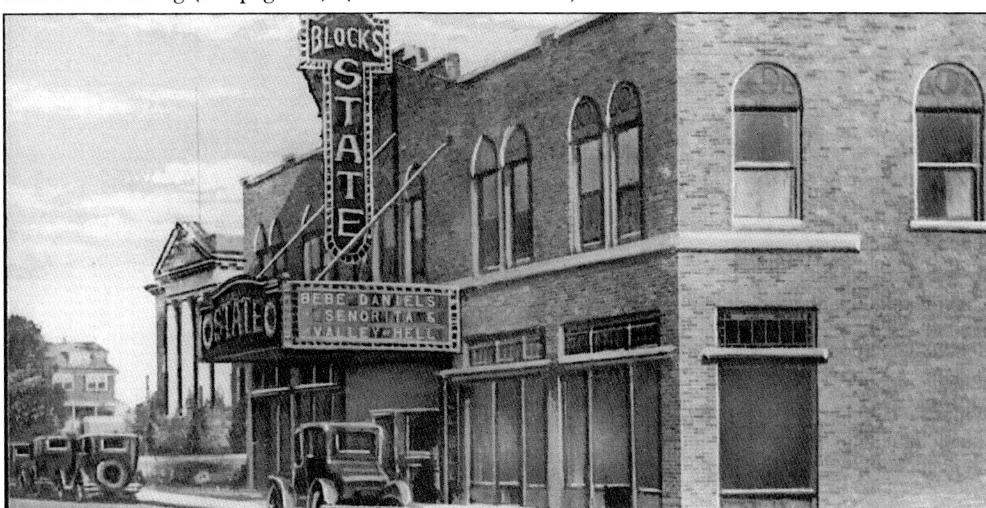

STATE THEATER, C. 1930. This building was torn down in the 1960s, but memories of the State Theater are not easily forgotten: Saturday afternoon matinees, cartoons, newsreels, dish nights, double features, small, printed programs of "Coming Attractions," the times when the lights went on to collect money for charity, ticket lines stretching onto Eleanor Place, and, of course, "Spec," the theater's faithful manager and ticket taker who kept his watchful eyes on all.

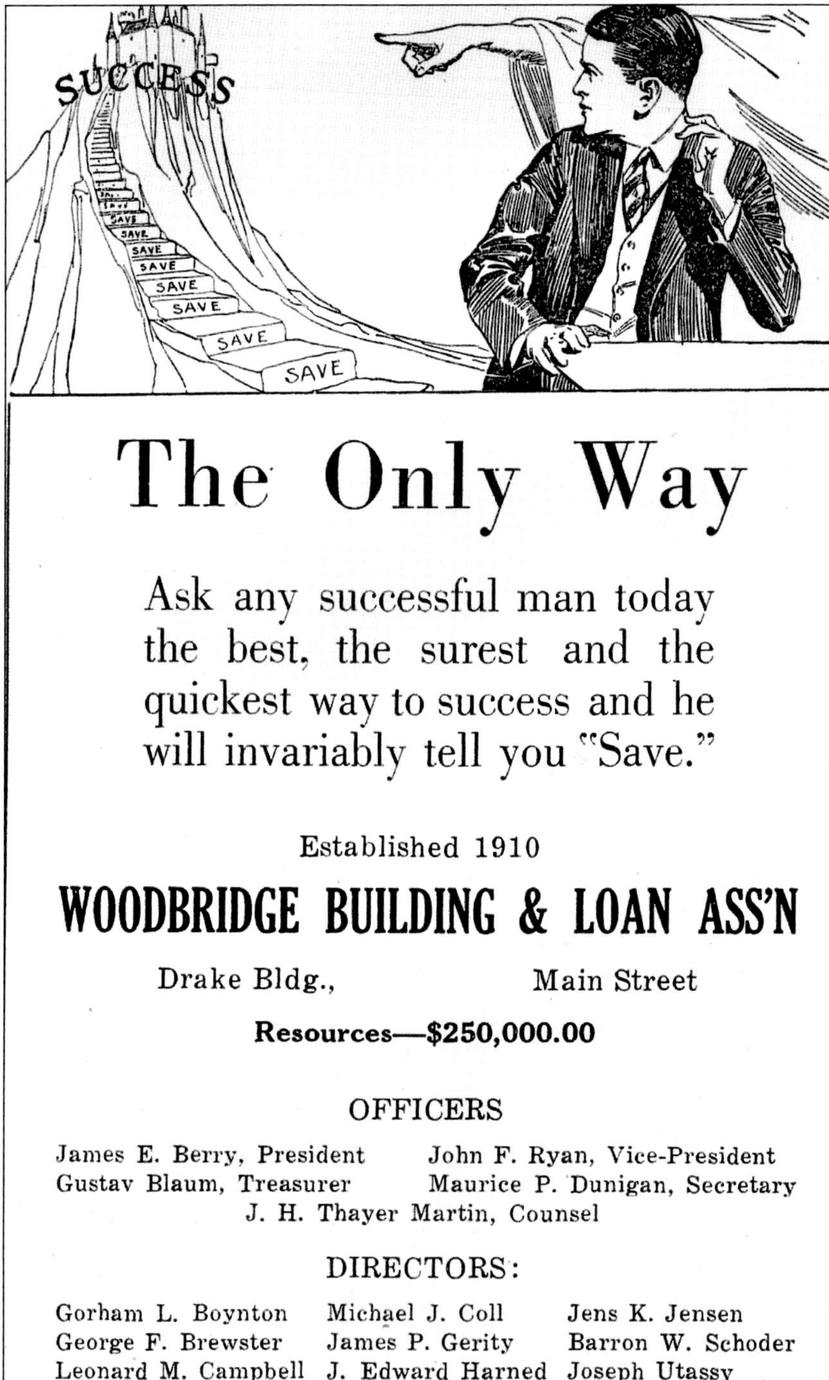

PATHWAY TO FINANCIAL SUCCESS, 1924. A mysterious guiding hand points the way to "success" through saving with the Woodbridge Building and Loan Association of Main Street. This advertisement is from the "Official Booklet" published for the dedication of the Memorial Municipal Building in June 1924. The ad reflects the brief years of prosperity that followed the end of World War I.

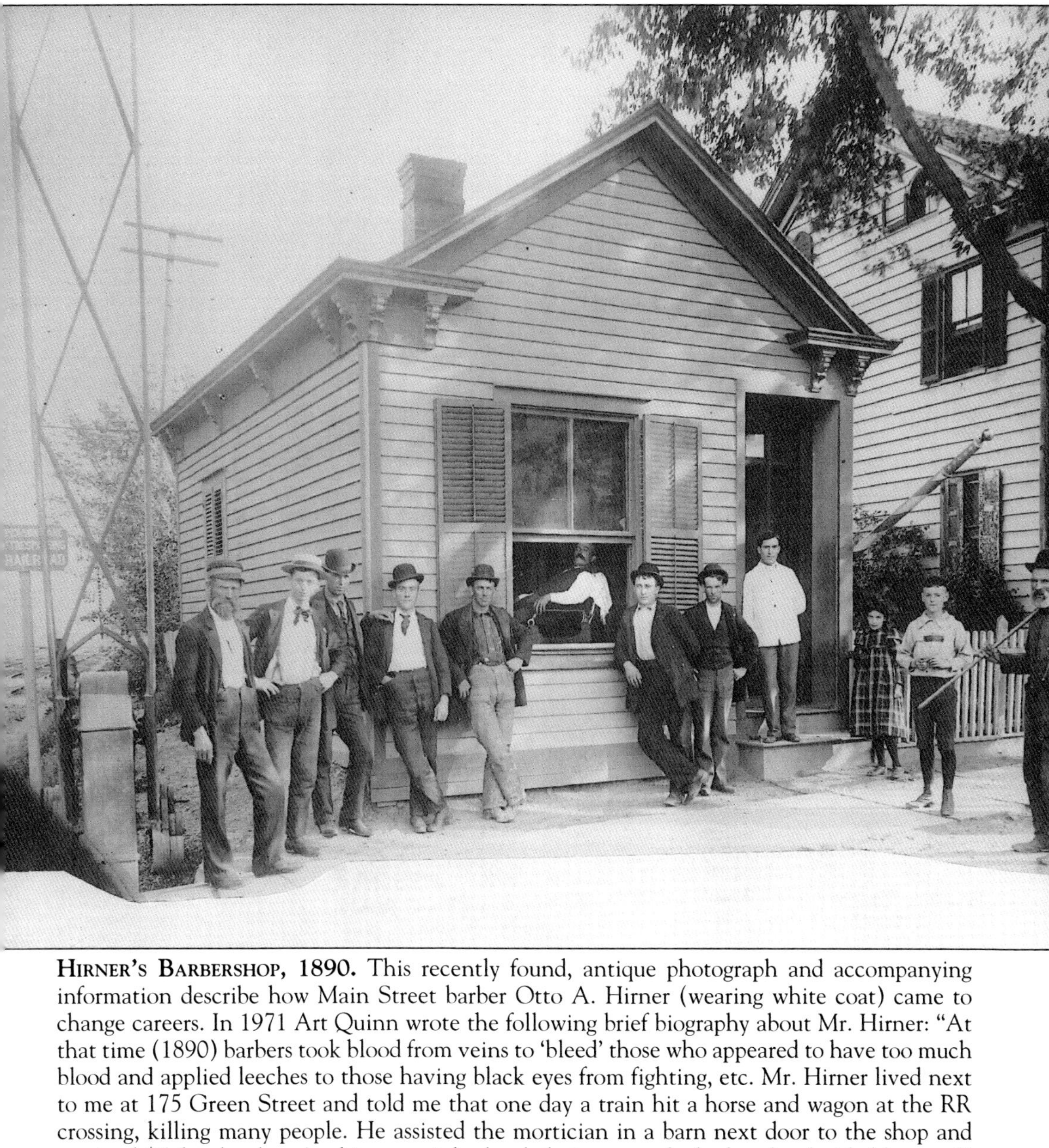

HIRNER'S BARBERSHOP, 1890. This recently found, antique photograph and accompanying information describe how Main Street barber Otto A. Hirner (wearing white coat) came to change careers. In 1971 Art Quinn wrote the following brief biography about Mr. Hirner: "At that time (1890) barbers took blood from veins to 'bleed' those who appeared to have too much blood and applied leeches to those having black eyes from fighting, etc. Mr. Hirner lived next to me at 175 Green Street and told me that one day a train hit a horse and wagon at the RR crossing, killing many people. He assisted the mortician in a barn next door to the shop and received $5 for the day. As this was triple the daily income of a barber, he decided he would become a mortician! He hung out a sign . . . He was a very nice person—never got 'old' in his manner—was very interested in everything and well liked by all. Was nicknamed 'Unk' Hirner. Guess it was because he was like an uncle to people. Mr. Hirner was in excellent shape until he had an operation in 1961. He died a few months later from complications." Mayor Greiner learned the mortuary business from Mr. Hirner and later started the Greiner Funeral Home on Green Street. (Chris Quinn.)

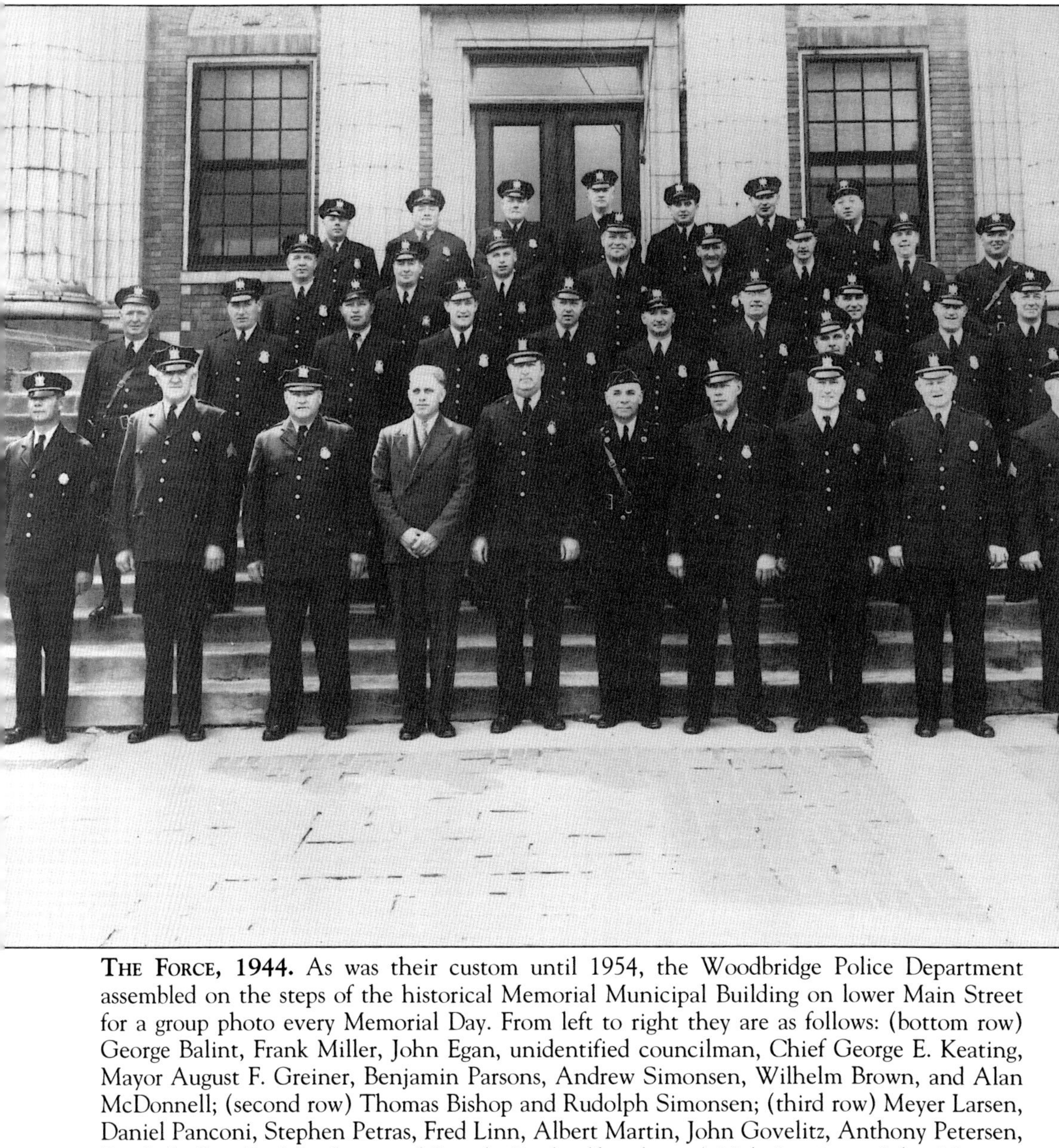

THE FORCE, 1944. As was their custom until 1954, the Woodbridge Police Department assembled on the steps of the historical Memorial Municipal Building on lower Main Street for a group photo every Memorial Day. From left to right they are as follows: (bottom row) George Balint, Frank Miller, John Egan, unidentified councilman, Chief George E. Keating, Mayor August F. Greiner, Benjamin Parsons, Andrew Simonsen, Wilhelm Brown, and Alan McDonnell; (second row) Thomas Bishop and Rudolph Simonsen; (third row) Meyer Larsen, Daniel Panconi, Stephen Petras, Fred Linn, Albert Martin, John Govelitz, Anthony Petersen, Frank Szallar, Fred Leidner, and Joseph Grady; (fourth row) Nels Lauritzen, John Manton, Horace Deter, William Romond, Martin Thullesen, Elmer Krysko, Kenneth Van Pelt, and Joseph Farkas; (top row) Closindo Zucaro, Joseph Casale, Henry Dunham, Joseph Sipos, Charles Wagonhoffer, John Ondeyko, and William Majoros. Joe Dalton, Richard Levi, Tom Lockie, and Carl Sundquist were on duty at the time of the photo. Steve Fiertag and Arnt Petersen were serving in the armed forces. (Bernie Anderson Sr.)

Four

Faces and Places: 1861–1940

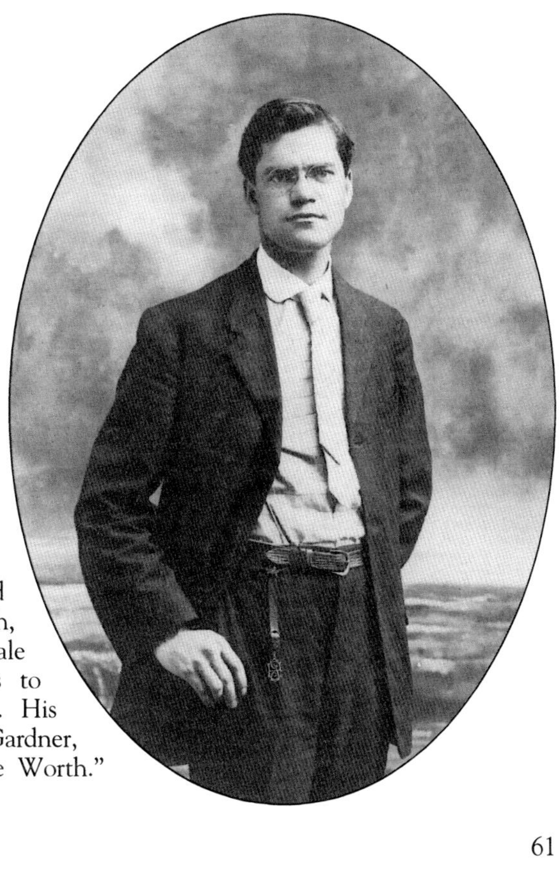

Freeman Worth Gardner, c. 1904. Through his dedication to and extensive study of local history, Freeman Worth Gardner (1884–1943) became the township historian and a well-known genealogical researcher. A bachelor, Mr. Gardner was employed in the offices of the Pennsylvania Railroad, and with his PRR pass he traveled throughout the country. After his death, his niece, Mrs. Harry Baker of Ridgedale Avenue, donated his voluminous files to the NJ Historical Society in Newark. His nephew, local resident Burnham Gardner, affectionately remembers him as "Uncle Worth." (Burnham Gardner.)

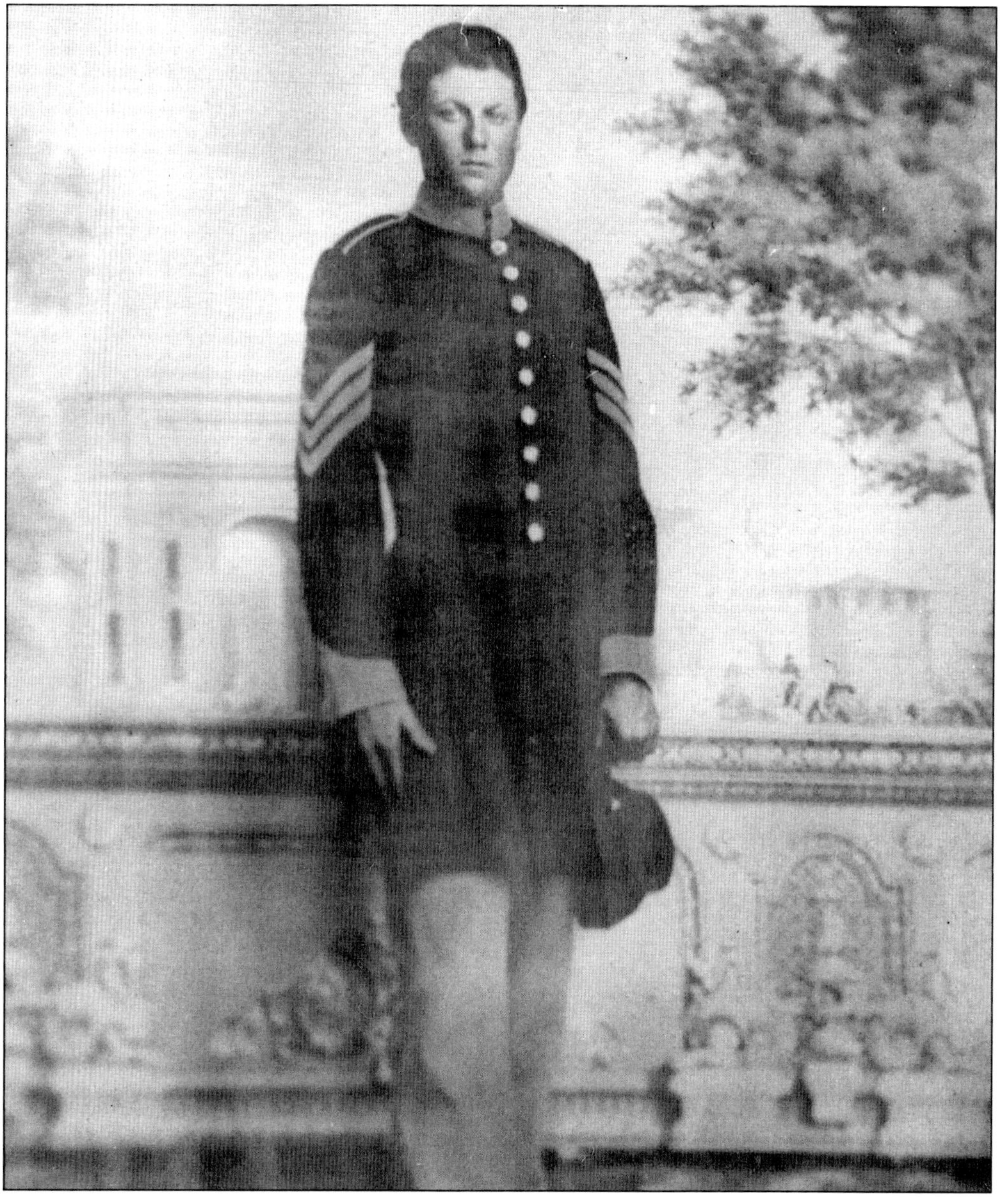

CIVIL WAR VETERAN. Woodbridge resident John F. Lee enlisted with Company H of the Fifth NJ Volunteers, nicknamed the "Pike Guard" by Union general Joseph Hooker. John Lee was wounded at Gettysburg on July 2, 1863, while his regiment was on picket duty at Emmittsburg Road and was taken prisoner by the Confederacy. Released later that year, John returned to his regiment. He was awarded a medal for conspicuous gallantry for saving the regimental colors of the Fifth NJ Volunteers at Gettysburg. John served his entire term with his regiment, which fought 32 engagements, including the 1862 Battles of Williamsburg, Savage's Station, and the Peninsular Campaign in Virginia. After the war, John returned home and joined the William C. Berry chapter, Grand Army of the Republic, Post No. 85. (The chapter was named in memory of local industrialist William H. Berry's son, a lieutenant with the Fifth NJ Volunteers, who was killed at Williamsburg.) John F. Lee died in 1910 and is buried in the Presbyterian Church Cemetery. (Ed McGuinn and George Ryan.)

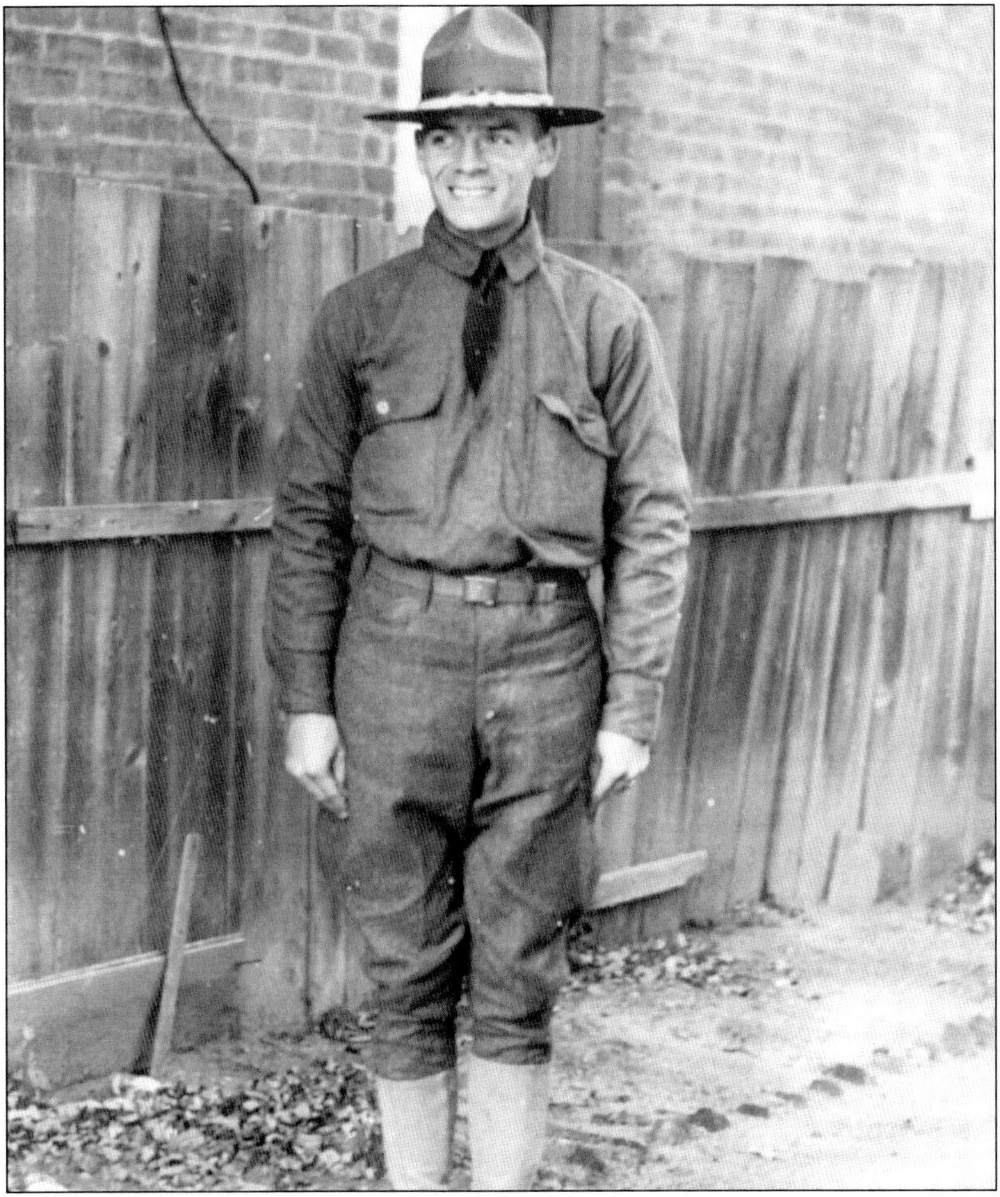

YOUNG AUGIE GREINER, C. 1917. August Furman Greiner, Republican mayor of Woodbridge from 1934 to 1951 and owner of the Greiner Funeral Home on Green Street, served with the American Expeditionary Forces of World War I. Greiner took office during the Great Depression and initiated a refinancing plan that saved the township from bankruptcy. Other changes that took place during his 18 years as mayor included the reopening of the Woodbridge National Bank in 1936 (which had been closed for several years), the purchase of the first ambulance, and the establishment of the township first aid squads. Mayor Greiner led Woodbridge through the difficult years of World War II and later assisted veterans resettling into civilian life in the township. In April 1951, he announced that he would not run for another term. Augie Greiner was a popular township personage who was returned to office many times by both Democrats and Republicans. He remained an active citizen and businessman in town until his death in 1965. (Nancy Burk Vasconcellos.)

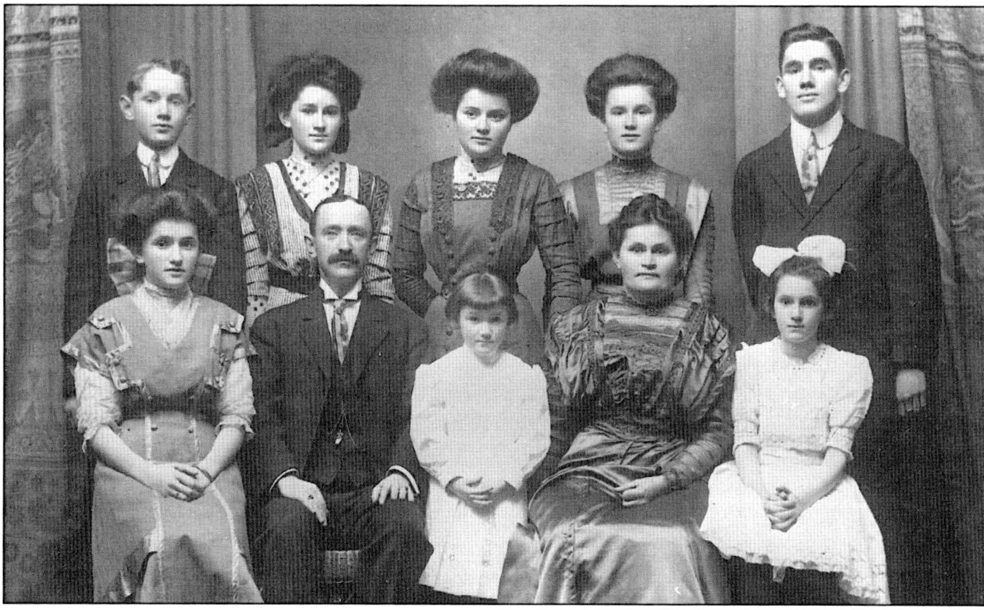

Farrell Family, c. 1908. Charles S. Farrell was employed as assistant superintendent of the Port Reading Coal Docks. From left to right, the Farrells are as follows: (seated) Gertrude; Charles; Margaret (later Mrs. Leonard Murphy); Charles's wife, Josephine Berton Farrell; and daughter Josephine (Mrs. Robert Ringwood); (standing) Charles Jr., who died in World War I; Leona (Mrs. Larry McLeod); Elizabeth (Mrs. Owen S. Dunigan); Theresa (Mrs. Leon Campbell); and Samuel. Many Farrell descendants still live in the area. (Robert Ringwood.)

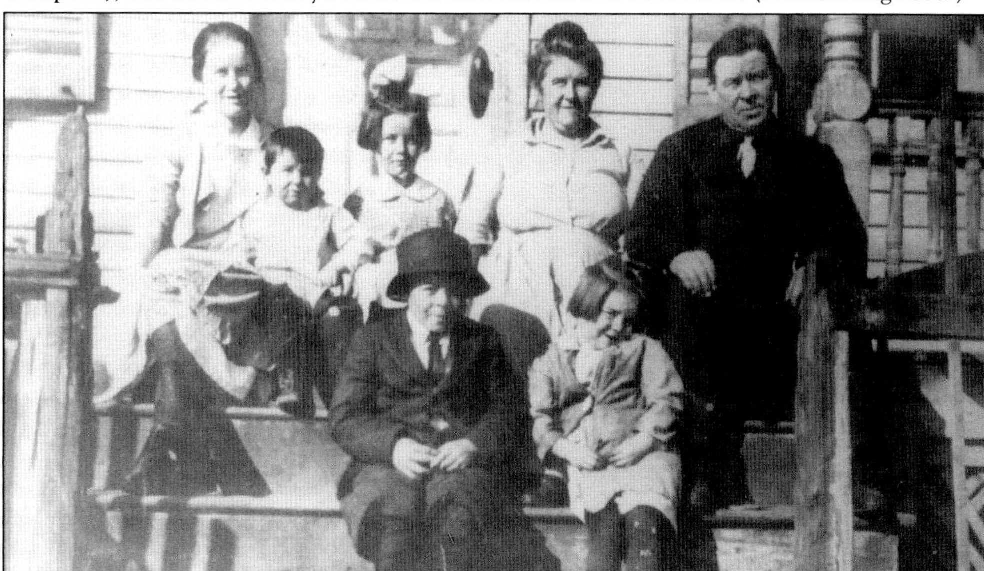

William Gerity's Family, c. 1917. From left to right are as follows: (front row) David and Anna (later Mrs. Dennis Kelly); (back row) Marie (Mrs. Leo Moffitt); Leon J.; Jane (Mrs. Thomas McDonough); William's wife, Mary Pender Gerity; and William. The family gathers on the porch of their home, probably on Second Street. William's father and mother emigrated from Ireland and settled on Fulton Street in 1871. For many years Leon J. Gerity and his family have operated their funeral home on Amboy Avenue. (Pat McDonough Brisson.)

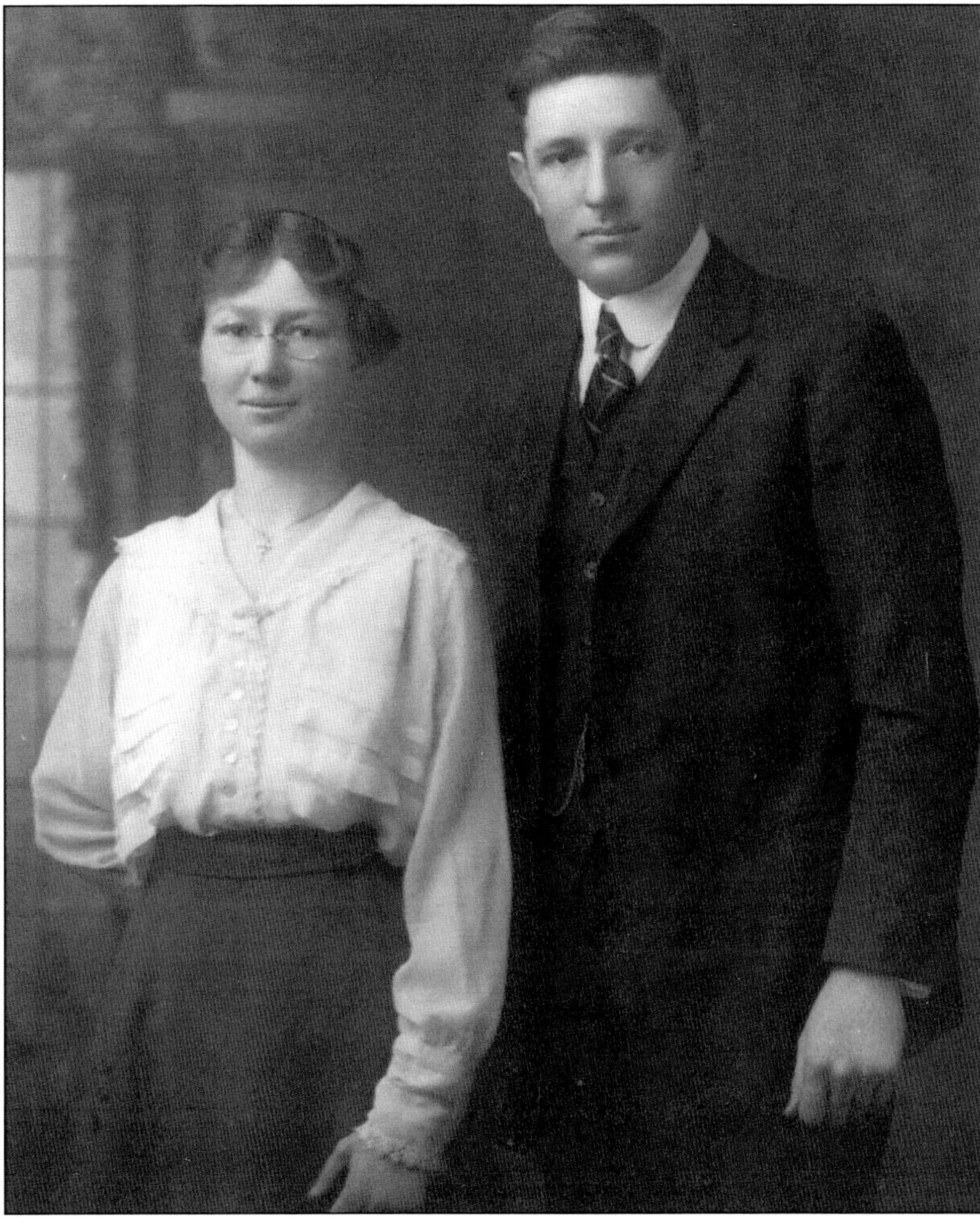

WOODBRIDGE NEWLYWEDS, 1917. Thora Louise Thomsen McEwen (1893–1990) and Joseph McEwen (1888–1961) were married at the First Presbyterian Church on September 29, 1917. Lifelong Woodbridge residents, both were first generation citizens. Thora's family came from Denmark, while Joseph's emigrated from England and Ireland. The couple had four children: Joseph, Robert (co-author of this book and *Woodbridge, Volume One*), Kathryn, and Jeannette. As of 1998, their family tree has expanded to 13 grandchildren and 18 great-grandchildren. Thora had the distinction of being one of the five graduates in the 1911 Class of Woodbridge High School (WHS). Joseph, a mason and builder, completed his apprenticeship as a mason at the age of 18 and built his first four-family house at age 20. As a young man in 1911, he supervised and worked on the construction of the parish house of the First Presbyterian Church on Rahway Avenue.

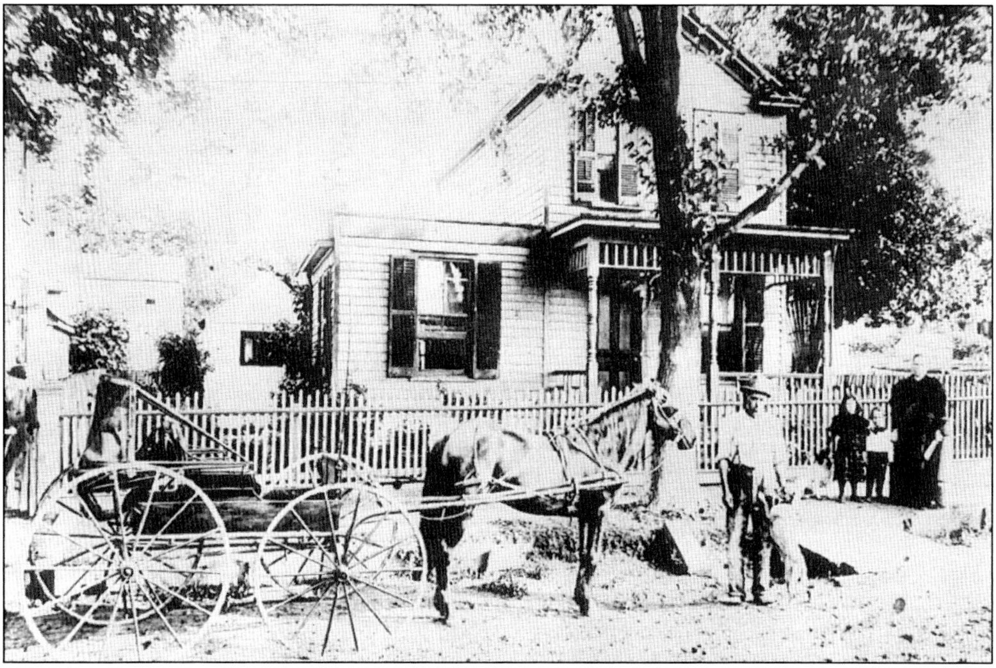

EARLY HOMESTEAD, C. 1900. The Deters of 63 Caroline Street portray a quiet picture of small town family life with their horse and buggy, two dogs, and cozy frame house, complete with picket fence. Built in 1864, the house is now owned by the Mecsics family. (Ruth Mecsics.)

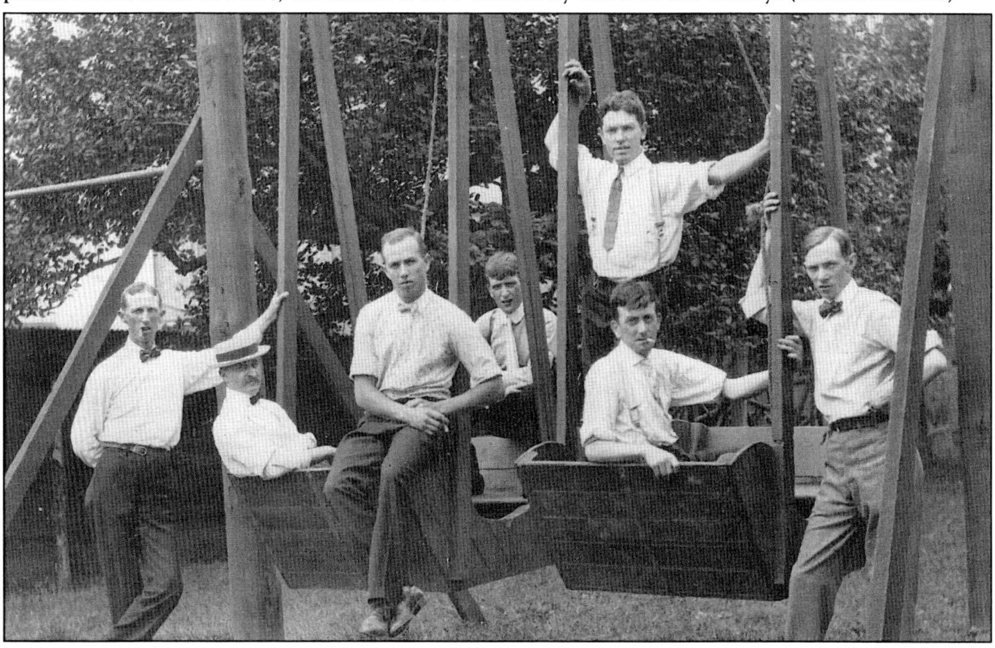

SUMMER OUTING, C. 1910. From left to right, Joe Dunigan, John Leisen, Owen Dunigan, J. Buttler, John Brown (standing), John Corgin, and Maurice P. Dunigan stop the swings for a photo opportunity at Washington Hall on upper Grove Street. A once popular picnic spot for the firemen's annual outing and other community get-togethers, Washington Hall has long since disappeared. (William "Barry" Dunigan.)

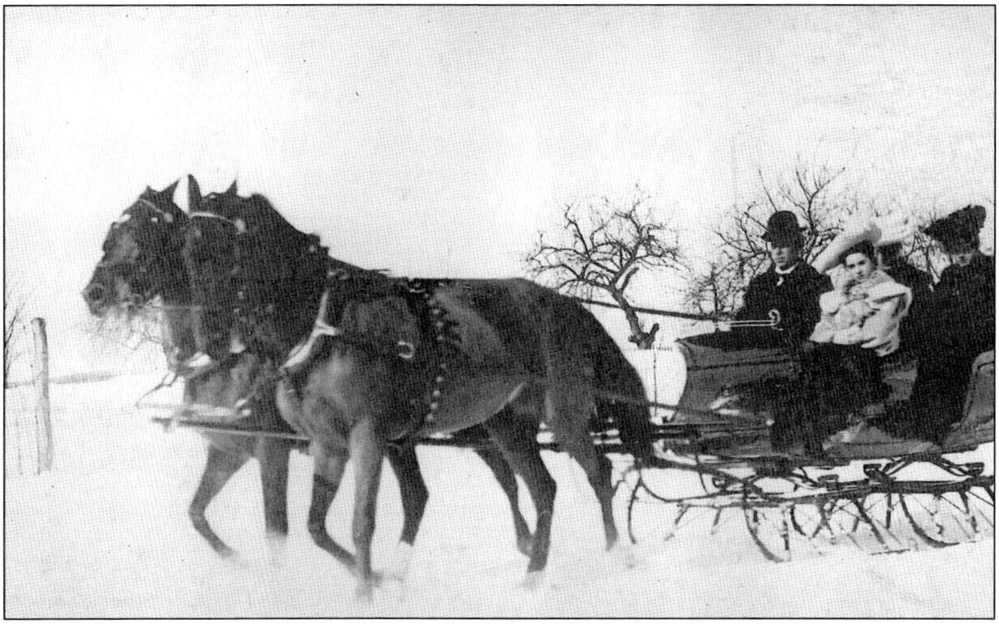

The Horses Know the Way, c. 1890. Bundled up for a wintry sleigh ride, Tom Dunigan and his family must have enjoyed the jingle of sleigh bells and the crunch of runners on the snow, sounds not often heard nowadays. Tom was the son of Bernard Dunigan, the first of his family to arrive in Woodbridge. (William "Barry" Dunigan.)

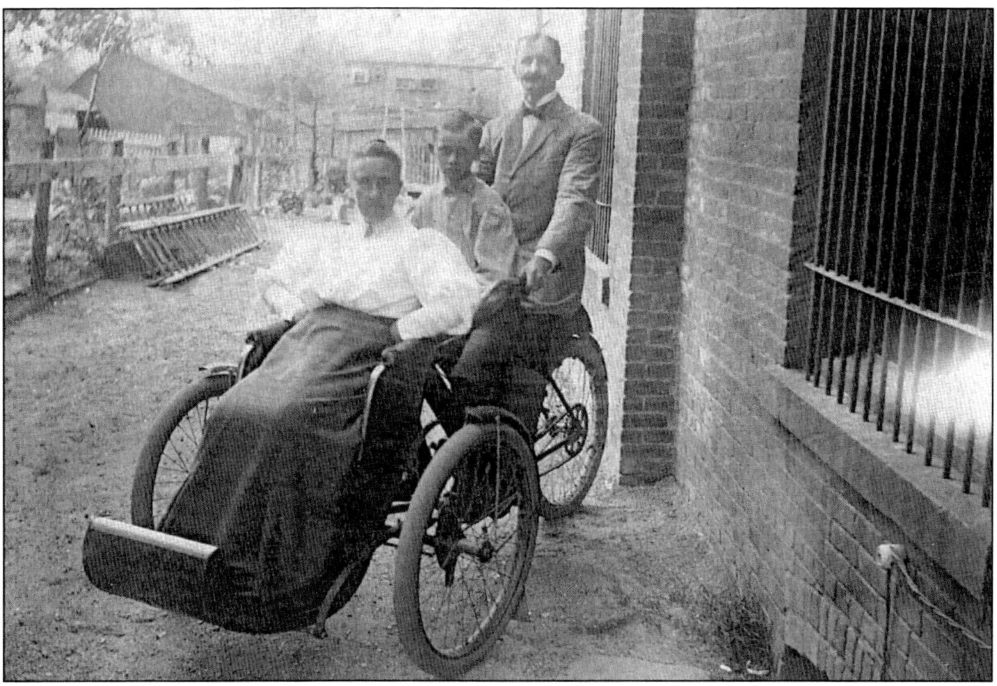

On a Bicycle Built for Three! c. 1900. Charles Edward Peterson (at the handlebars), his wife, Charlotta Olivia, and their son Titus (nicknamed "Jim") are ready for an invigorating spin about town. Titus saw service on the battleship *Arizona,* before World War II. (Raymond and Joan Peterson.)

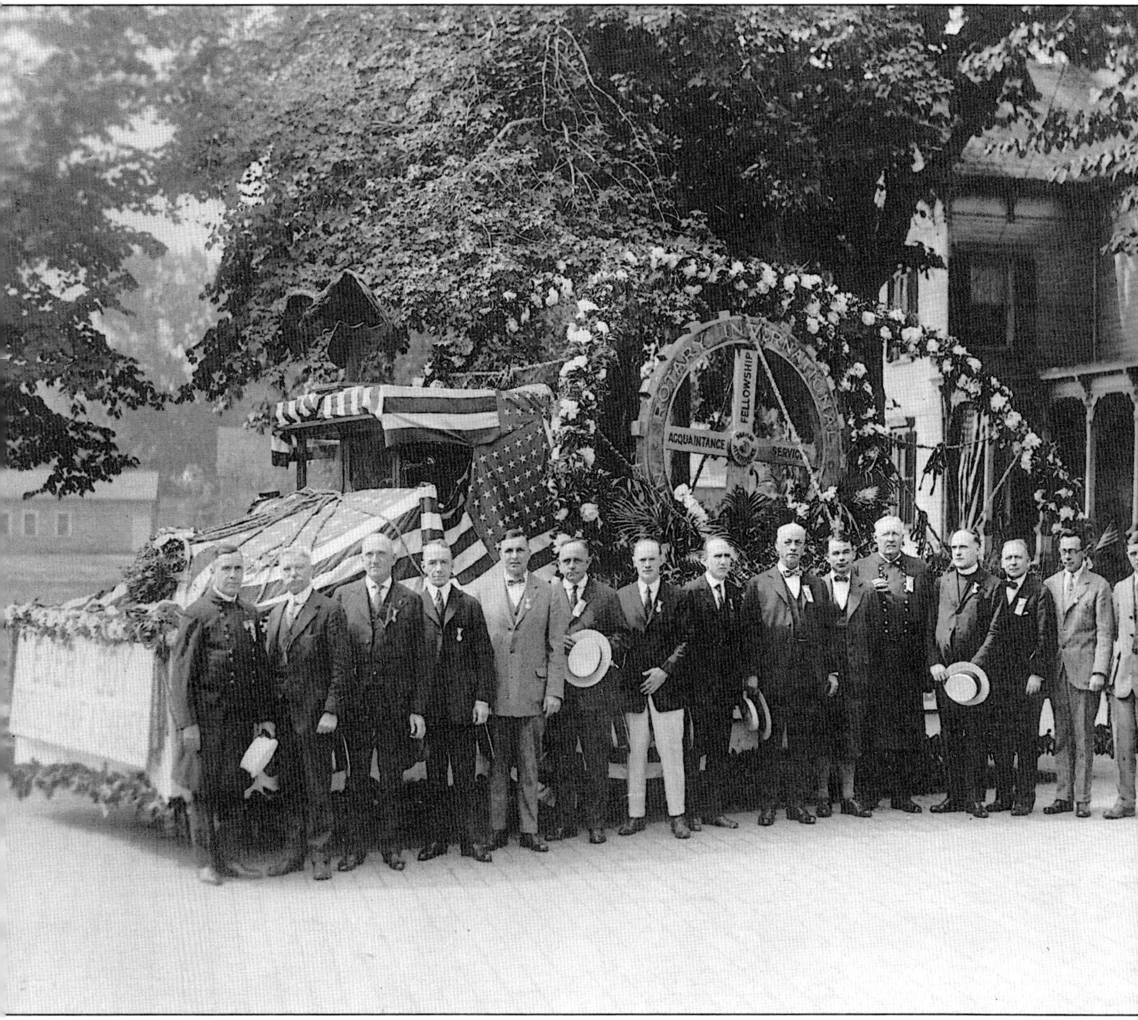

ROTARIANS ALL, JUNE 14, 1924. Organized in Woodbridge in 1923, Rotary Club members assemble near the home of Gus Campbell on Grove Street before marching in the Township's 255th Anniversary Parade. Standing by their elaborately decorated float of fresh flowers, which received honorable mention, are, from left to right, Robert Hirner (funeral home director), Ira T. Spencer (physician), Andrew Keyes (road contractor), John Serena (hardware store owner), Walter H. Warr (coal businessman), Gorham Boynton (lumber businessman), Edward Harned (insurance agent), Raymond Jackson (druggist), Fred Anness (hollow tile businessman), John M. Kreger (clay mining engineer), David Brown (retired businessman), Father Meyers, Hugh Williamson Kelly (the *Independent* newspaper owner), Oscar Wilkerson (Security Steel Co. owner), and Charles Lewis (marine construction businessman). The International Rotary Club was founded in 1905 by a Chicago lawyer, Paul P. Harris, to develop high ethical standards among business and professional people who serve the community. Since Mr. Harris scheduled members to meet in rotation at their places of business, the club became known as the "Rotary Club." (The Rotary Club of Woodbridge.)

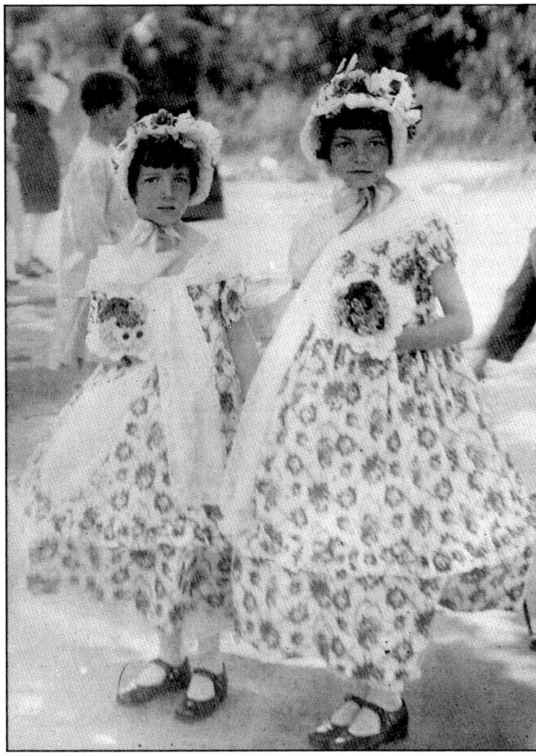

SUNBONNET GIRLS, C. 1927. Jean (left) and Evelyn Kreger took first prize in the "prettiest" category of the Woodbridge Baby Parade. They wore lacy bonnets and printed dresses with hoopskirts made by their mother, Evelyn. The girls won a kitchen table and benches. Evelyn and Jean were winners again later, when they dressed as Raggedy Ann and Andy and took first prize for the "funniest costumes." (Jean Kreger Jost.)

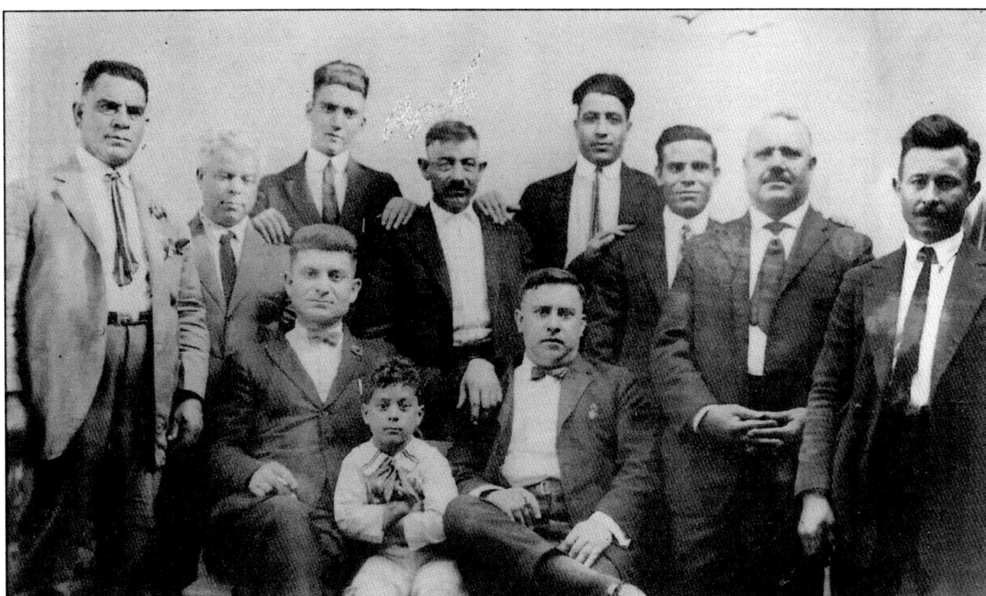

ITALIAN-AMERICAN CLUB, C. 1921. From left to right, the members of this community organization are as follows: (seated) F. Cacciola; Richard Janni, who must have been the very youngest member; and Anthony Barcellona; (standing) A. Marino of Fords; Carmelo Janni; Angelo Carcuri; Vincent Manganaro; M. Trabonella; Sam Ferraro; C. Simmone; and Charles Bellanca. The club held their meetings at Barcellona's Barber Shop on Main Street. (Mickey Manganaro.)

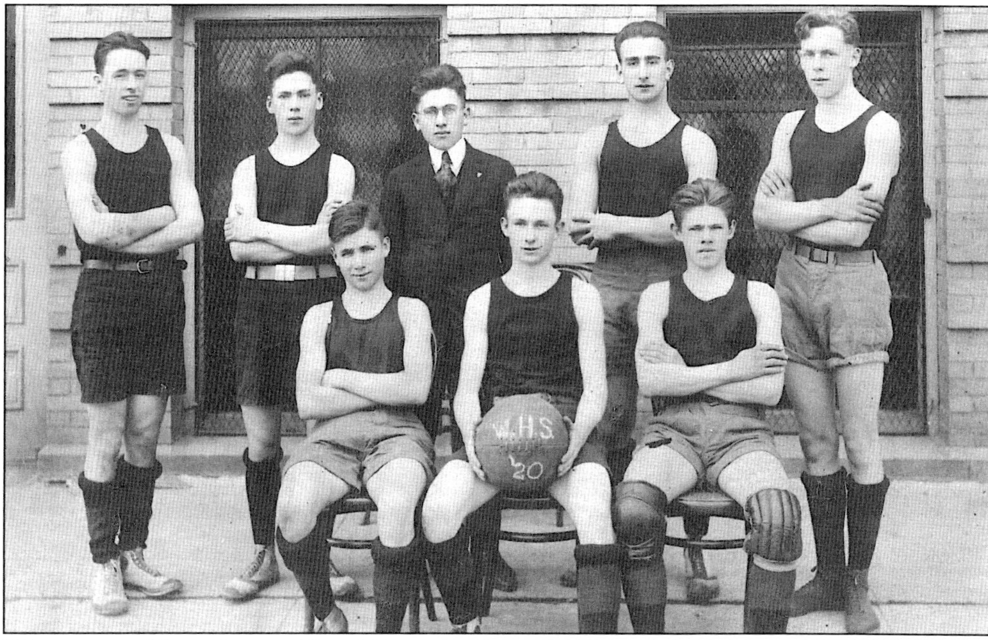

WOODBRIDGE HIGH SCHOOL BOYS' BASKETBALL, 1920. From left to right are as follows: (front row) Jacob Schwenzer, Russell Lorch, and Bill Martin; (back row) Victor Drummond, Ed Potter, coach Martin Brown, Lewis Nork, and Harry Tappen. They appear ready to take on all opposition. (Herbert Christensen.)

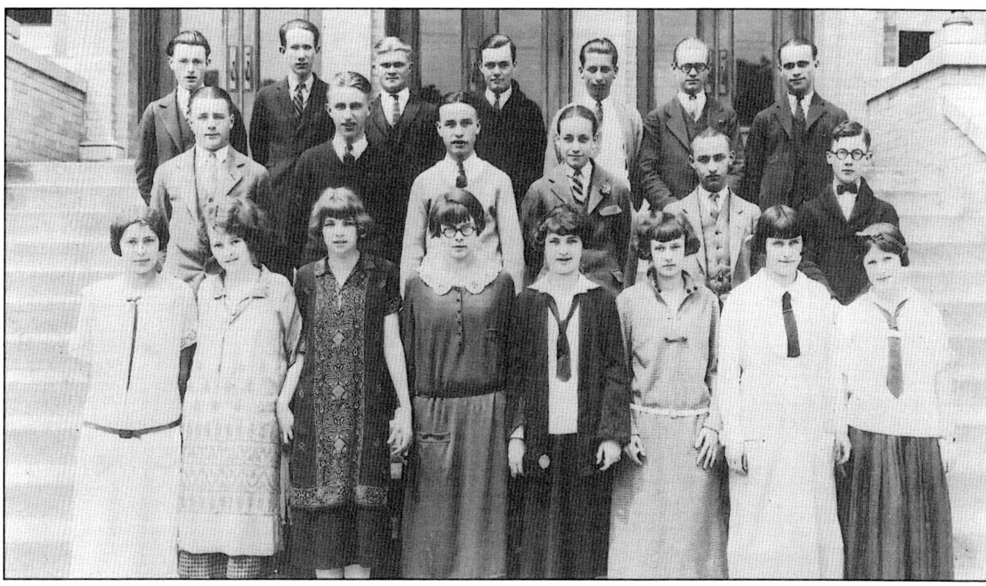

WHS JUNIOR PLAY CAST, 1924–1925. Assembled for an off-stage photo are the following, from left to right: (bottom row) Margaret Voorhees Booton, Genevieve Ryan Neary, Lois Wiant, Helen Dockstader Lauritsen, Pearl Filer Sandahl, Evelyn Schoonover, Alba Formodoni, and Helen Harned; (middle row) Vincent Tomsen, Charles Jacobs, Thomas Desmond, Edward Kaus, Elmer Vecsey, and Kenneth Caufield; (back row) Bob May, John Strohm, Edward Augustine, Stanley Kjeldsen, Arthur Anderson, Allen Thergeson, and teacher Richard Stauffer. (William "Barry" Dunigan.)

BELOVED TEACHER, 1960. Martha J. Morrow, head of the Social Science Department at WHS, was active in Republican politics and community affairs. The Township honored her by naming the footbridge over Heard's Brook near South Park Drive the "Martha Morrow Bridge." In 1986 the Woodbridge Free Public Library Board of Trustees dedicated their downstairs meeting room to her in "appreciation of her outstanding efforts on behalf of library development."

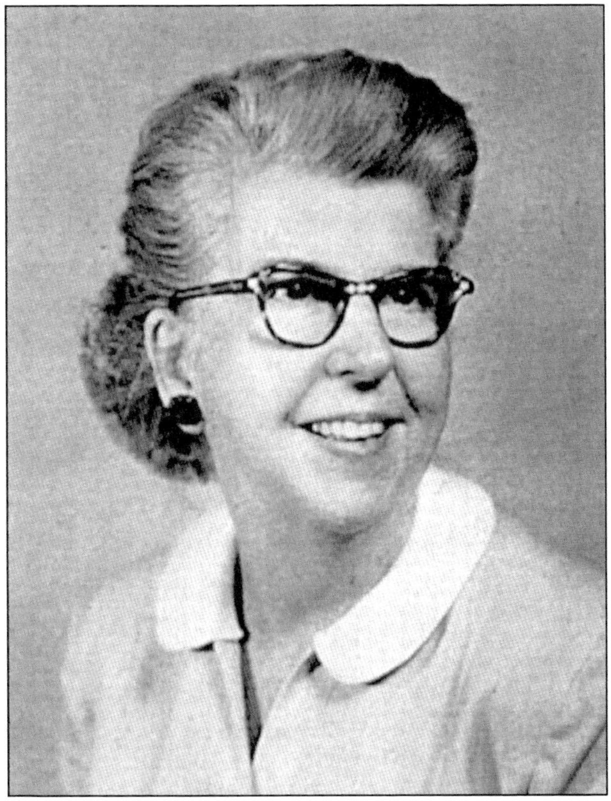

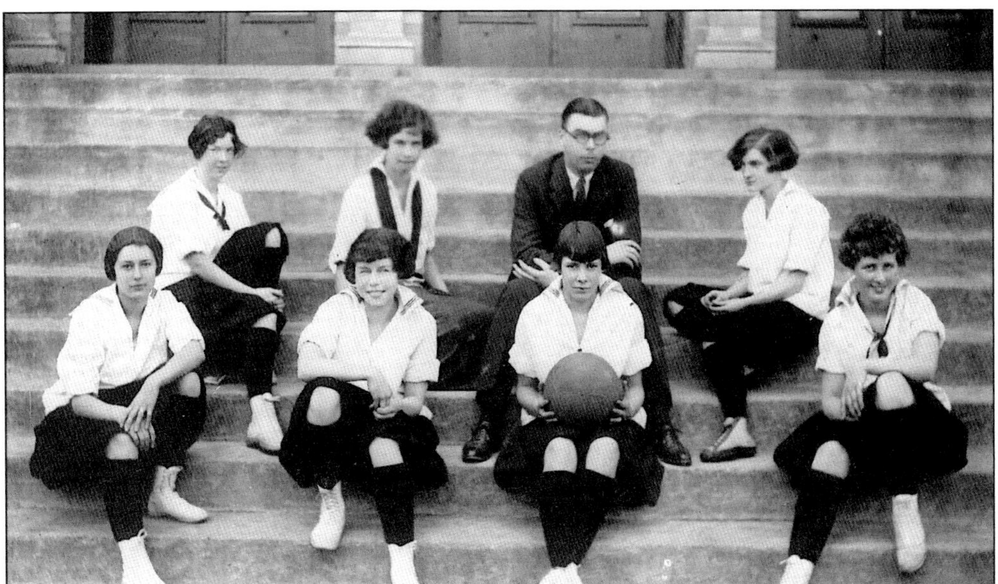

WHS GIRLS' BASKETBALL, 1924. Seated on the high school front steps with their coach Bryan Rothfuss, the team members are from left to right, as follows: (bottom row) Margaret Voorhees, Dot Nelson, Captain Florence Voorhees, and Helen Johnson; (top row) Carol Martin, Grace Rankin, and Olive Sandholt. Grace Rankin served as captain for the 1926–1927 season. (Margaret Voorhees Booton.)

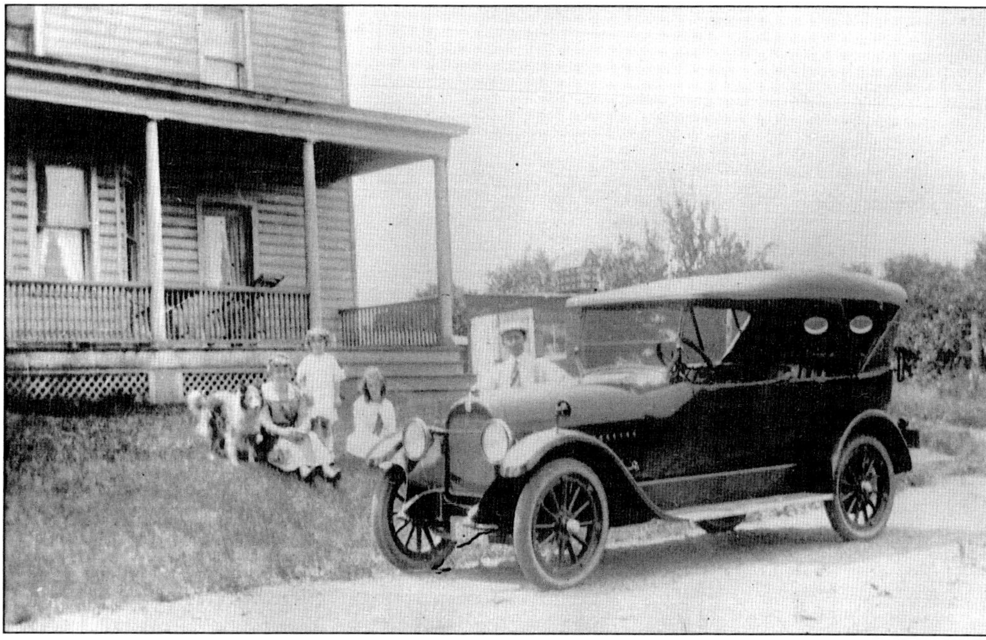

Nielsen Family, c. 1915. Although Jurgen Nielsen was a local blacksmith (see page 103), he and his family obviously enjoyed owning a "horseless carriage." Jurgen stands by his automobile, while his wife, Jensine, their daughters, Dagmar (seated) and Jeanette, and their dog relax on the front lawn. (Carol Agesen Dunigan.)

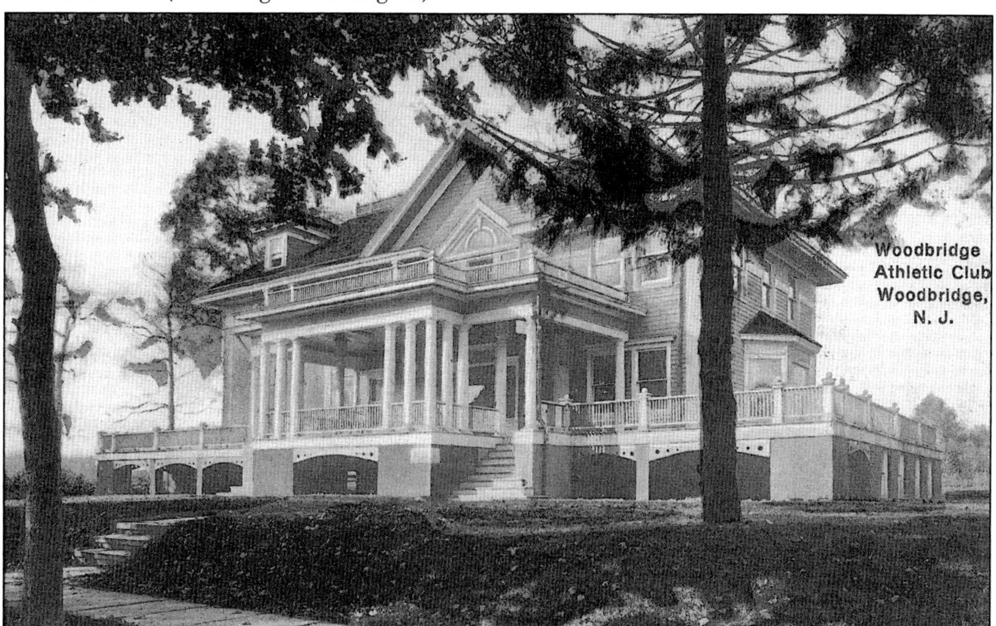

Woodbridge Athletic Club, c. 1920. Located on Grove Avenue at the Cedar Street corner not far from the old Woodbridge High School on Barron Avenue, this impressive, pillared structure was a social gathering place for its members, who enjoyed dancing in the ballroom, bowling, billiards, and tennis. When the club closed, the building was turned to face Cedar Street and now houses several apartments.

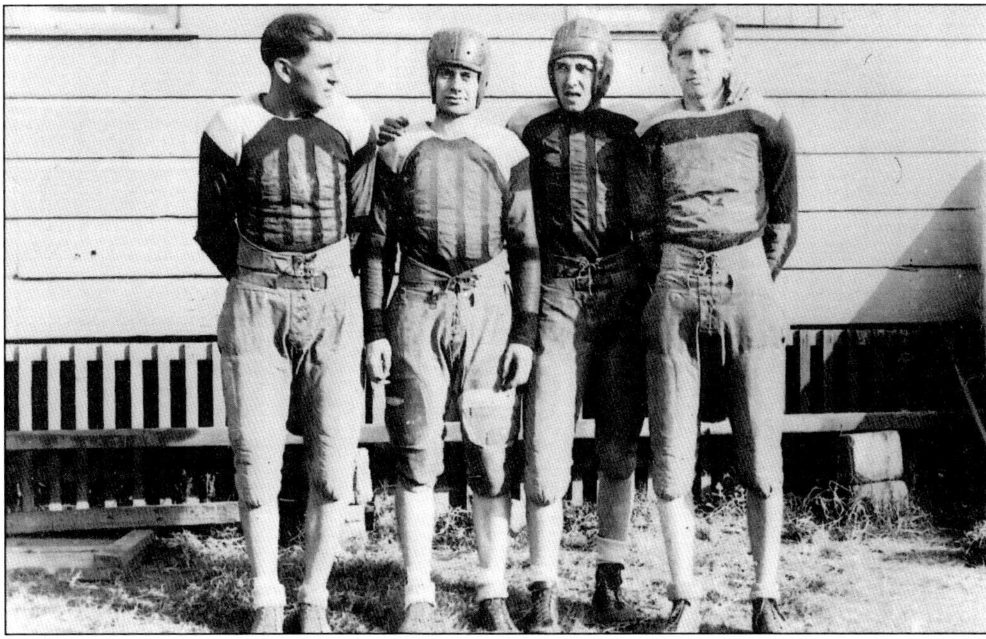

WHS VARSITY FOOTBALL, 1931. From left to right as follows: (top photo) backfield players George Gerek, Andy Jandrisevits, Frank Jost, and Francis Parsons; (bottom photo) linesmen Ned Pomeroy, Thomas Marcous, Ed Nahaus, James Lee, John Aquila, John Blair, and Francis Barna stand ready to play ball against Leonardo High School on their opponents' home field. Heinie Bankert coached the 1930 and 1931 WHS teams. (John Blair.)

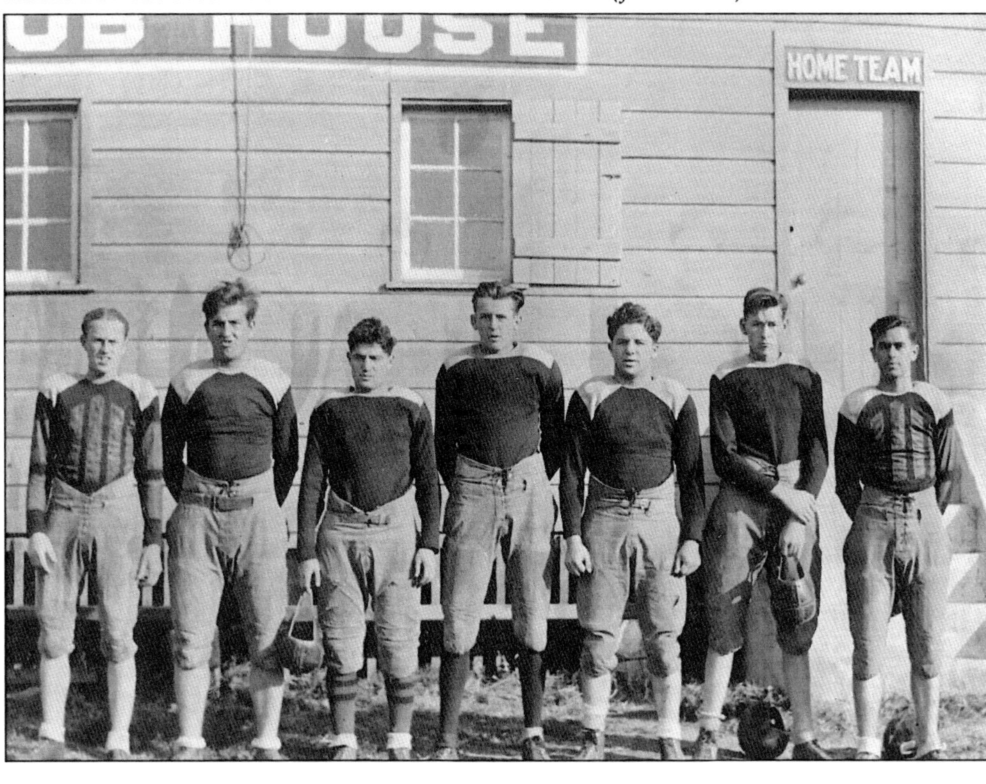

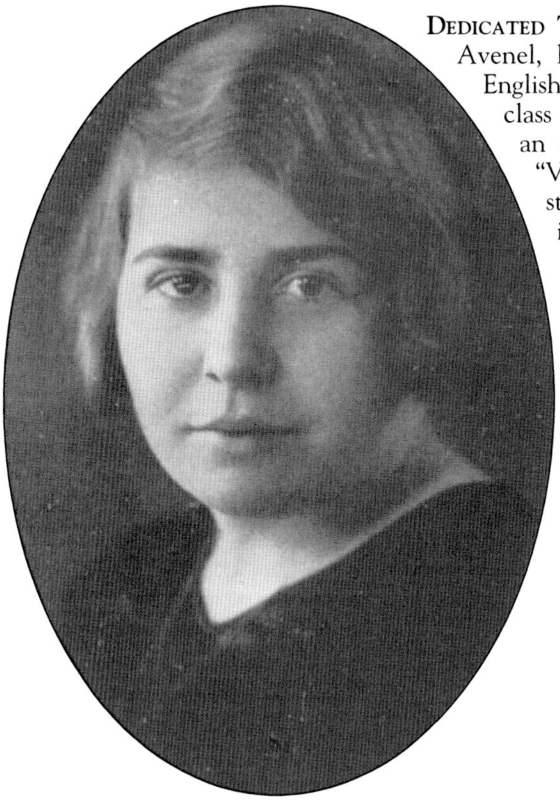

Dedicated Teacher, 1929. A. Alida van Slyke of Avenel, head of the Woodbridge High School English Department, directed many senior class and drama club productions and played an integral part in the life of the school. "Vannie" expected her students to always strive for excellence and pulled no punches in telling them so.

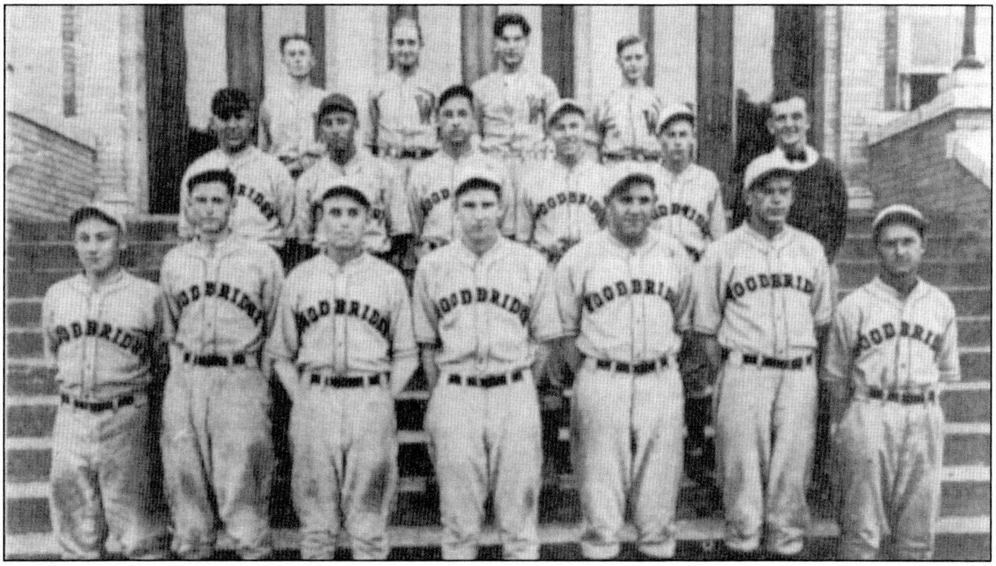

WHS Red Ghosts of 1934. Newspaper headlines proclaimed that "Woodbridge Had Best Club Since the Championship Team of 1925." Coach Frank W. Kirkleski's winners closed their 1934 baseball season by defeating powerful South River High. From left to right, players are as follows: (front row) L. Simonsen, C. Burger, J. Kurucza, Captain F. Jost, J. Wukovets, A. Kluj, and T. Balog; (center row) Coach Kirkleski, A. Barcellona, D. Scutti, J. Karnas, E. Simsonsen, and Manager J. Zilai; (top row) A. Jeglinski, H. Skay, R. Arkey, and R. Larson.

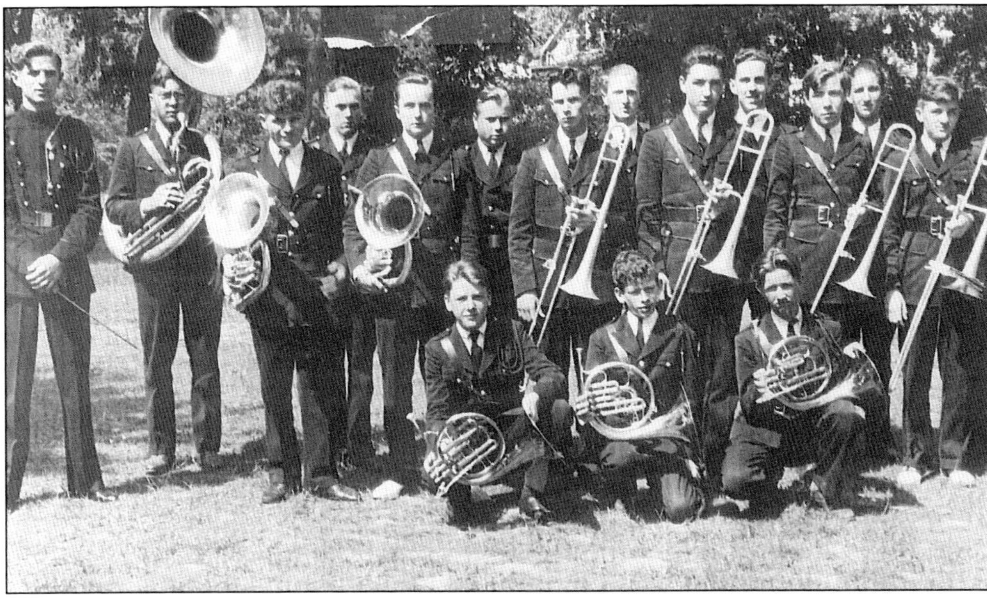

Brass Players, 1939. From left to right the Woodbridge High School band brass section, shown tuning up for the Memorial Day parade, are as follows: (kneeling) Ray Schmidt, Elmer Aldington, and an unidentified player; (standing) drum major Paul Chovan, unidentified player, Fred Melocco, Kenneth Petersen, Jack Rebeck, John Katko, Bill Rebeck, John Klug, William Harned, John Kuhlman, "B-flat" Johnson, Richard Murphy, and George Merrill. (Ann and Paul Chovan.)

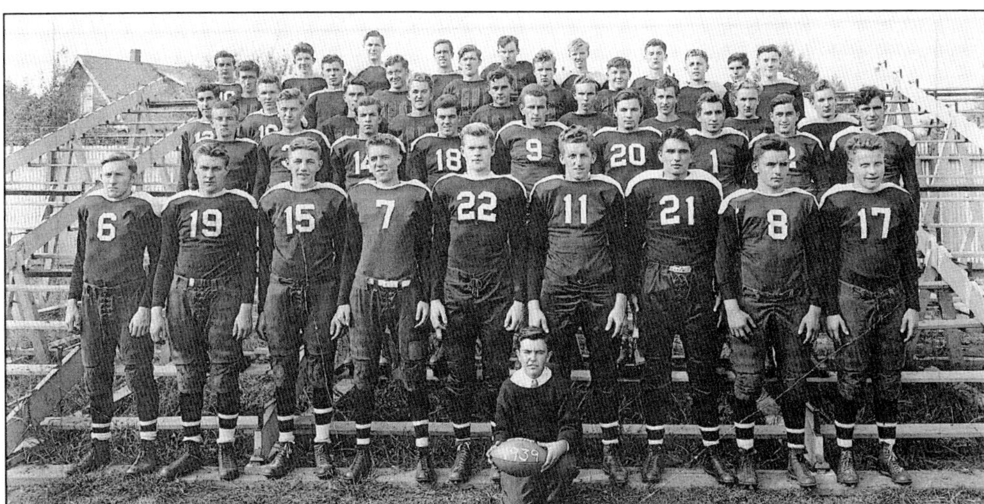

WHS 1939 Football Champs. From left to right, the players are as follows: (front row) W. Finn, W. Flowers, W. Aquila, A. Ur, W. Holub, J. Trosko, G. Gyenes, N. Semak, R. Daub, and Manager. F. Yacovino (in front); (second row) B. Trosko, M. Remar, J. Bedi, J. Royle, E. Bartha, J. Cipo, G. Wasilek, A. Pellegrino, and S. Pochek; (third row) N. D'Aprile, A. Toke, A. Cilo, J. Serko, S. Kozar, J. Nahay, S. Bakos, and others; (fourth row) A. Vahaly, W. Ferrick, L. Barna, B. Hanson, L. Balint, C. Horowitz, J. Dietrich, and W. Currie; (top row) J. Hladik, J. Grant, E. Chovan, T. Jones, D. Galbraith, J. Parker, S. Melocco, and unidentified player.

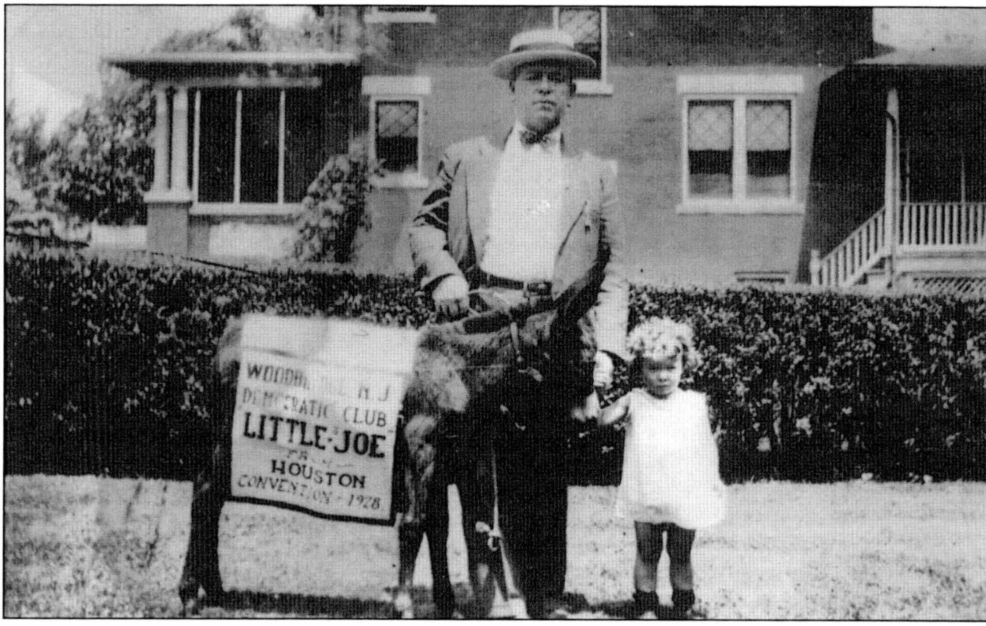

A True Democrat, 1928. Mayor William (Billy) Ryan, who has just returned from the Democratic Convention in Houston, stands outside his home on King George Road with one of his four children and Little Joe, a real, live donkey. Billy Ryan served as township mayor from 1926 to 1933. The donkey first appeared as the Democratic Party symbol in a political cartoon by Thomas Nast published in an 1870 issue of *Harper's Weekly*. (Paul Nagy.)

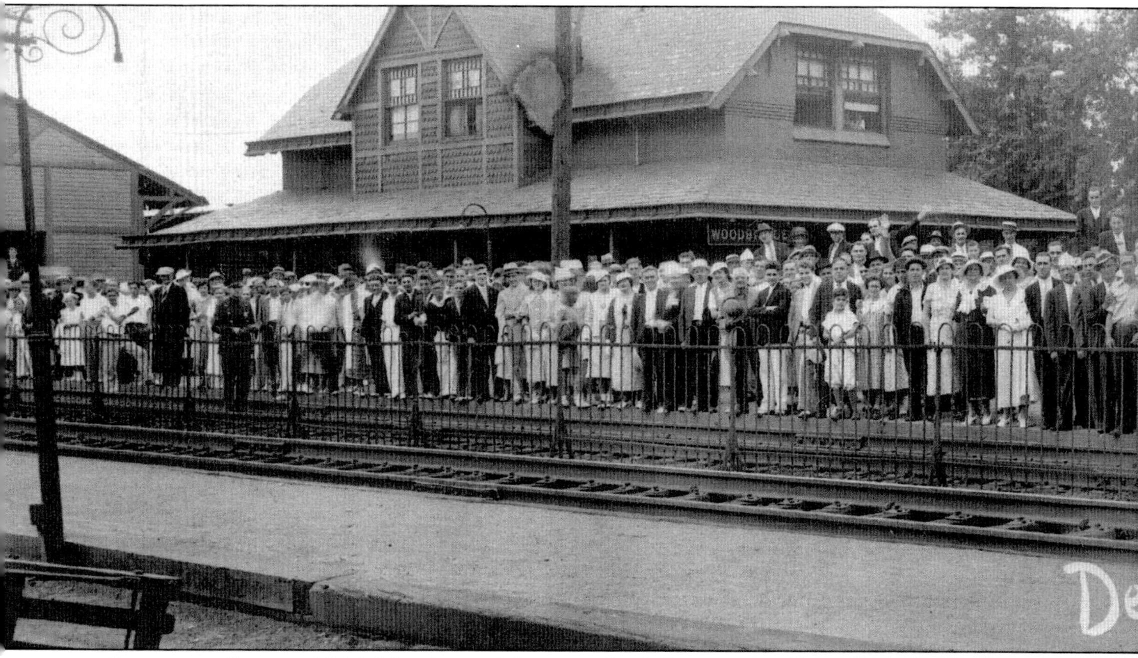

Down the Shore, 1934. Members of the township's Democratic Party line the platform of the old Woodbridge railroad station as they await the Jersey shore train to Sea Girt. Even on what was probably a hot August day, most gentlemen are wearing suits and neckties, while the ladies

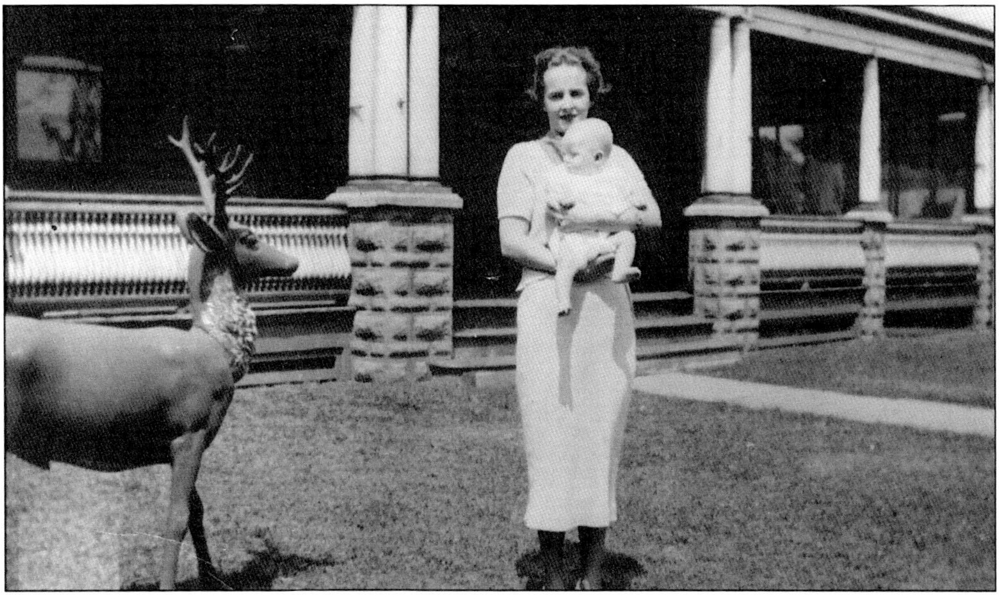

DUNNE HOUSE, C. 1935. Jean Dunne Adams and her son, James Rivers Adams, stand by the expansive front porch of 34 Green Street, the home of James and Florence Dunne. The house was easily recognized by the life-sized cast-iron statues of a deer and a greyhound on the lawn. When the house was torn down, the deer was moved to the Elks' Club property on Rahway Avenue, but mysteriously disappeared some years ago. Perhaps someone thought the deer didn't look enough like an elk. The case remains open! (William "Barry" Dunigan.)

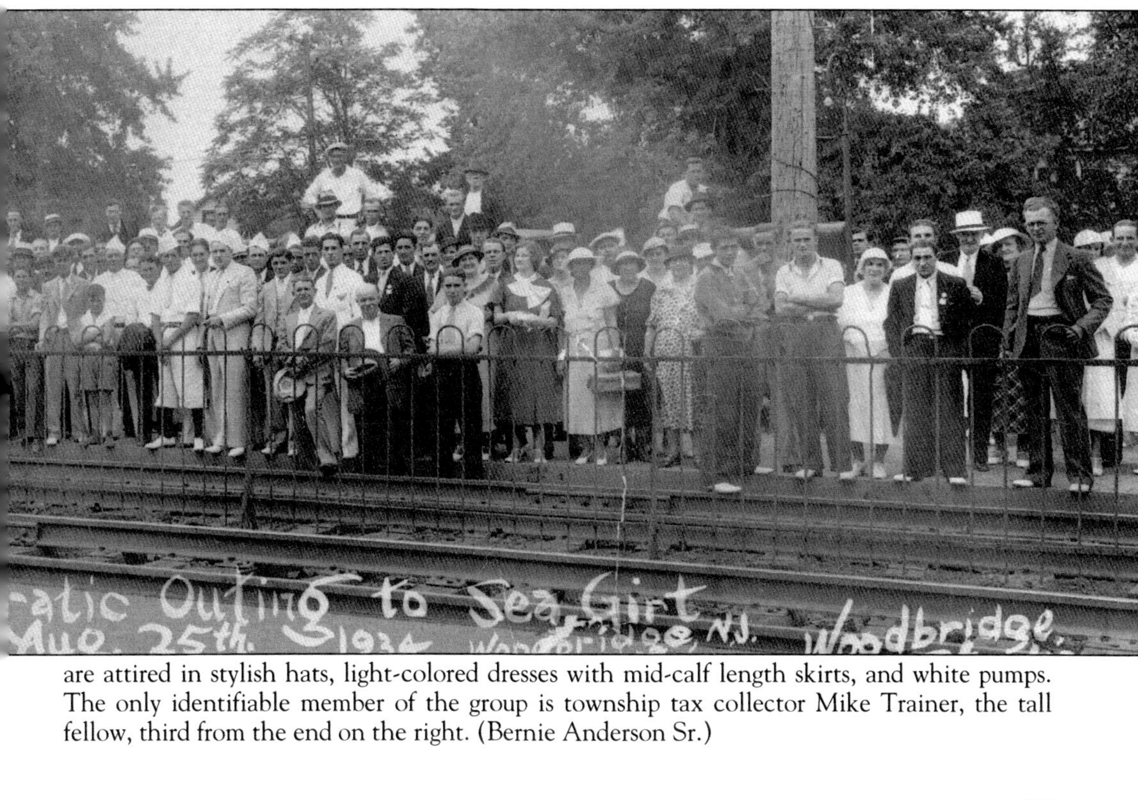

are attired in stylish hats, light-colored dresses with mid-calf length skirts, and white pumps. The only identifiable member of the group is township tax collector Mike Trainer, the tall fellow, third from the end on the right. (Bernie Anderson Sr.)

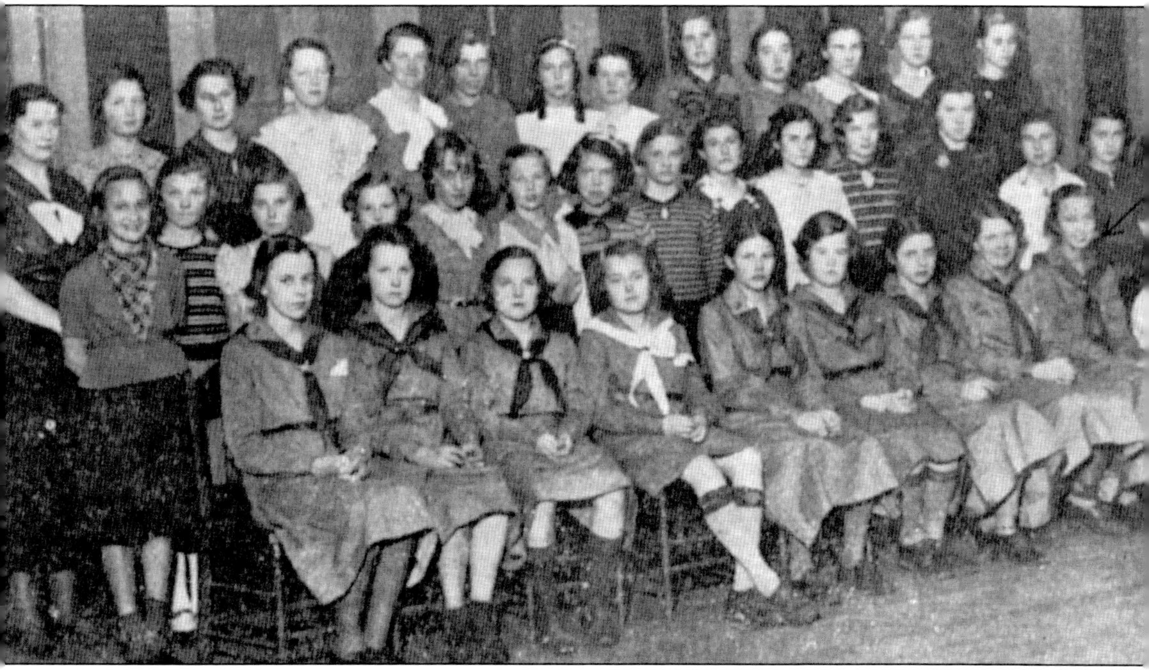

Clover Troop, Number One, 1935. The Woodbridge Girl Scouts gathered here for a troop shot are, from left to right, as follows: (bottom row) Olive Camp, Dorothy Marratt, Lillian Gillis, Barbara Briegs, Patricia Burns, Janet Shain, Doris Burns, Helen Woodruff, Marie Baldwin, and Marian Woodley; (second row) Ruth Woodley, Ann Muller, Dorothy Landt, Jean Aaroe, Vivian Stetin, Laverne Hunt, Dolores Melberg, Ethel Logan, Marie Smanko, Ruth Ely, Eleanor Logan, Mary Maner, Margaret Janick, Emma Earley, and Lillian Edwards; (top row) Mrs. James Chalmers, Mary C. Clark, Anna Schwenzer, Marie Larson, Alice Skay, Helen Darcey, Betty Tighe, Nora McGuirk, Emily Binder, Dorothy Misdom, Louise Galaida, June Young, and Elizabeth Baker.

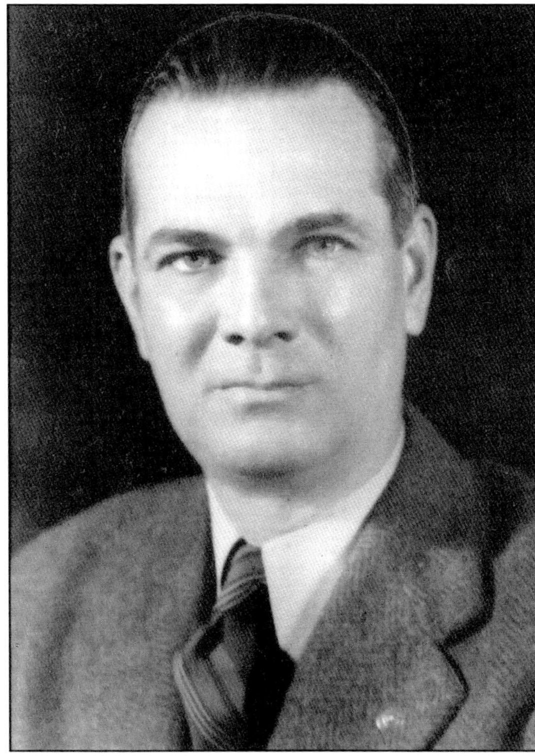

LEON J. MCELROY (1896–1958). Throughout his life Leon McElroy was certainly one of Woodbridge's movers and shakers. He graduated from WHS and New York Law School and served as township attorney (1933–1947) and later as postmaster. An active Republican, his many affiliations included the Knights of Columbus, the Kiwanis, the American Legion, the board of education, and the fire company. McElroy also wrote *A History of Woodbridge and Vicinity*, to be published in 1999 by the Historical Association of Woodbridge Township. He was married to Kathryn Gundrum of South Amboy and had two children, Joseph and Rosemary. (Joseph McElroy.)

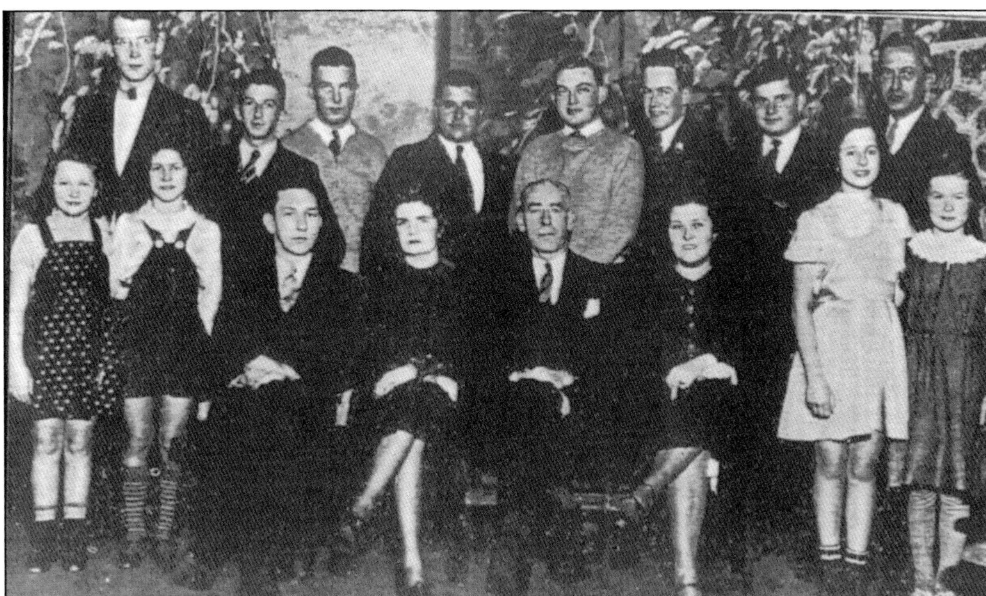

ST. JAMES' JESTERS, FEBRUARY 1936. These players in a minstrel show sponsored by the Holy Name Society and Sodality of the Blessed Virgin of St. James Catholic Church are, from left to right, as follows: (front row) Gloria Paul, Dorothy Walsh, Bernard Quigley, Margaret Dalton, Eugene Bird, Susie Murphy, Dorothy Shawl, and Dorothy Langan; (back row) Clair Bixel, Leon Gerity, Barney Concannon, John J. Keating, Daniel Cosgrove, Thomas Smith, James Mesics, and Vincent Weaver. Al Ritter directed the production.

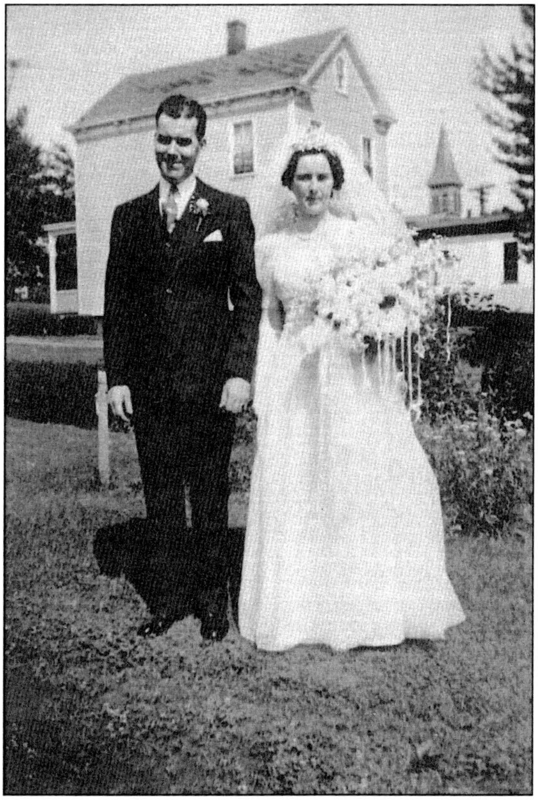

Summer Wedding, June 29, 1940. Jane M. Gerity of 314 Amboy Avenue, daughter of Mary and the late William Gerity, married Thomas McDonough of Elizabeth at a nuptial Mass at St. James Church with Rev. Charles G. McCorristin officiating. The couple was photographed at the Gerity home with a glimpse of St. James' steeple in the background. According to the marriage announcement in the *Independent-Leader*, "the bride wore a gown of frosted organdy, made in simple lines . . ." (Pat McDonough Brisson.)

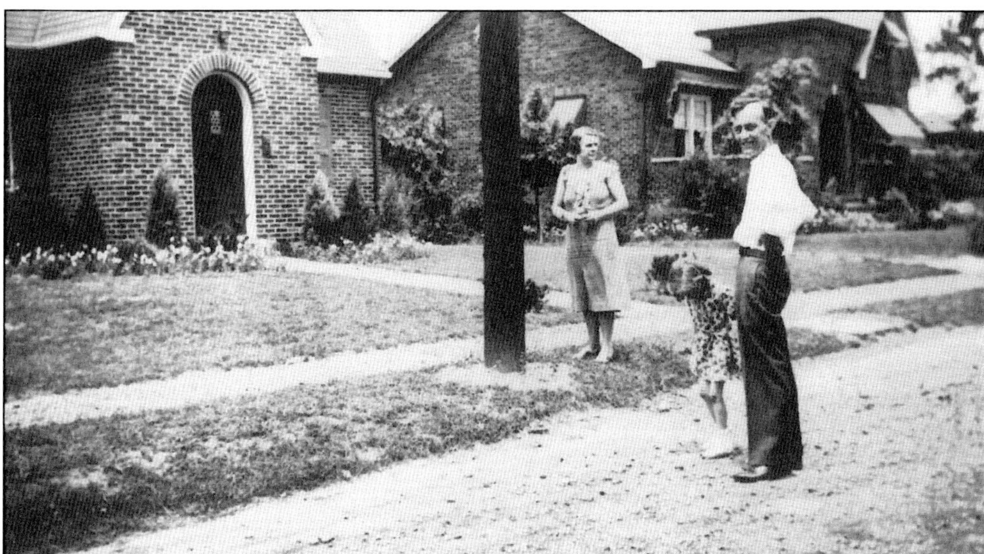

On North Park Drive, c. 1938. Jane and Frank Smith with granddaughter Patsy MacManus pose outside their home at 210 North Park Drive. Patsy, now Pat Ritt of Hemet, CA, remembers her grandmother's story about the naming of North Park Drive. When the builder told her that the new street had not yet been named, Jane Smith suggested "North Park Drive" since it was on the north side of Woodbridge Park. (Pat MacManus Ritt.)

Five

FACES AND PLACES: 1941–1997

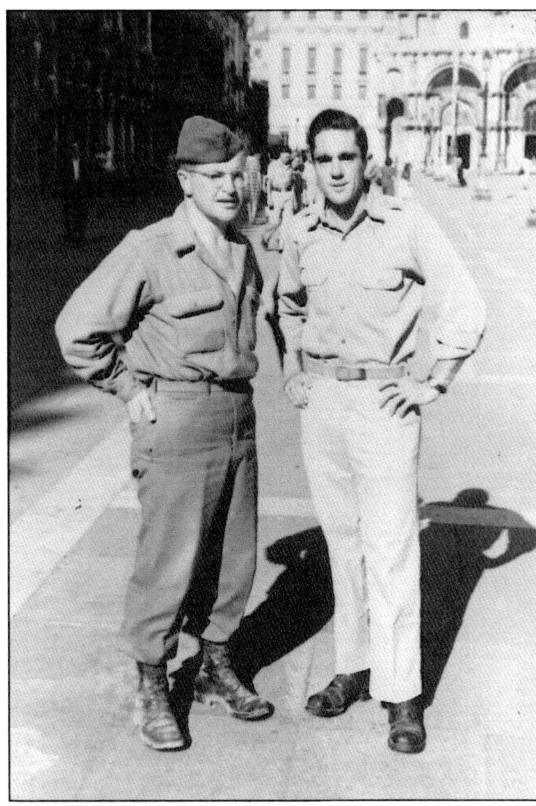

CHANCE MEETING, AUGUST 1945. Township residents George Molnar (left) and Maynard B. Winston met by accident in Venice while serving in the U.S. Army. After World War II George was employed as a reporter and photographer at the *News Tribune*. Maynard, who died in 1997, worked as a supervisor for American Cyanimid and served on the Township Committee. (Mary and George Molnar.)

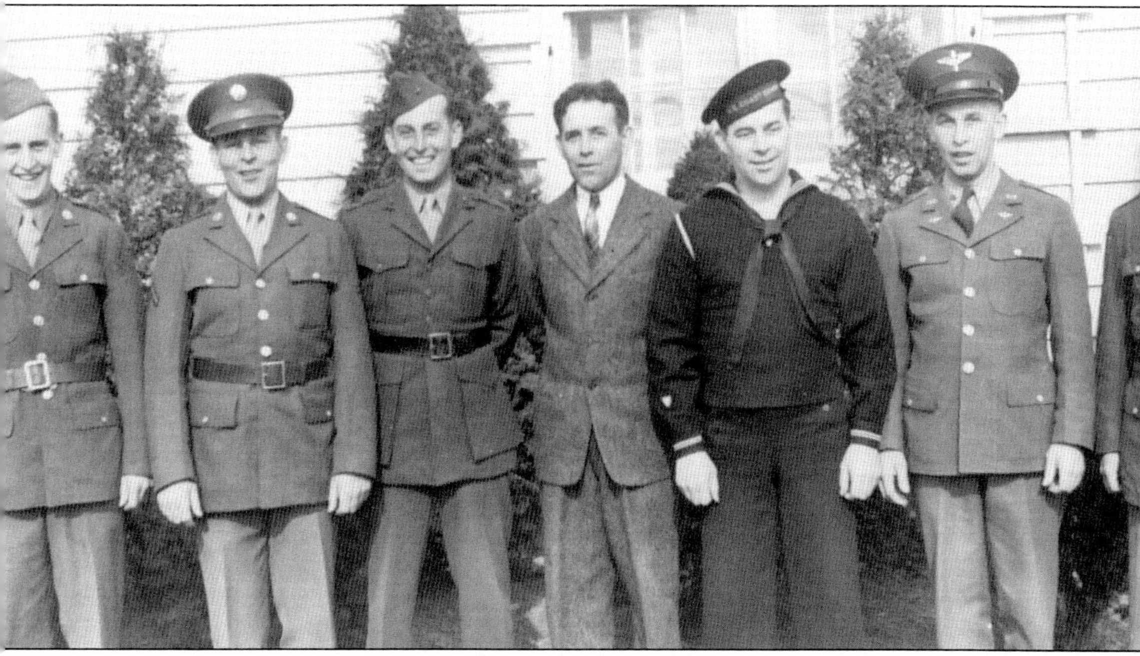

Family Reunion, March 1943. All seven brothers of the Urban family were reunited at home on Maple Avenue for the first time since six of them were called to active service during World War II. From left to right are Julius (125th Armored Battalion in North Africa and Italy), John (car and truck pool battalion in Texas), William (U.S. Marine Air Corps Reconnaissance Group flight engineer in the Pacific), Albert (employed by NJ Shipbuilding in Perth Amboy building victory ships), Peter (U.S. Coast Guard stationed at Sandy Hook, NJ), Theodore (major in the 8th Air Force Fighter Group, where he took part in 98 missions, downing four German planes), and Nicholas (Signal Corps at Fort Monmouth, NJ). Theodore also served in the Korean War and was awarded the Distinguished Service Medal. The two Urban daughters, Marion and Emma, lived in Newark, NJ, with their families. Their father, Michael, also helped in the war effort working for NJ Shipbuilding. Although in ill health, Mrs. Urban lived to see all her boys return home safely. She died a few months later. After the war, Peter became the *Perth Amboy Evening News* sports editor, and Nick became a well-known, local photographer. (Nicholas and Peter Urban.)

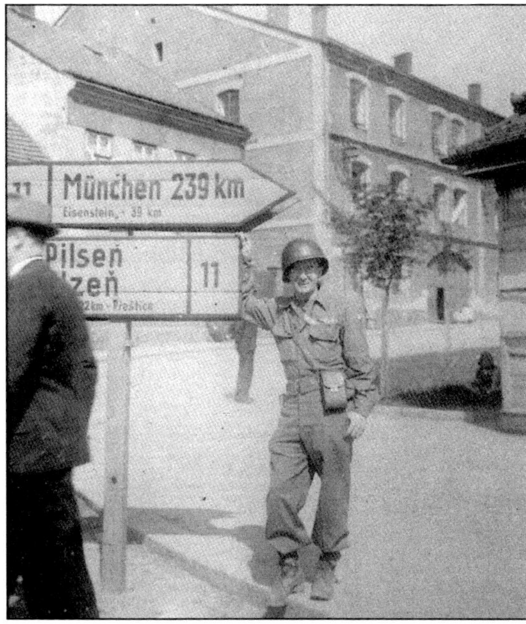

WOODBRIDGE SOLDIER, MAY 1945. James Patrick Gerity grew up in town and worked for the American Smelting and Refining Co. in Perth Amboy before joining the Army in 1943. Jim took part in the June 1944 D-Day invasion and is pictured here in Klatovy, Czechoslovakia, at the end of the war. Jim's letter home describing his D-Day experiences was published on the front page of the *Independent-Leader* as "Report from Normandy." (Pat McDonough Brisson.)

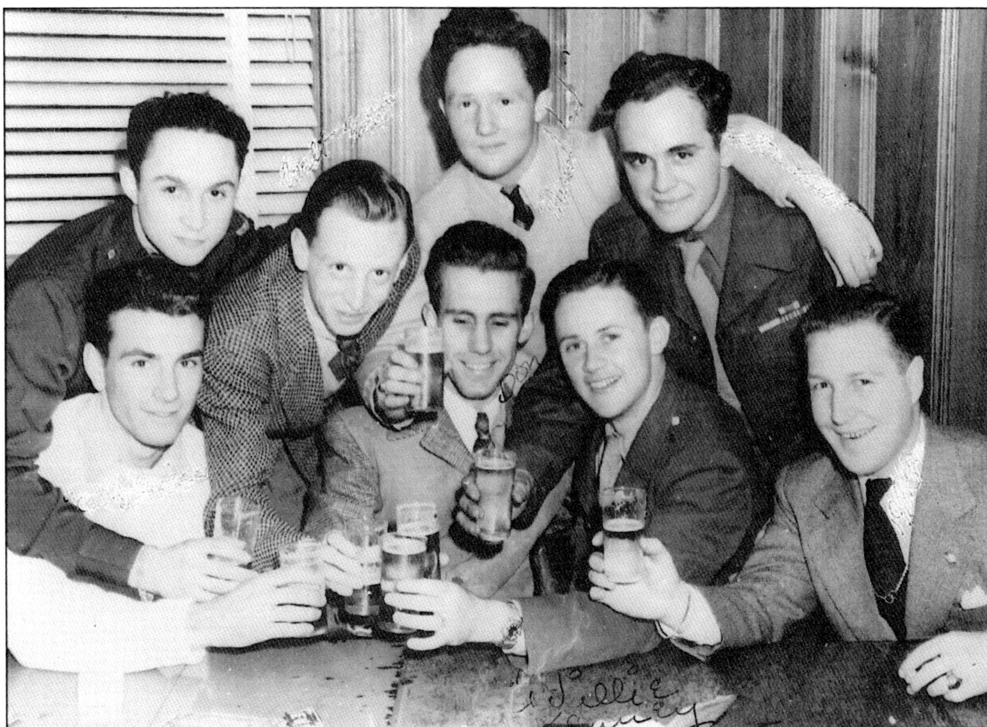

POSTWAR REUNION, 1946. Eight Woodbridge High School buddies from the class of 1942, seven of them veterans of World War II, met at the Log Cabin in Clark for a reunion. They made toasts to lasting friendship and to the fact that they had survived the war. From left to right, they are Johnny Venerus (white shirt), George Stillwell (in uniform), Walter Drews (checked jacket), Don Kerr (seated center), Bob McEwen (top center), William Kenny (seated in uniform), Steve Machat (top in uniform), and Arthur Locker (right). (George Stillwell.)

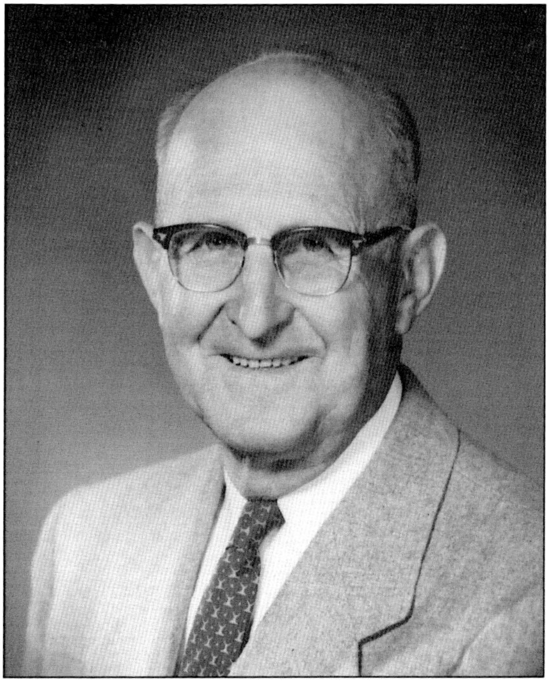

Andrew P. Aaroe (1893–1976). Born in New Jersey to Danish parents, Andy Aaroe, a well-known builder, was active in the United Brotherhood of Carpenters and Joiners of America, and served as president and business agent of Local No. 65 in Perth Amboy during the 1940s. A member of the board of education for 21 years, he served as president from 1946 to 1956 and was instrumental in obtaining proper equipment for Woodbridge schools' sports teams. (Donald Aaroe.)

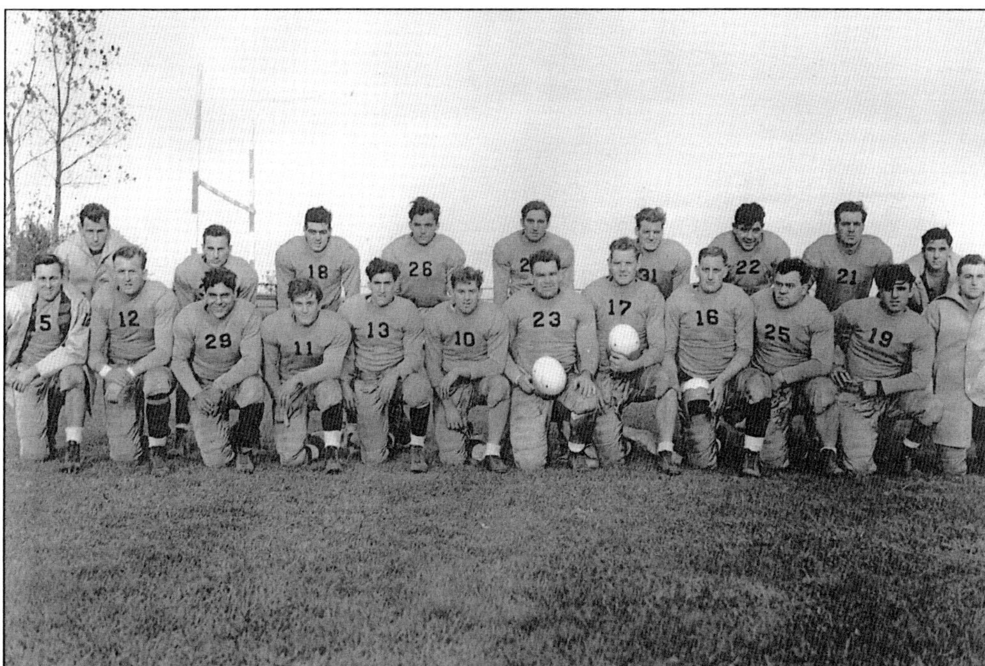

The Golden Bears, 1941. The Woodbridge High School alumni football team are, from left to right, as follows: (front row) John Cassidy, James Lee, P. Barbato, John Dubay, Nick D'Aprile, John Govelitz, William Patrick, Norm Kilby, Fred Leyh, George Markulin, Steve Pochek, and Albie Leffler; (back row) Ernie Bartha, Tuto Zuccaro, Johnnie Royle, Nick Semak, George Wasilek, Ray Voelker, Percy Wukovetz, Earl Smith, and Bob Schwenzer (see following two pages). (Nick Urban.)

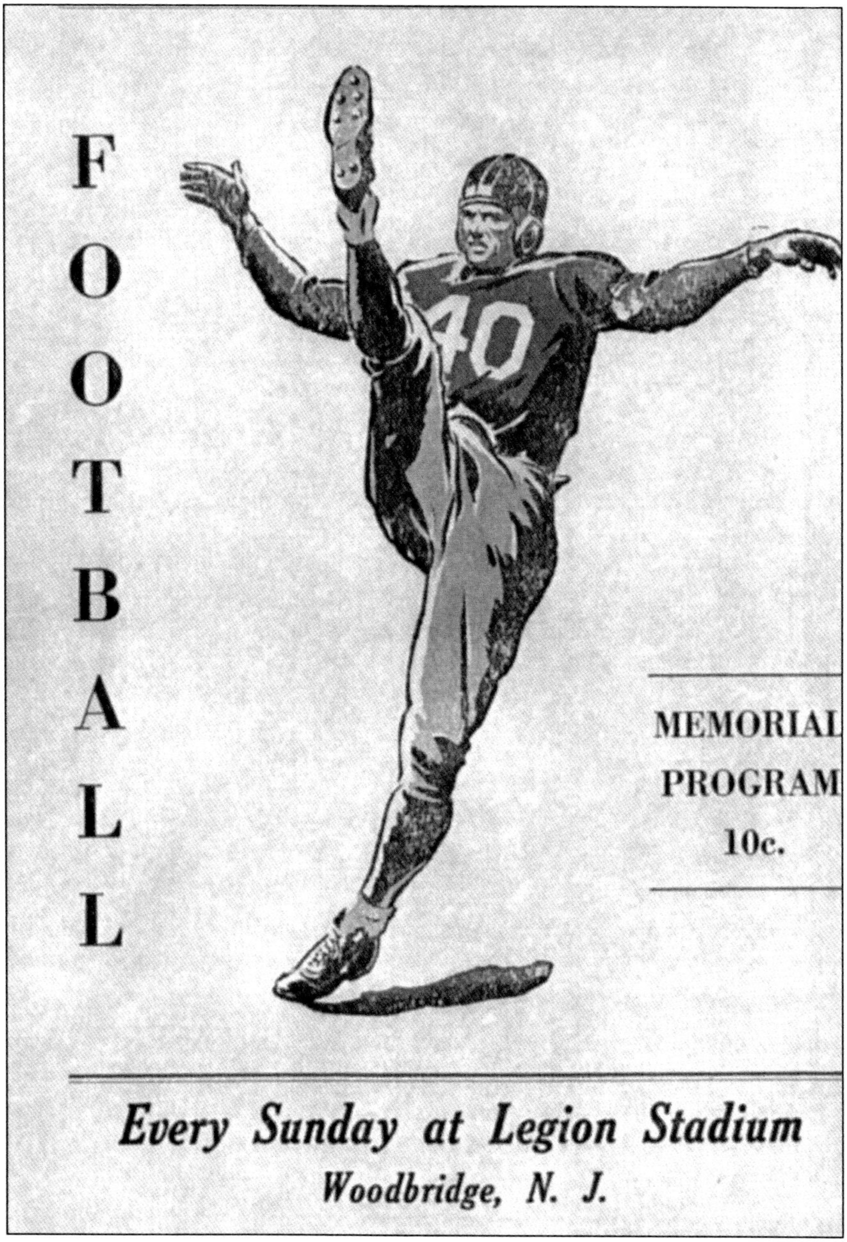

GOLDEN BEARS PROGRAM, 1946. Through the initial suggestion of Board of Education President Andy Aaroe, the Woodbridge Alumni Golden Bears semi-pro football team became a reality in 1940. Organized by Tony Cacciola, Clair Bixel, and Andy Gadek, the Golden Bears provided young men of the township the chance to play football after high school and for fans to see their former high school stars in action. In 1940, their first season, the Golden Bears came through undefeated with a tie by the South River Eagles. In 1943 the team disbanded for the duration of World War II, fielding a team again in 1945. This memorial program, with its distinctive golden-yellow cover, represented a first rate semi-pro team. The Bears won nine out of ten games in the 1946 season. They lost 19-6 to the Perth Amboy Alumni, but later that season posted a 6-0 victory over their old rivals.

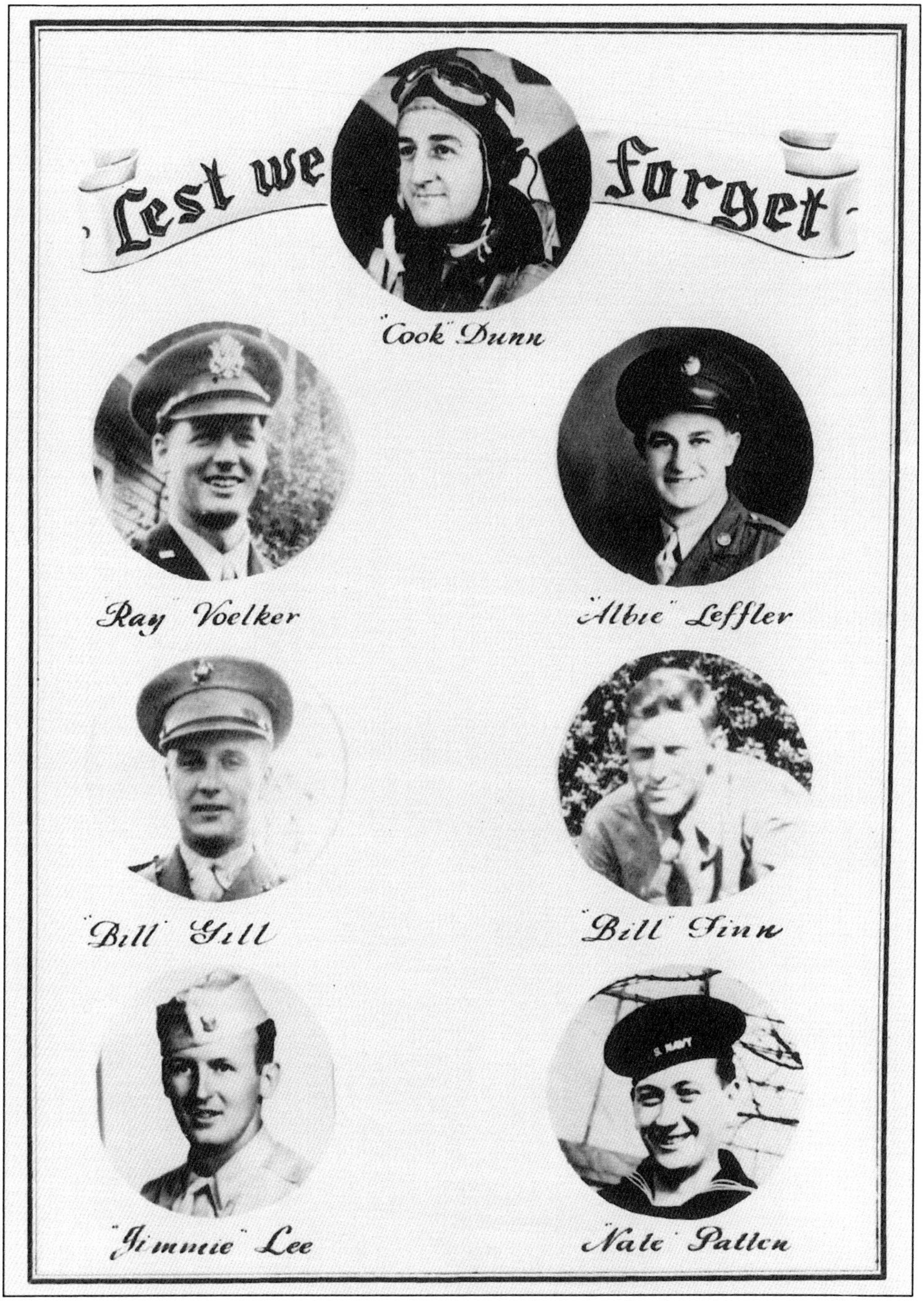

GOLDEN BEARS MEMORIAL. In their 1946 program, the Woodbridge Alumni Golden Bears football team included a special page remembering their players who were killed in World War II: James P. Lee, William J. Gill, Raymond F. Voelker, John B. Dunn Jr., Albert J. Leffler, William J. Finn, and Nathan H. Patten. In his two seasons with the Bears Al Leffler scored 17 touchdowns. The Golden Bears played ball for 11 seasons and were considered one of the toughest semi-pro teams in the state. Attendance at the games declined in the 1950s when college and professional football games became popular on television. (Nick Urban.)

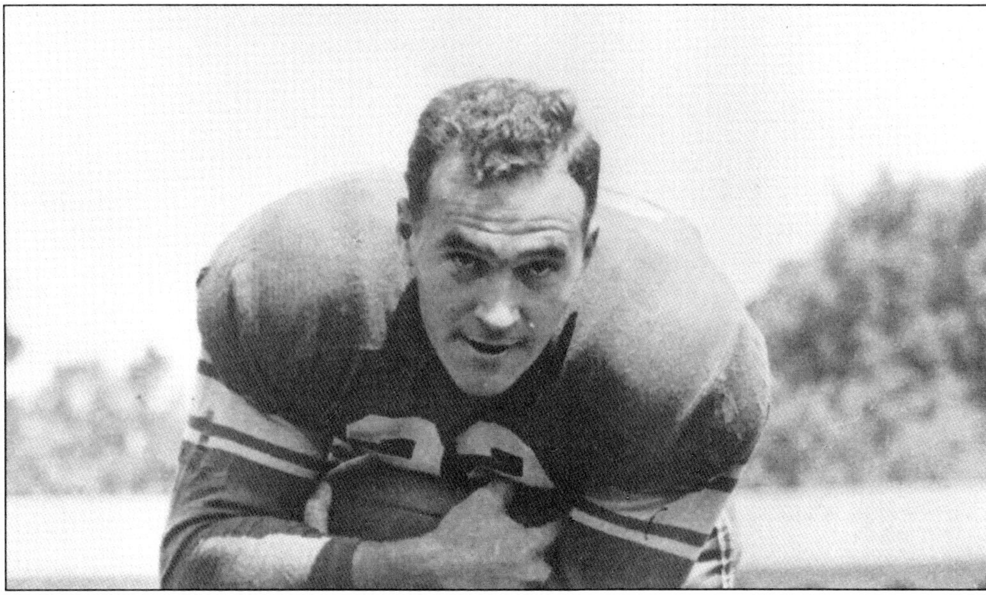

Gridiron Hero. Star fullback on WHS's football team and class of 1938 graduate Johnny "Gutch" Korszowski of Hopelawn is shown here at the College of William and Mary, c. 1940, where he played football after high school. Johnny served as a naval officer in World War II. He played professionally with the Buffalo Bills of the old All-American Pro-Football Conference and later coached high school football in Richmond, VA. (Lou Creekmur.)

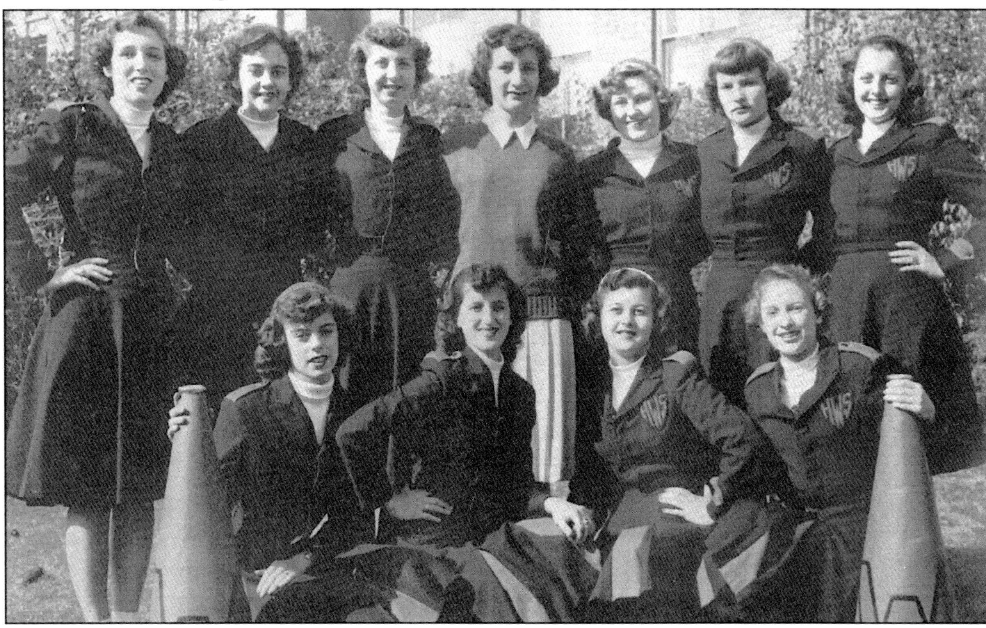

Woodbridge High School Cheerleaders, Fall 1948. From left to right are as follows: (front row) Marie Terzella, Dorothy Minucci, Eleanor Tasnady, and Cathryn Puckett; (back row) Elizabeth Tarnick, Dolores Lott, Eleanor Kudrick, advisor and physical education teacher Jeanne Giroud, Betty McElroy, Geraldine Thullesen, and Rae Marsh. The squad is gathered in their new uniforms on the high school lawn on Barron Avenue before a football game. (Virginia B. Troeger.)

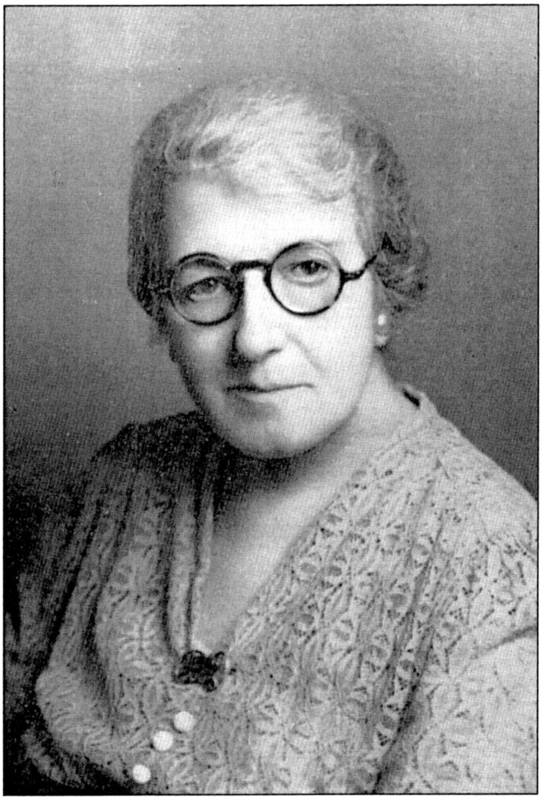

WOODBRIDGE HISTORIAN, C. 1940. Amy Edgar Breckenridge authored a historical booklet, *Disappearing Landmarks of Woodbridge*, in the 1940s. She and her husband, John, were active community and church leaders. Mrs. Breckenridge was a longtime Red Cross production chairperson, and a member of the Daughters of the American Revolution (DAR) and the First Presbyterian Church. Her husband served as township mayor from 1918 to 1919. Mrs. Breckenridge died in 1945.

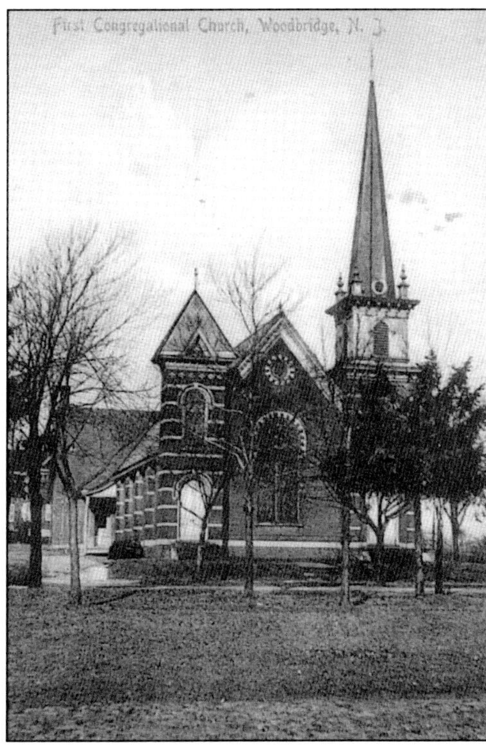

CONGREGATIONAL CHURCH, C. 1940. This house of worship, located at the corner of Grove and Barron Avenues, was founded in 1874 by local residents who broke away from the First Presbyterian Church because they were dissatisfied with the Presbyterian form of worship. Before they constructed this building, the group held services in the old Masonic Hall on Green Street. Today the church is known as the United Church of Christ.

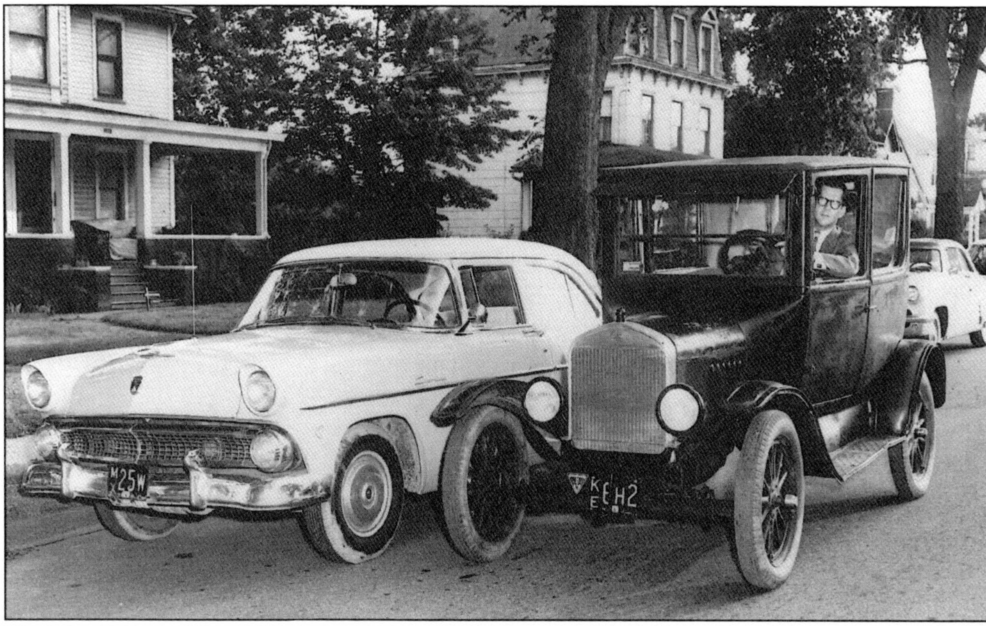

CAR BUFF, AUGUST 1956. Accountant Art Quinn, who lived on upper Green Street, proudly displays his 1924 prized, antique Model-T Ford along with his brand new Ford. For a study in contrast, just look how tall and square early cars were. Art Quinn died in 1995; his son Chris now resides in the family home on Green Street. (Art Quinn.)

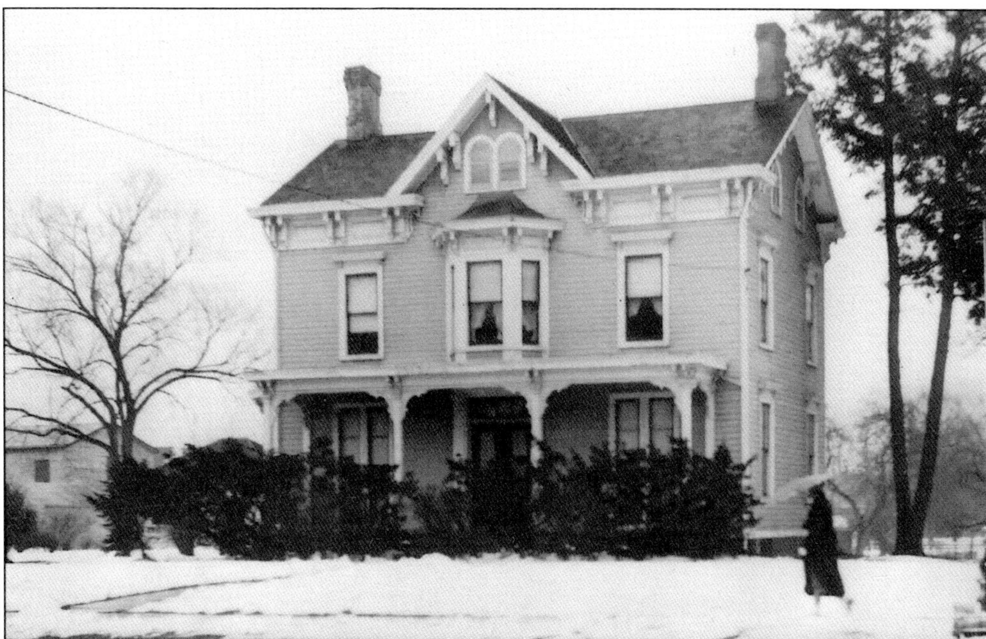

HARNED HOUSE, C. 1950. William Lawrence Harned, vice president of the Woodbridge Trust Company, and his wife, Lulu, resided in this gracious Green Street homestead for years. It was later owned by William's son, W. Leon Harned, also a banker, and his wife, Helen Valentine Harned, who is pictured on page 91. At one time the large backyard was filled with fruit trees, a grape arbor, and a goldfish pond. (William Harned.)

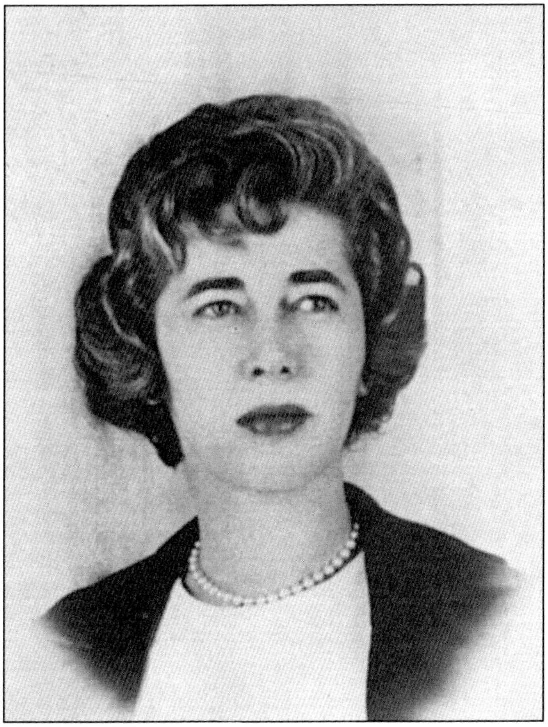

WELL-KNOWN EDUCATOR C. 1960. Mary Patricia Connolly taught history at Woodbridge High School for many years and became the first principal of John F. Kennedy High School in Iselin, when the school opened in September 1964. Miss Connolly, a graduate of Goucher College in Maryland, was a lifelong resident of Grove Street.

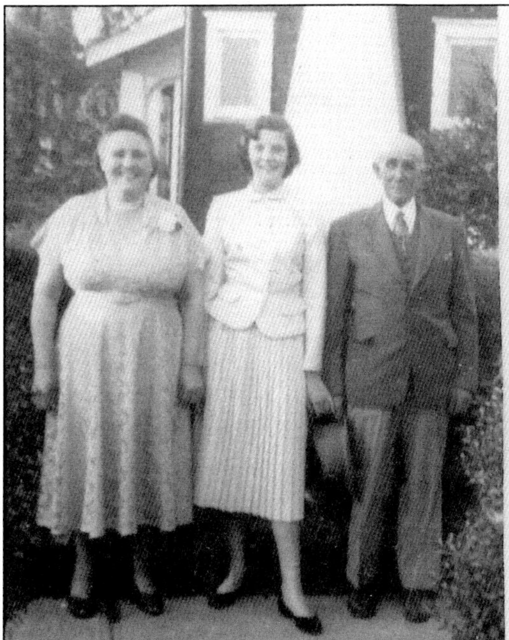

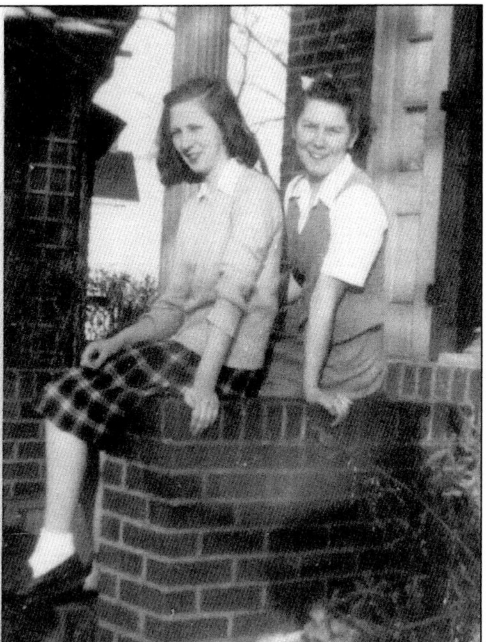

LINDEN AVENUE RESIDENTS. *Left:* Thomsen Christensen, the brother of Chris and Peter, founders of Christensen's Dept. Store, raised and sold chickens, eggs, and vegetables. He is pictured here with his wife, Betty, and younger daughter Lydia, *c.* 1957. *Right:* Thomsen's older daughter Bertha "Chris" (left) is seated outside her home in 1947 with Virginia Remais, who later married Thomsen's son Daniel. (Lydia Christensen Yates.)

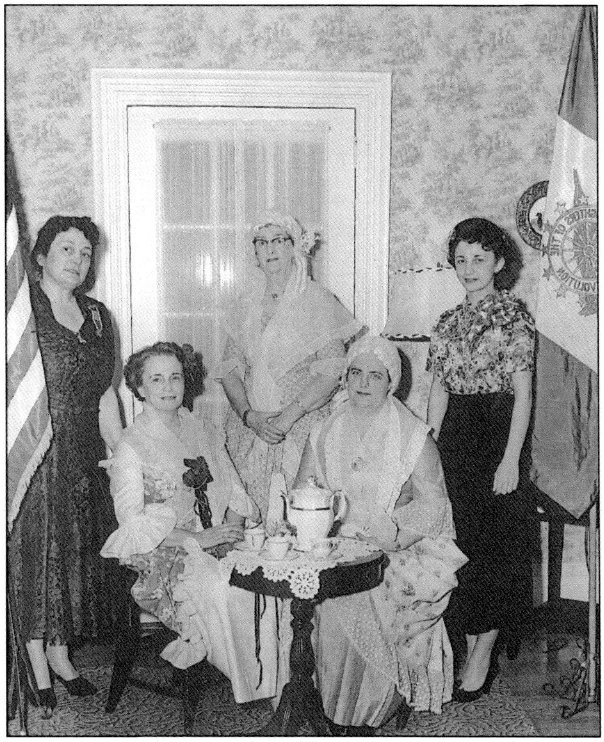

DAR Good Citizen Award. In February 1953, the Janet Gage Chapter of the Daughters of the American Revolution honored their Good Citizen of the Year, Margaret Kertesz (right), a senior at WHS. The afternoon meeting at Evelyn Kreger's home was highlighted by a "White House tea with Dolly Madison in 1810." From left to right are DAR members Miriam D. Bergen, Isabel Rankin, and Hilda Demarest, and guest Edna H. Traill of Fords. (Virginia B. Troeger.)

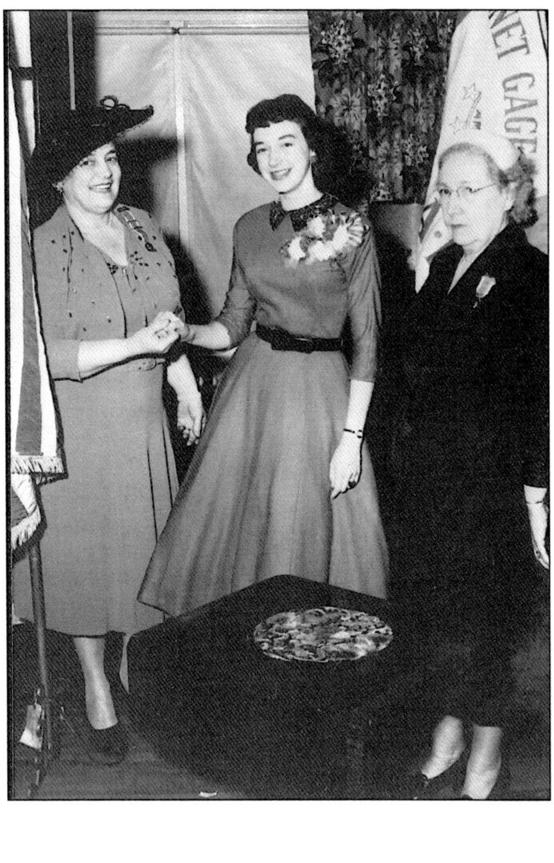

DAR Award, February 1956. Nancy Sloan (center) of Sewaren receives the chapter's Good Citizen of the Year Award from Miriam D. Bergen (left) and Helen Valentine Harned. The Janet Gage Chapter of the DAR was an active organization in Woodbridge until dwindling membership in the 1960s forced the group to disband. Remaining members joined the Matochshoning Chapter in Metuchen. (Virginia B. Troeger.)

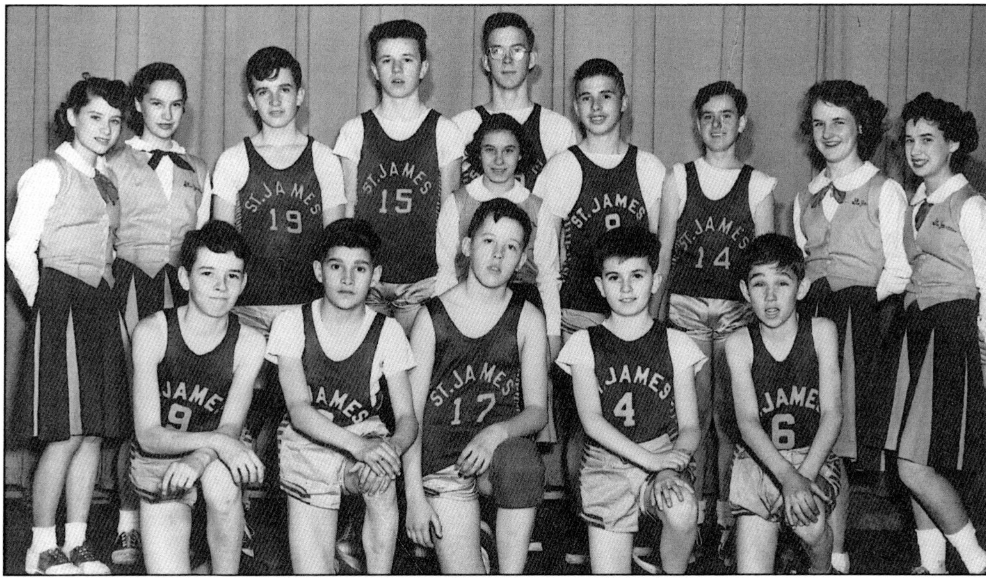

St. James Basketball Team, 1950–51. The Catholic Youth Organization (CYO) cheerleaders and players are, from left to right, as follows: (front row) William "Barry" Dunigan, John Schwartz, Robert Gerity, Allen Jordan, and Jack Nagy; (back row) Claire Blume, Carol Yuhasz, Raymond Terpanick, Lee Jordan, Thomas Bader, Theresa White (in front of Tom), Howard Trumble, Larry Kerner, Carol Tiernan, and Joan Farley. CYO coach James Keating is not pictured. (William "Barry" Dunigan.)

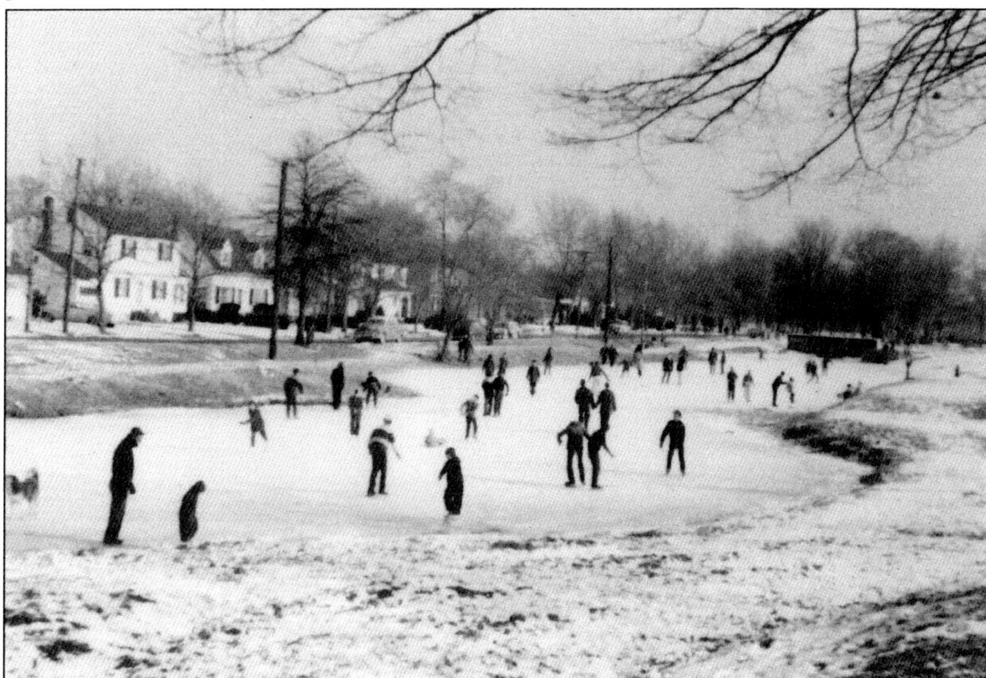

On the Ice, c. 1959. Through the years the pond at South Park Drive has been a popular skating site whenever the weather cooperates. North Park Drive houses face the pond, which flows into Heard's Brook through Woodbridge Park. (Lydia Christensen Yates.)

WHS HEAD TWIRLER. Nancy Younger Dunham, class of 1954, was the second head twirler for WHS. A twirling squad was organized in 1952 under the direction of Irene B. Shay. Nancy, a squad member in 1953–54, worked closely with Mrs. Shay to create innovative formations for half-time festivities during football games. Since there were no funds for uniforms, each girl purchased the fabric and paid a seamstress to make her uniform. (Nancy Younger Dunham.)

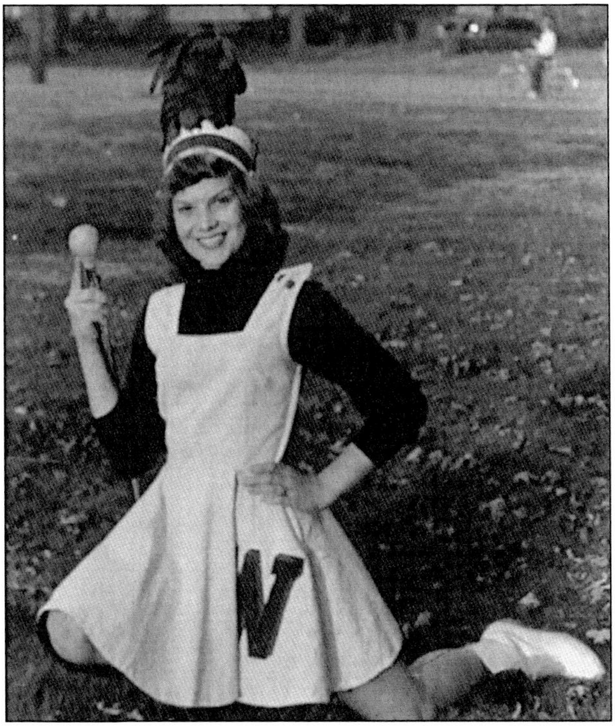

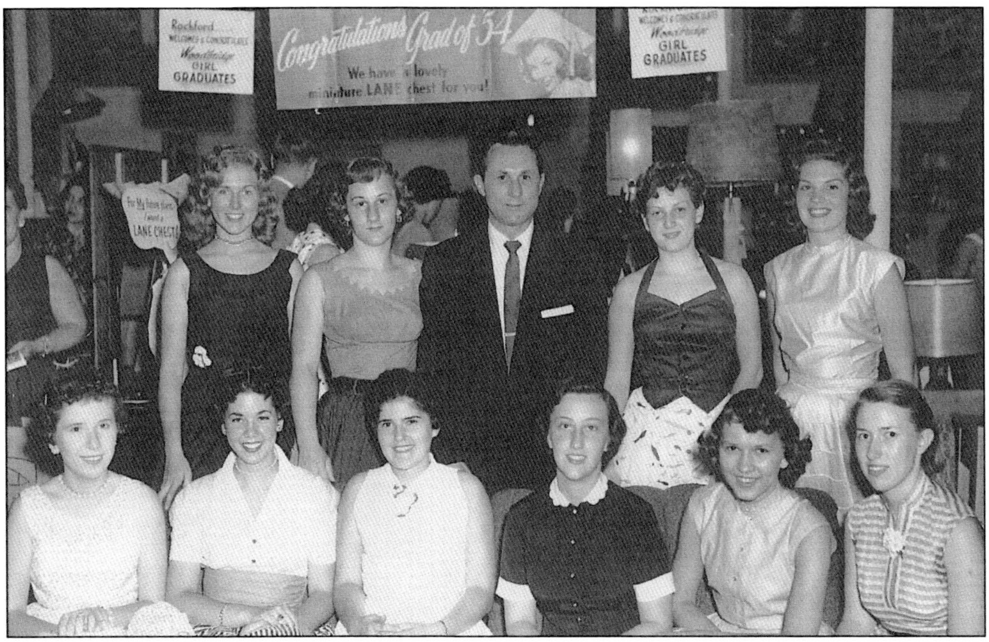

GRADUATES WELCOMED, 1954. As a sales promotion, the Rockford Furniture Co. invited WHS senior class girls to its store on Route Nine. They received miniature, Lane Company cedar "hope" chests and took part in a raffle to win a full-size chest. Participants are, from left to right, as follows: (front row) G. Krisak, G. Parkstrom, J. Sohnle, S. Petoletti, B. Vetesy, and C. Delisle; (back row) P. Lease, C. Martinello (emcee and local disc jockey), unidentified, L. Samson, and N. Younger. (Nancy Younger Dunham.)

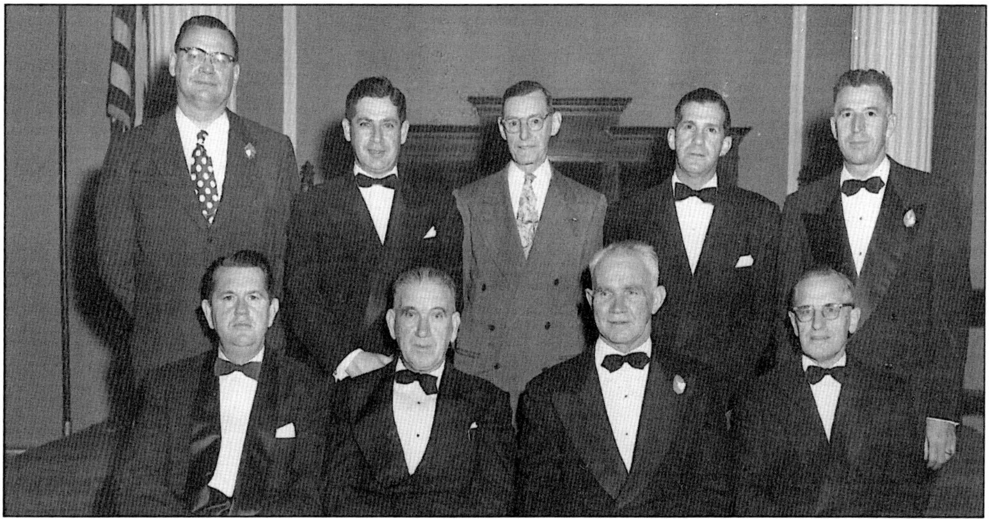

MASONIC OFFICERS, 1954. From left to right are as follows: (front row) Lou Wainwright (secretary), Mitch Cairns (vice president), Niels Kjeldsen (president), Charles Kuhlman (treasurer); (back row) Fred Kahlning, Nate Bernstein, William Turner, Art Rousset (financial secretary), and George Baker. This group served as officers for the Masons of the Americus Lodge No. 83, which met at the Craftsmen's Club on Green Street. In later years the Woodbridge Masons became part of the Perth Amboy Lodge. (William Tolia.)

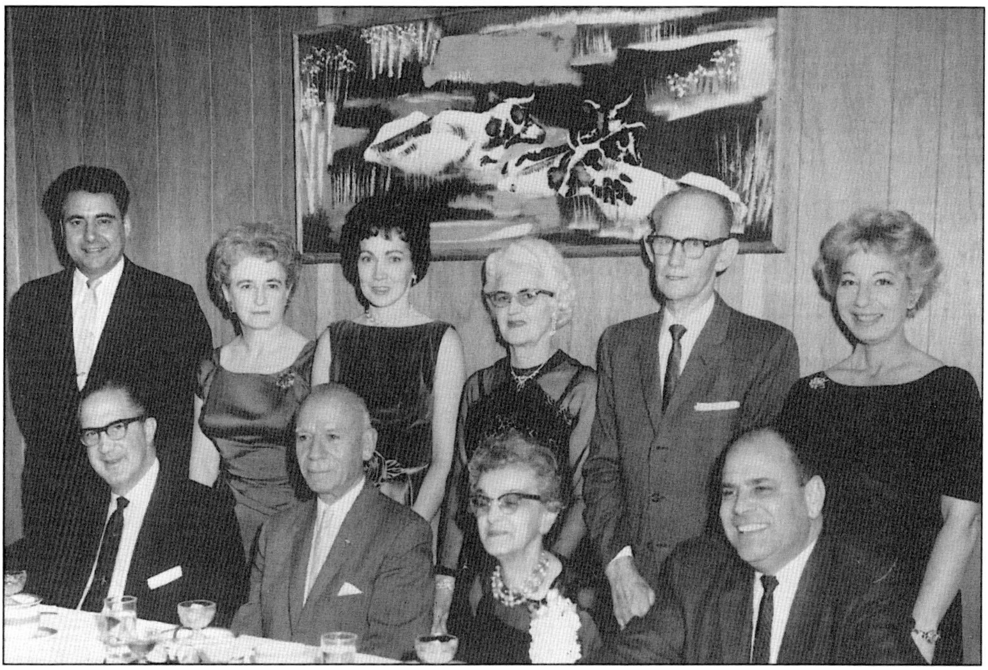

TOWNSHIP DINNER, NOVEMBER 1962. Retiring Assistant Welfare Director Carrie Mundy was honored at the Log Cabin Restaurant for her long years of service. Four Woodbridge mayors were in attendance. From left to right, are as follows: (front row) Mayor Walter Zirpolo (1962–67), Mayor August Greiner (1934–51), Carrie Mundy, and Mayor Fred Adams (1960–61); (standing) Mayor Ralph Barone (1967–71), Sophie Zullo D'Apolitto, Midge Pannone, Marion Dunham, Welfare Director John Omenheiser, and Jean Shane.

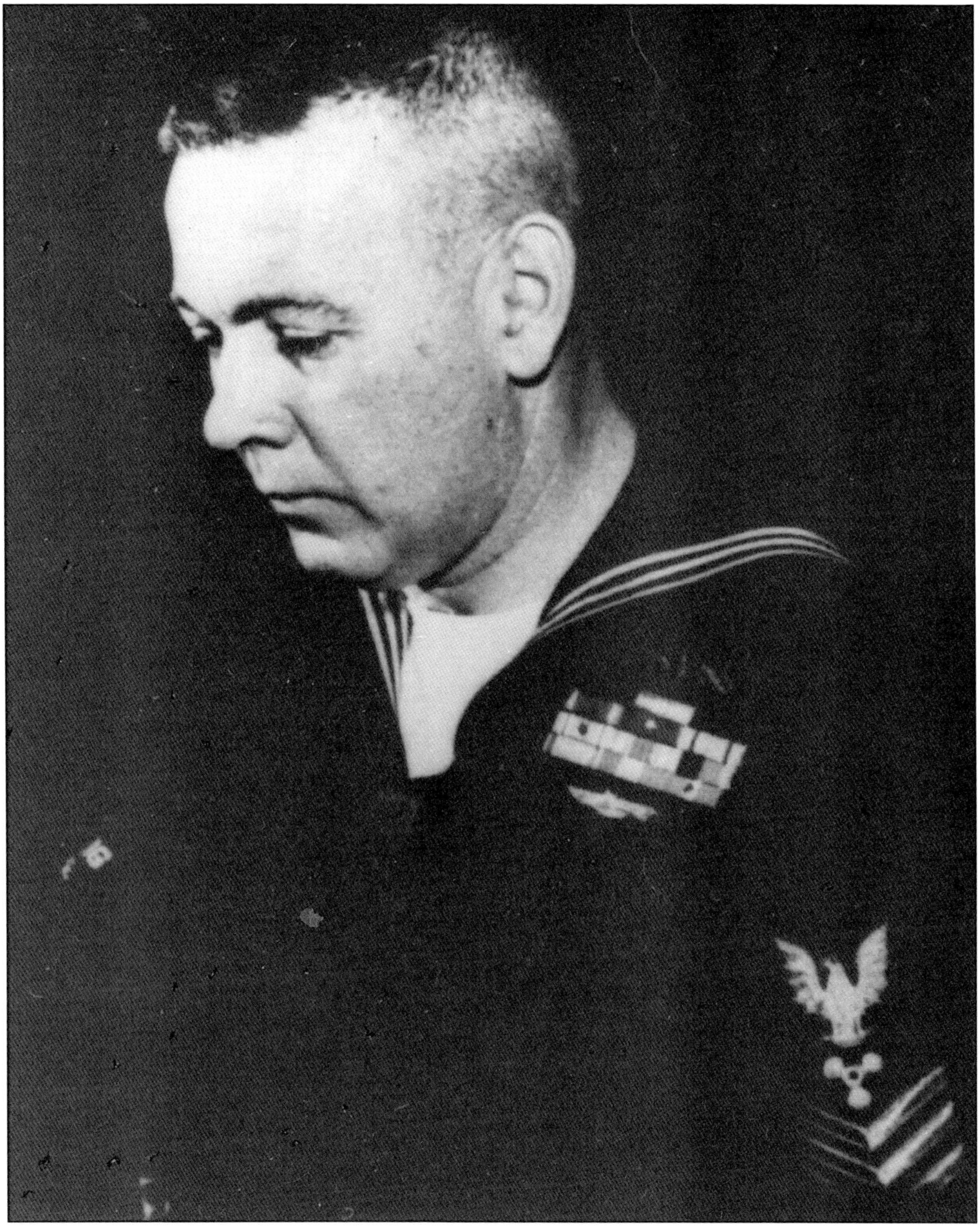

USS *Nautilus* Navy Man. Woodbridge resident Philip J. Boyle served as part of the original crew of the world's first nuclear-powered submarine, the USS *Nautilus*, SSN571. He was still aboard when the submarine transited for the first time under the North Pole from the Pacific Ocean to the Atlantic Ocean on August 3, 1958. After surfacing in Greenland the sub continued on to England, where the crew was awarded a Presidential Unit Citation by the American Ambassador. New York City welcomed the *Nautilus* crew with a ticker-tape parade. Township Mayor Hugh Quigley presented Boyle with a plaque, and the Middlesex Knights of Columbus honored him at a dinner. Boyle, who made the Navy his career, enlisted in January 1943 during World War II and served until May 1964. His last tour of duty was as a Navy recruiter stationed in Perth Amboy. Mr. Boyle died on March 10, 1999. (Philip J. Boyle.)

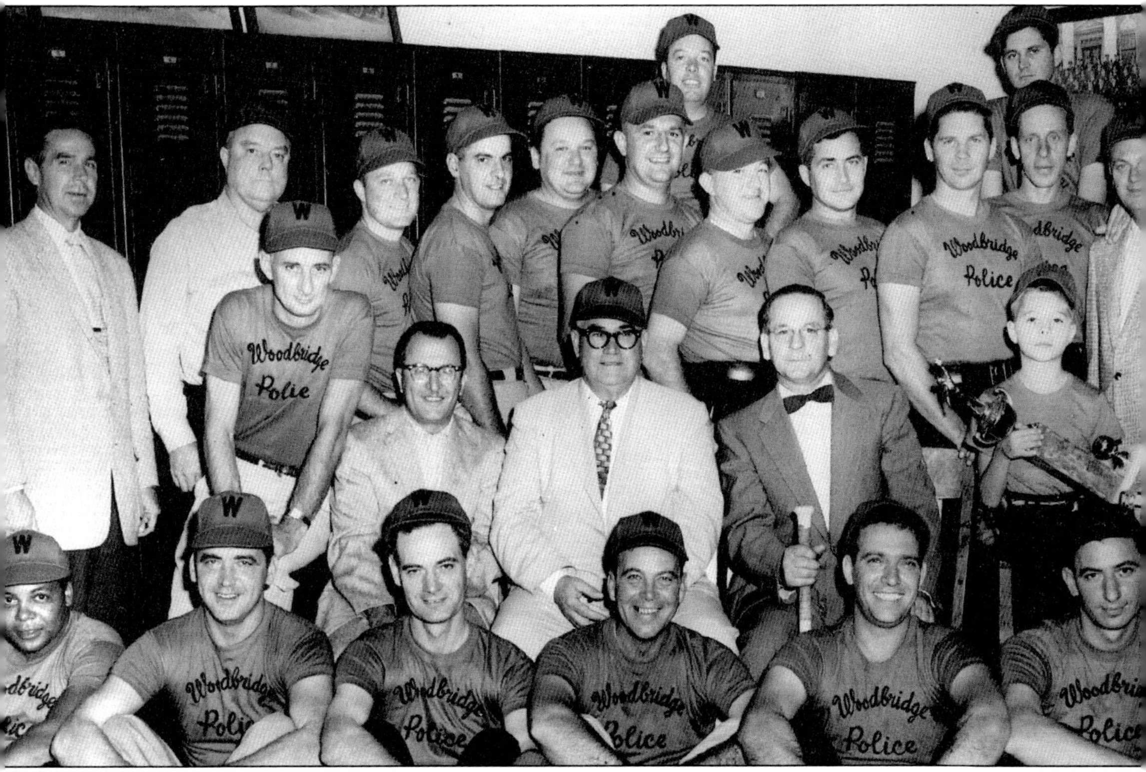

"Batter Up!" 1957. The Woodbridge Police Baseball Team are, from left to right, as follows: (first row) Larry Jefferson, Ziggy Wojcik, John Yuhasz, Joe McLaughlin, Sal Grillo, and Steve Yuhasz; (second row) Ed Feeney, unidentified, Chief Jack Egan, unidentified, and Robby Ohlson; (back row) Ken Van Pelt, Henry Dunham, Tony O'Brien, Phil Galasso, Joe Nagy, Ed Preputnick, Jack Waldman (behind Ed), Gene Martin, Bill Burns, Bob Ohlson, Joe Dombrowski, Alex Yaczina (behind Joe), and Charlie Bahr. Sponsored by the Policeman's Benevolent Association (PBA), the team played in the town league and against local factory teams. And, yes, the township policemen are still playing baseball! (Catherine Clark Burns.)

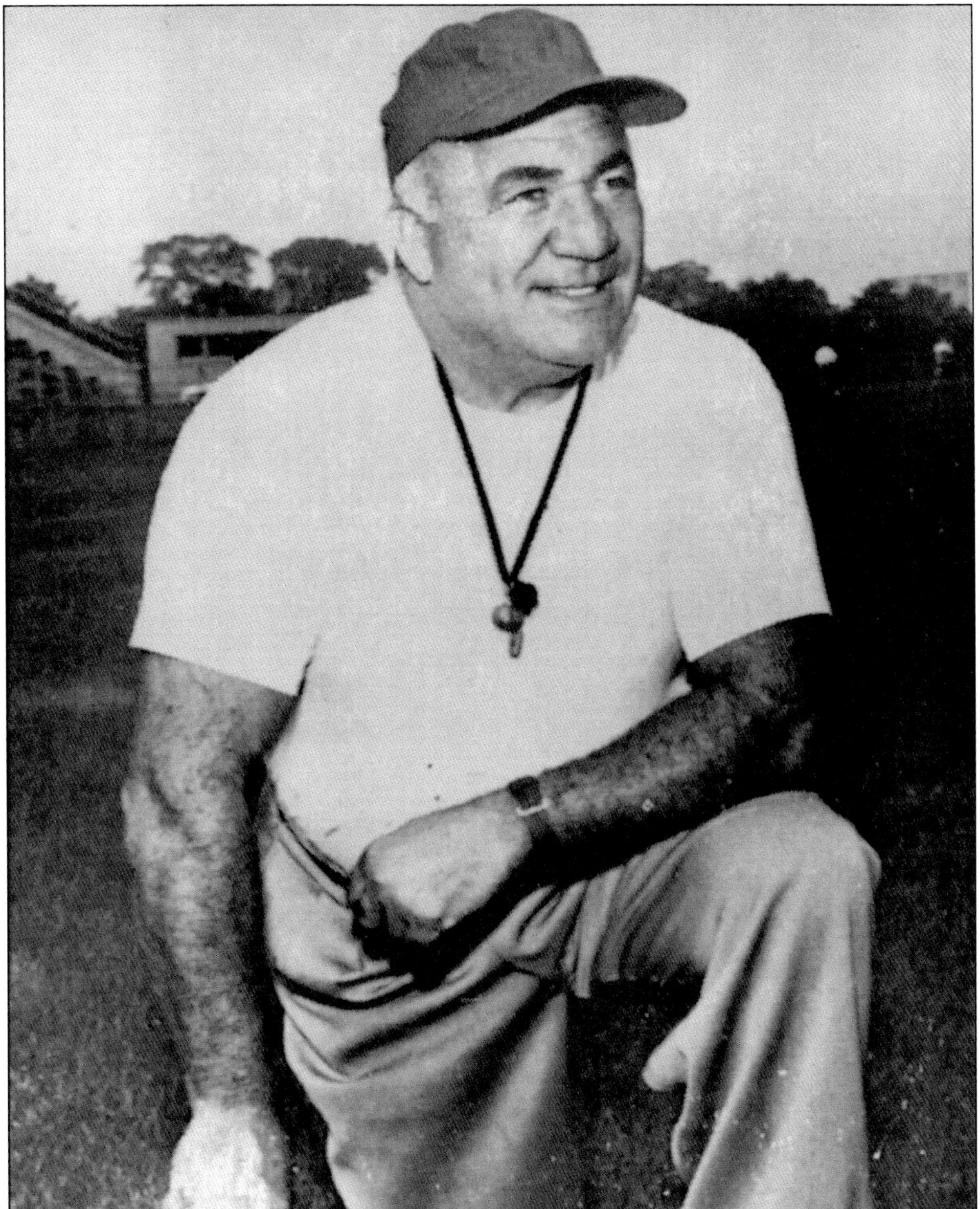

THE COACH, 1960. WHS football coach and physical education teacher Nicholas Anthony Priscoe was honored in October 1960 at a testimonial dinner celebrating his 25 years as a township educator. By the time of this banquet Nick was already a legend at Woodbridge High along with his famous quotation: "Remember the three C's, boys. Keep cool, calm, and collected." Board of education members saluted him by saying that "Mr. Priscoe has been an excellent influence upon the youth of the township and he can justifiably look with pride at the accomplishments of many a young man whose character he helped to build through the years." After graduating from Rutgers University, he joined the Philadelphia Eagles pro-football team and arrived in Woodbridge in 1935. Priscoe retired in 1973, and in 1979 township officials named the WHS stadium in his honor. He died two years later.

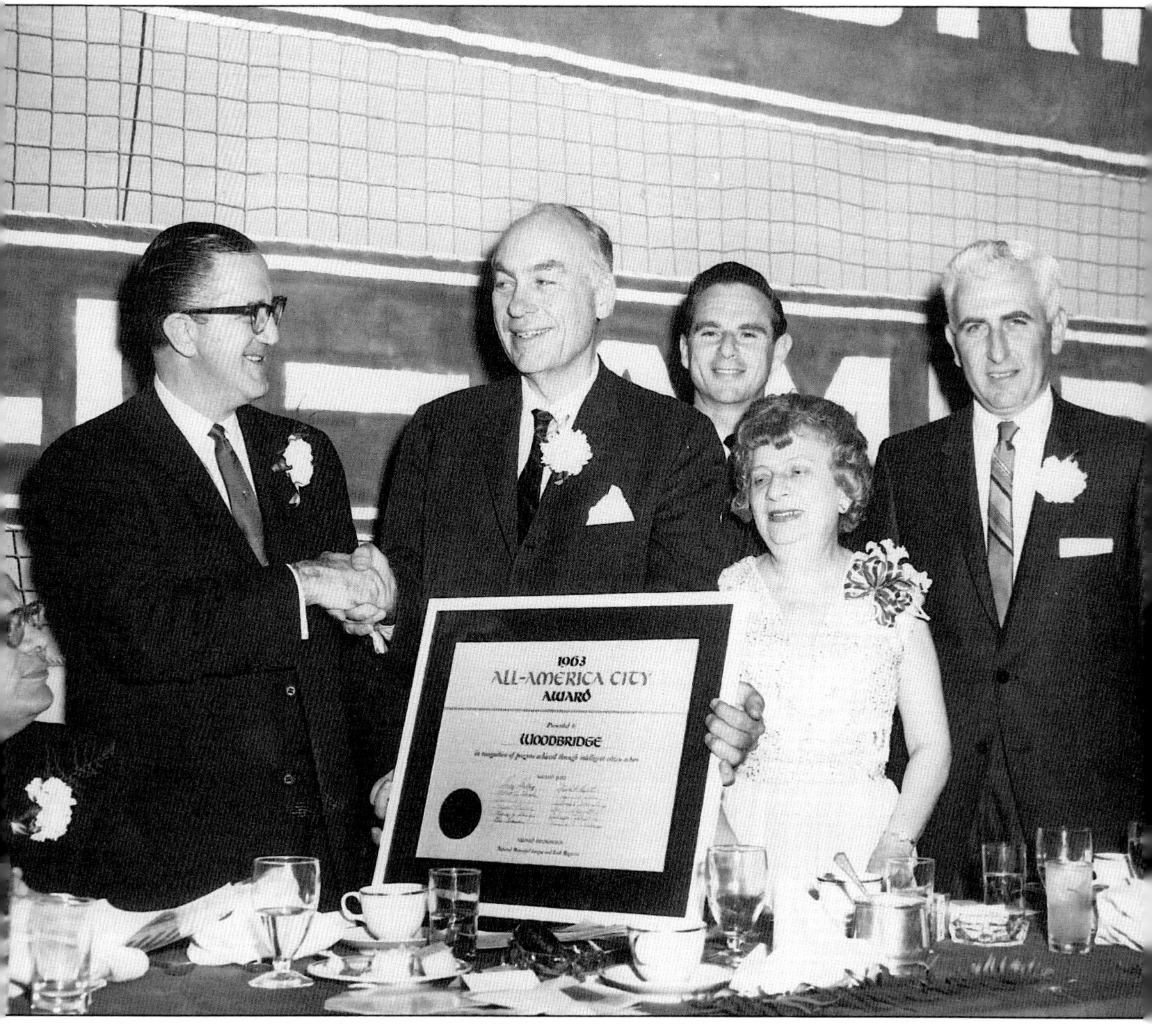

ALL-AMERICA CITY, APRIL 1964. The Jaycees and the Business and Professional Women's Club sponsored the township of Woodbridge in the prestigious All-America City competition conducted by *Look* magazine and the National Municipal League. After the township was judged a semi-finalist in November 1963, BPW member Ruth Wolk and Jaycee S. Buddy Harris traveled to Detroit to present the township's credentials to the All-American Cities jury, which was headed by Dr. George Gallup of the Gallup Poll. In March 1964 Woodbridge welcomed the big news that it had, indeed, won the award! The township held two special events, the raising of the All-America City flag at the Municipal Building on April 3 and a grand dinner-dance for 550 people at the National Guard Armory on April 18. This photo was taken at the Armory; it shows, from left to right, Mayor Walter Zirpolo accepting the official All-America City Award from Dr. Gallup, with Mr. Harris, Miss Wolk, and NJ Assemblyman Norman Tanzman looking on with admiration.

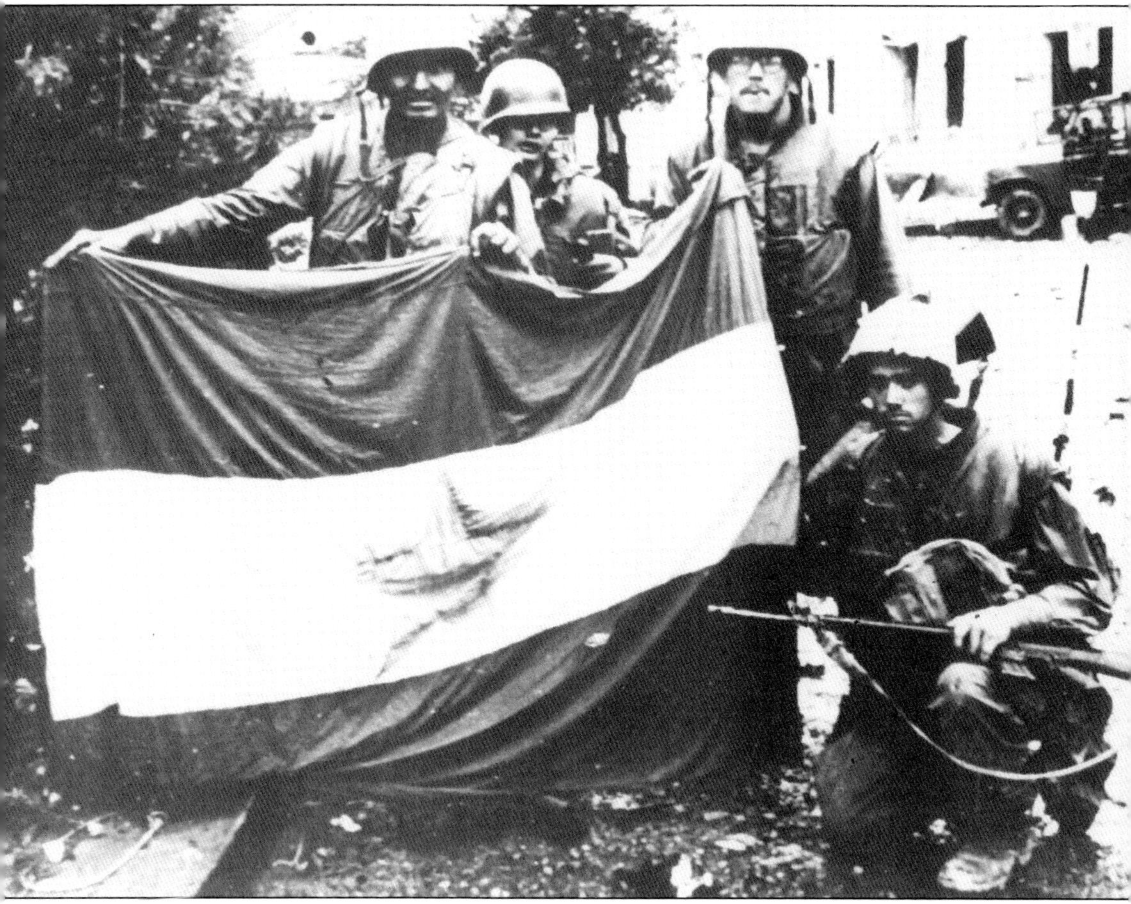

So Proudly He Served. Woodbridge resident Walter P. Kaczmarek served with the U.S. Marine Corps during the Vietnam War. On January 30, 1968, Communist troops attacked Saigon and other provincial capitals in an assault known as the Tet Offensive. On February 6, Walter (at left holding the flag), aided by two other Marines, made history by capturing the Viet Cong flag at Hue City while under heavy enemy fire. They then raised the American flag that presently is on board the U.S. Navy guided missile cruiser *Hue City*. (This photo showing three Marines with Walter was probably taken shortly after the flag raising.) In 1955, the United States agreed to train the South Vietnamese army. For the next 20 years, the U.S. was inextricably involved in the Vietnam War, with its personnel, military equipment, and money, making it the longest and most unpopular war in American history. (Walter P. Kaczmarek.)

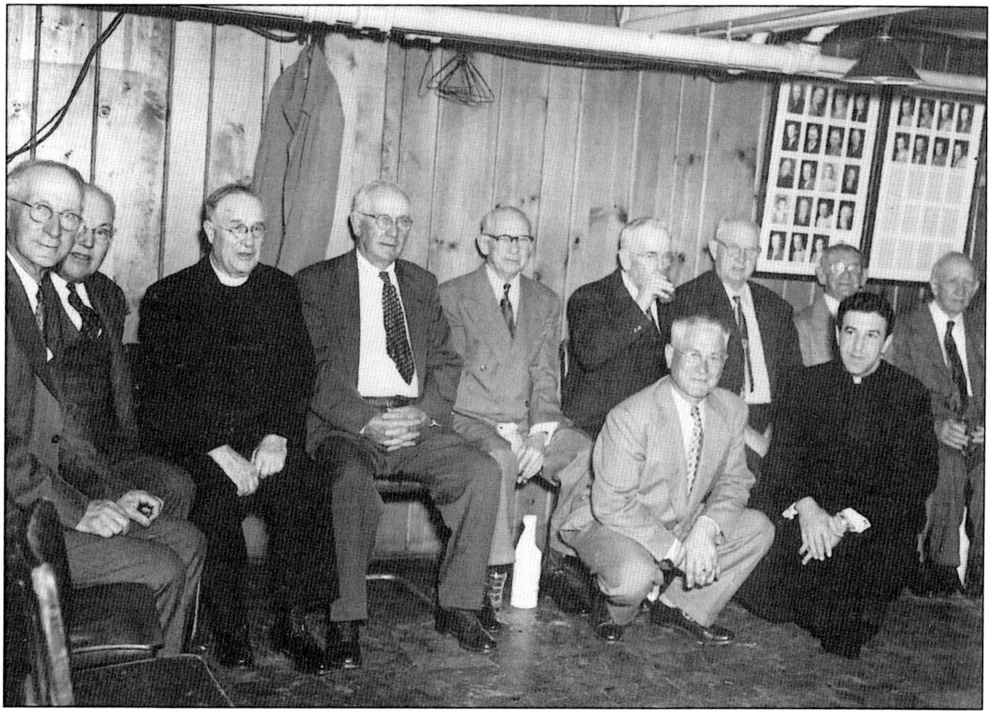

KNIGHTS OF COLUMBUS, C. 1965. The members shown here at their clubhouse on Main Street for Old Timers' Night are, from left to right, as follows: (front row, kneeling) Peter Fofrich and Father Gustave A. Napoleon; (back row) Bill Grace, Barney Dunigan, the Right Reverend Monsignor Charles G. McCorristin (pastor of St. James Church), Dick Grace, Maurice P. Dunigan, former Township Mayor William "Billy" Ryan, Michael Holohan, Fred Kath, and Thomas Gerity. (Philip J. Boyle.)

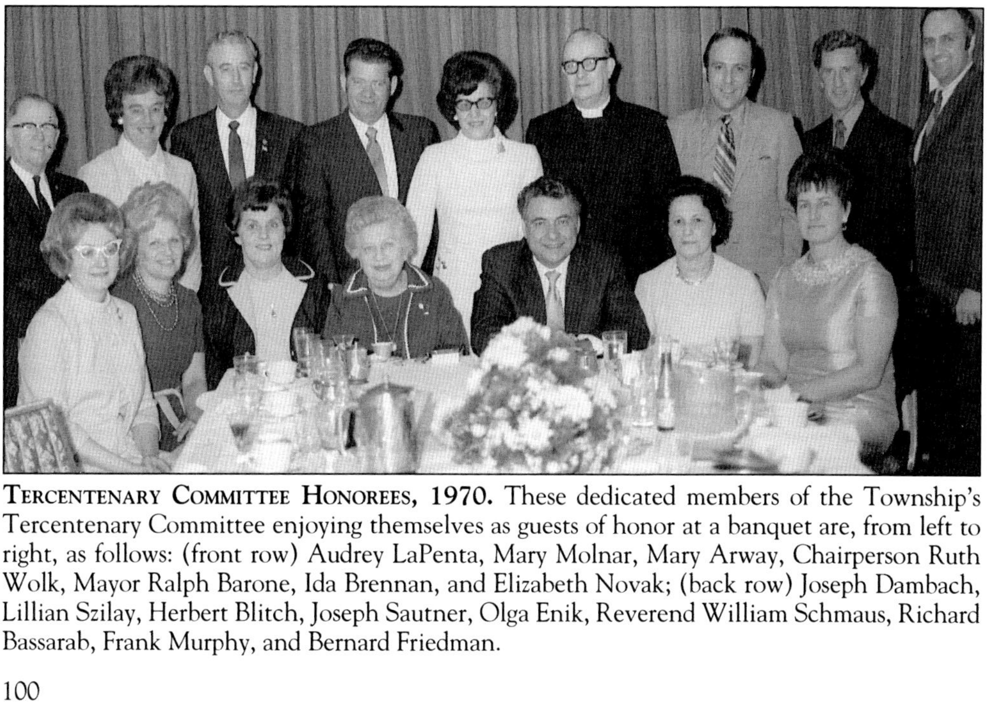

TERCENTENARY COMMITTEE HONOREES, 1970. These dedicated members of the Township's Tercentenary Committee enjoying themselves as guests of honor at a banquet are, from left to right, as follows: (front row) Audrey LaPenta, Mary Molnar, Mary Arway, Chairperson Ruth Wolk, Mayor Ralph Barone, Ida Brennan, and Elizabeth Novak; (back row) Joseph Dambach, Lillian Szilay, Herbert Blitch, Joseph Sautner, Olga Enik, Reverend William Schmaus, Richard Bassarab, Frank Murphy, and Bernard Friedman.

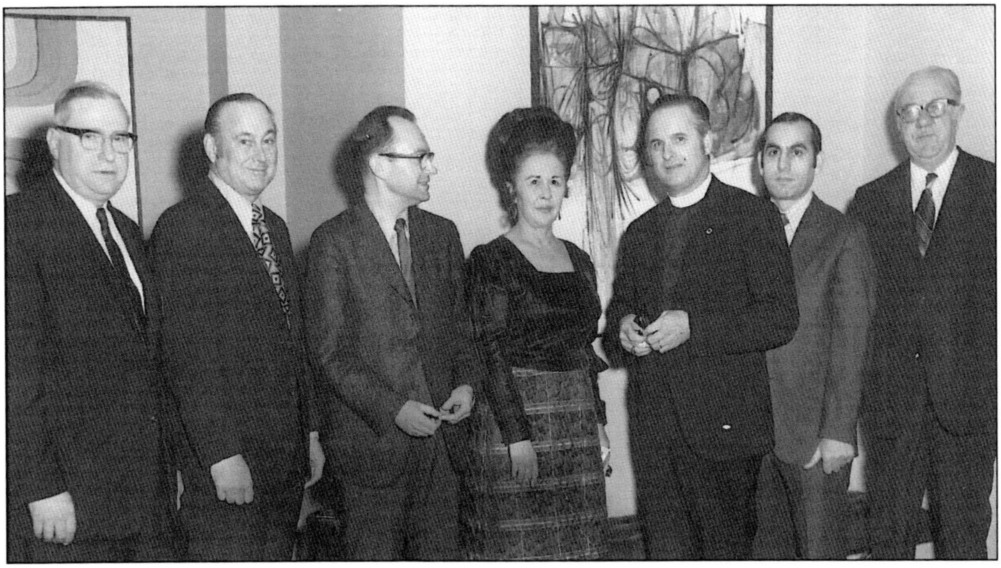

HISTORICAL SOCIETY, C. JUNE 1971. The organizers of the Woodbridge Historical Society are, from left to right, Clifford Bundy, Mayor John J. "Jack" Cassidy, unidentified guest speaker, Mary Bixel, Rev. Lewis Bender, Superintendent of Schools Dr. Fred Buonocore, and Housing Director Winfield Finn. Unfortunately, the society disbanded after a few years, but in 1984 other local residents founded the Historical Association of Woodbridge Township, an active, growing organization.

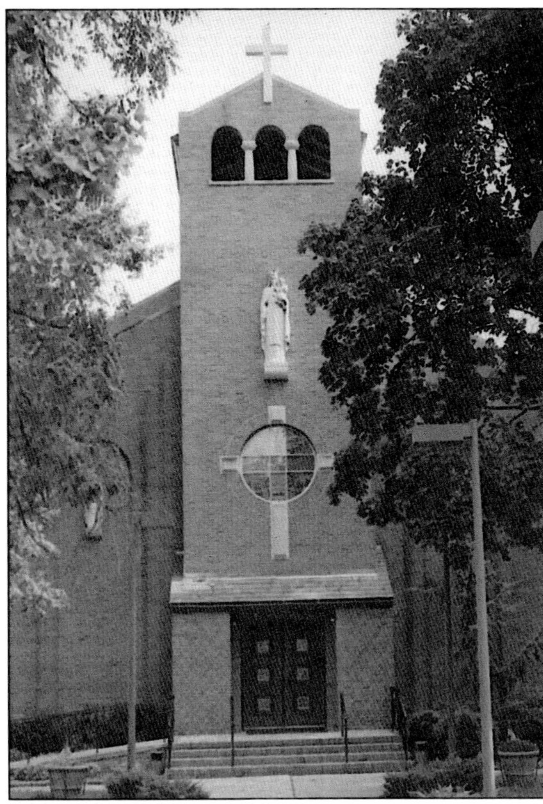

MT. CARMEL CHURCH. Local Hungarian immigrants founded the Roman Catholic Church of Our Lady of Mount Carmel on Amboy Avenue in 1920. From 1961 until 1970 the church maintained a parochial school. Two well-known Hungarian cardinals visited the parish, József Mindszenty in 1974 and Ladislaus Paskai in 1989. Through its dedicated pastors and members, Mt. Carmel remains an enduring house of worship. (Ray Schneider.)

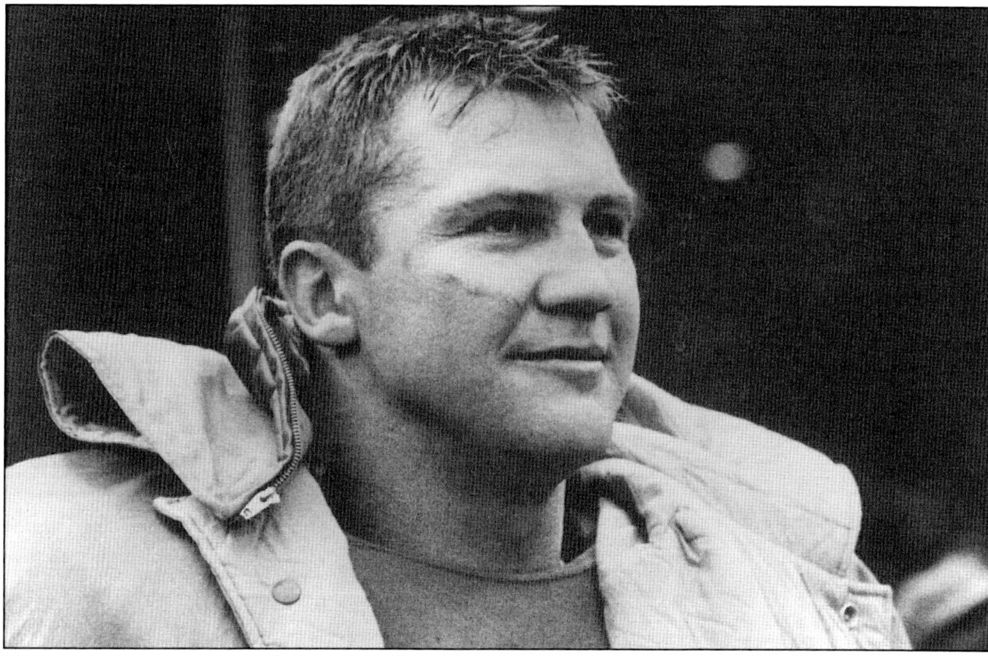

Man in Motion, c. 1955. Lou Creekmur, captain of the 1943 WHS football team, is shown here as a Detroit Lion. He became the Lions' regular offensive guard as a rookie in 1950. Lou made the Pro-Bowl squad for eight consecutive seasons and was named National Football League All-Star six times. (Lou Creekmur.)

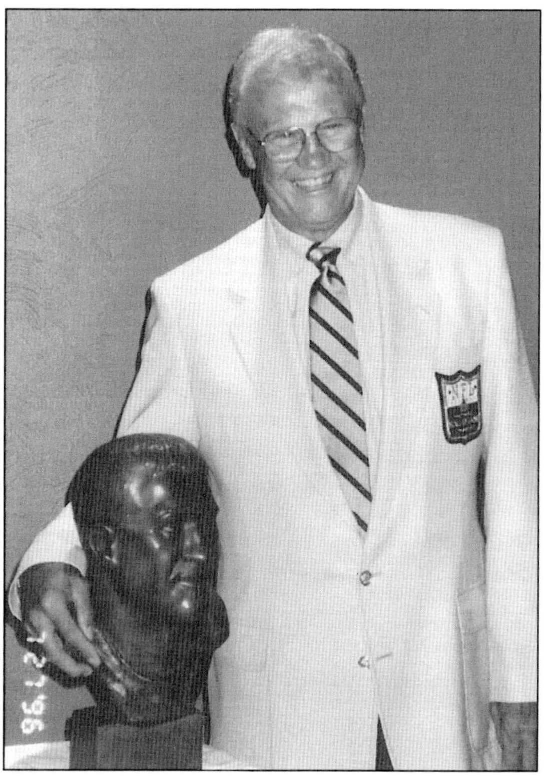

NFL Hall of Fame Inductee, July 1996. Lou Creekmur is pictured here at the time he was inducted into the Pro Football Hall of Fame in Canton, OH, an event Lou described as, "the biggest, wildest 'Wow' of my life!" Lou retired from the Detroit Lions in 1959, and has been affiliated with Ryder Truck Rentals for many years. He has made TV commercials for Nike and Cadillac and appears on six collectible sports cards. (Lou Creekmur.)

Six

WOODBRIDGE AT WORK

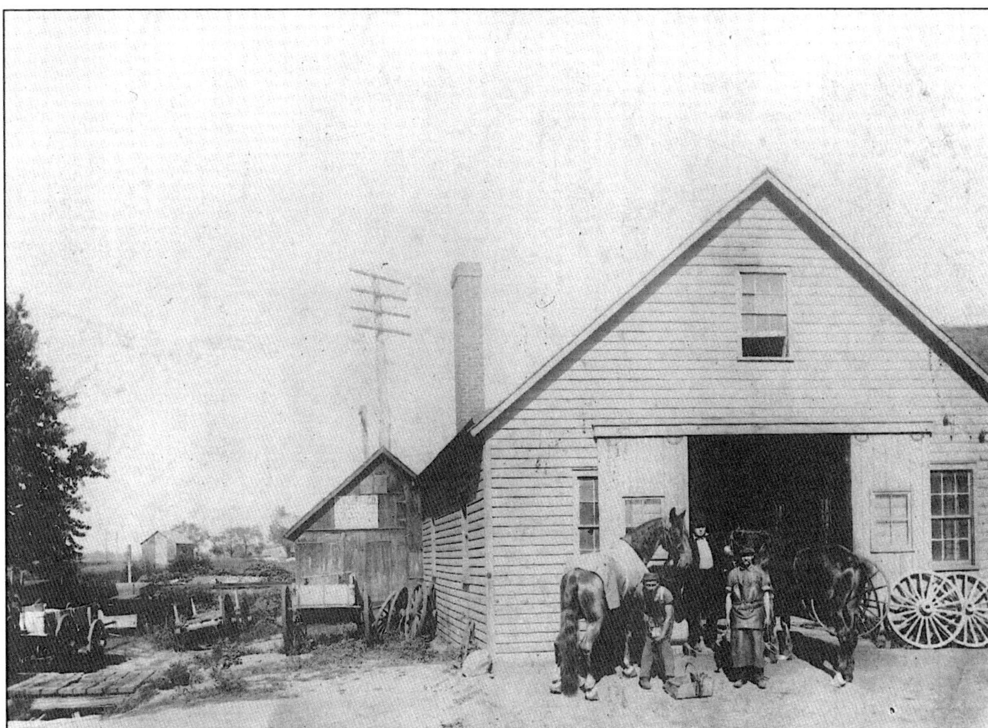

THE VILLAGE BLACKSMITH, C. 1910. Jurgen L. Nielsen (left) may not be working "under a spreading chestnut tree," as in Henry Wadsworth Longfellow's beloved poem, but he probably was a man "with large and sinewy hands" as the poet described his "smithy." Jurgen Nielsen and N. Johnson owned this blacksmith shop at Fulton and Albert Streets. The shop closed in 1930. The sign on the left building reads, "D. Wolff, Pianos and Furniture." (Carol Agesen Dunigan.)

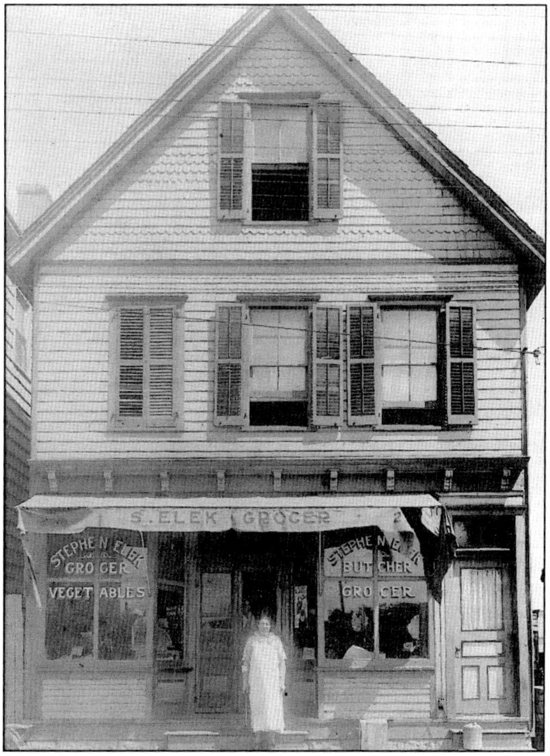

ELEK'S STORE, C. 1920. Julia Elek stands outside the grocery at 238 Fulton Street that she and her husband, Stephen, purchased from Simon and Leah Kahme in 1919. The store, which was patronized by residents from the Strawberry Hill area, opened at 5 a.m. and closed long hours later, seven days a week. In 1928 the grocery was rebuilt after a fire, and in 1946 it was sold to the Highway Authority for the construction of the NJ Turnpike. Julia Elek was the grandmother of local resident James Elek. (James Elek.)

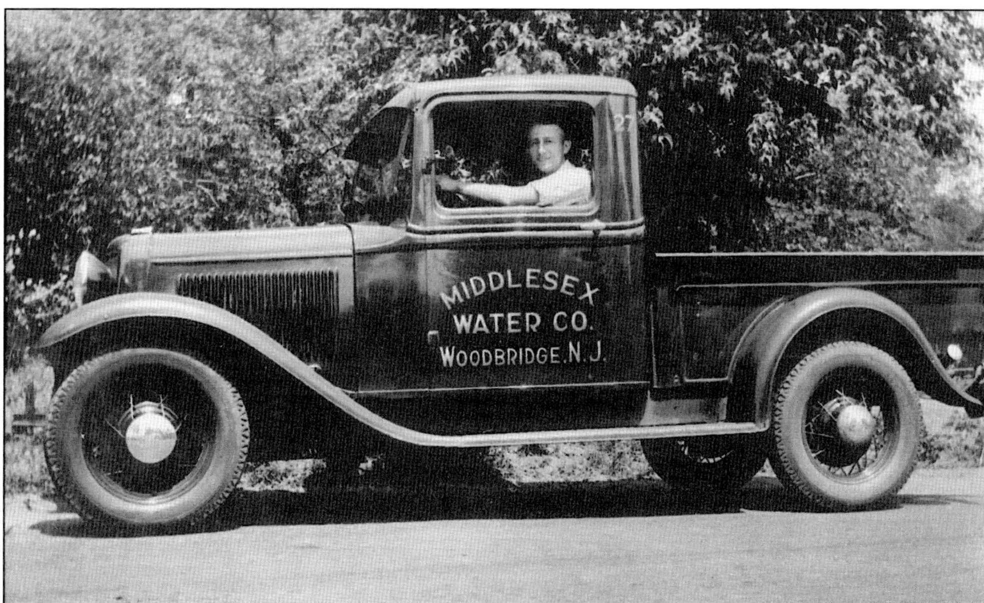

MIDDLESEX WATER CO., MAY 1934. Leon Silakoski Sr., behind the wheel of a company truck, worked for Middlesex Water for more than 50 years as a repairman and foreman. His brother Anthony, also an employee, was seriously injured in the 1940 United Railway Explosion. The water company maintained offices in the old National Bank building on Main Street until 1984, when its present complex opened in Iselin. (Middlesex Water Co.)

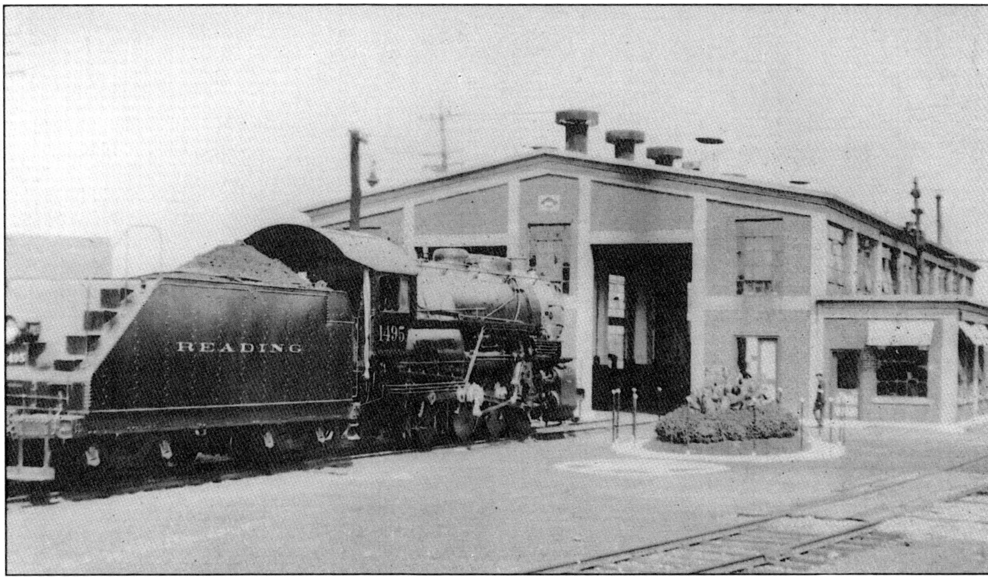

ROUNDHOUSE, C. 1925. Coal for heating power plant boilers was transported to the Port Reading Terminal by railroad cars. These coal cars were then moved to docks and emptied into barges for the trip to area electric power plants. Steam locomotive No. 1495 is typical of the small engines that remained at the terminal to move the coal cars. Behind No. 1495 is the roundhouse where these locomotives were maintained and repaired. (Fred McElhenny.)

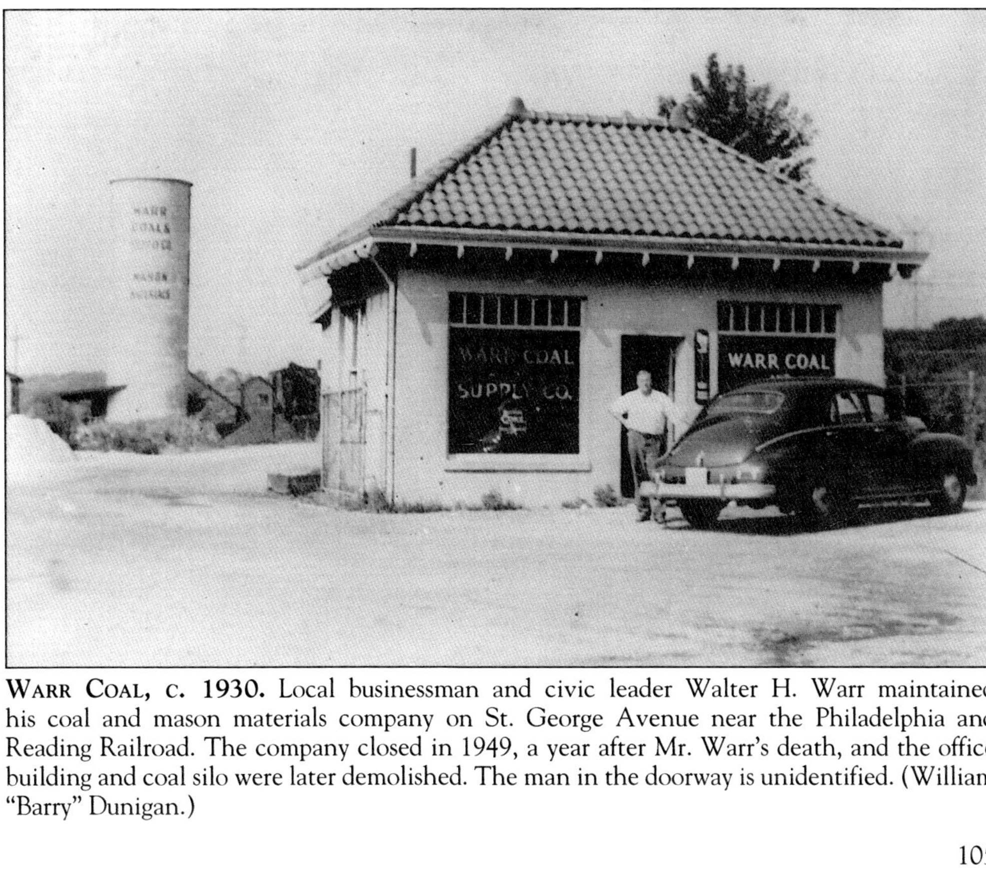

WARR COAL, C. 1930. Local businessman and civic leader Walter H. Warr maintained his coal and mason materials company on St. George Avenue near the Philadelphia and Reading Railroad. The company closed in 1949, a year after Mr. Warr's death, and the office building and coal silo were later demolished. The man in the doorway is unidentified. (William "Barry" Dunigan.)

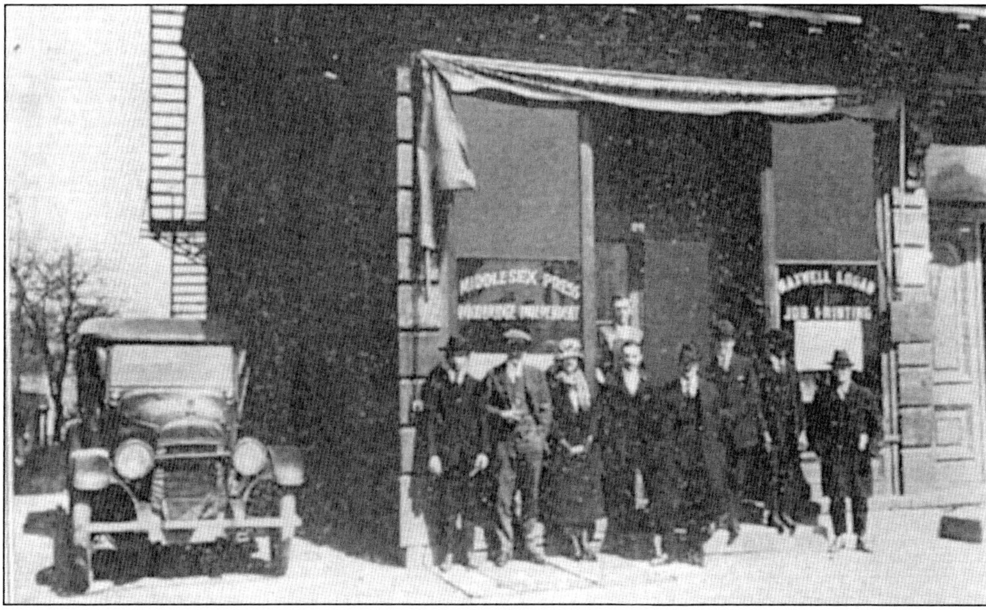

PRINT SHOP, 1924. Maxwell Logan started the Woodbridge *Independent* in 1919, putting it in competition with the older community paper, the *Leader-Journal.* Wider circulation may have allowed the *Independent* to tout, "The most widely read newspaper in Woodbridge." A staff of one woman and eight men formed the parent company, the Middlesex Press, which also did job shop printing.

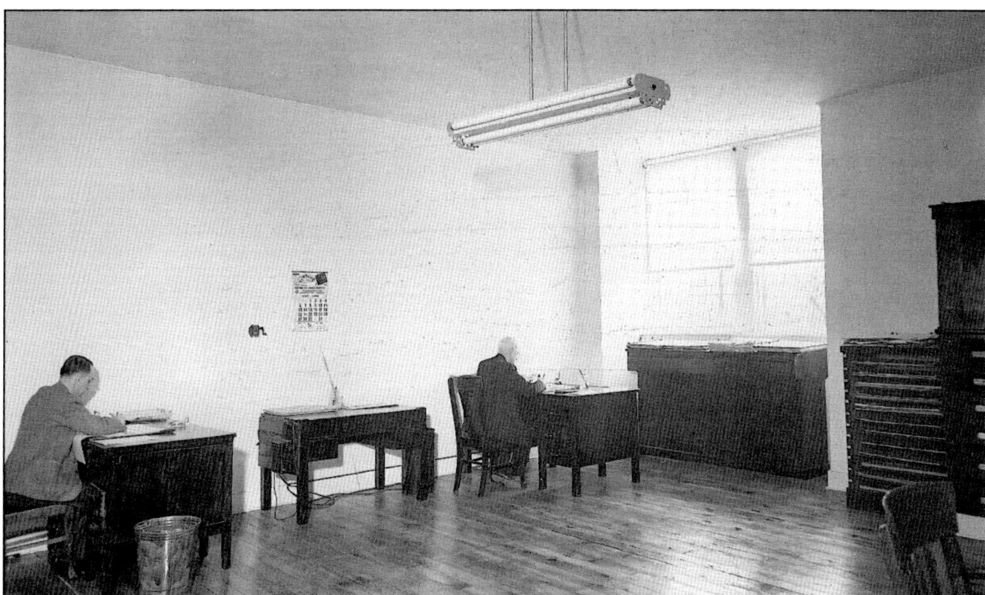

NEWSPAPER OFFICE, MAY 1946. In 1939 the *Leader-Journal* and the *Independent* joined forces under the title, *Independent-Leader,* with Hugh Williamson Kelly as president and Charles E. Gregory as managing editor. The war-imposed shortages of the preceding years may have limited this austere office to one telephone, one pencil sharpener, a wall calendar, and, apparently, no typewriters. (Nick Urban.)

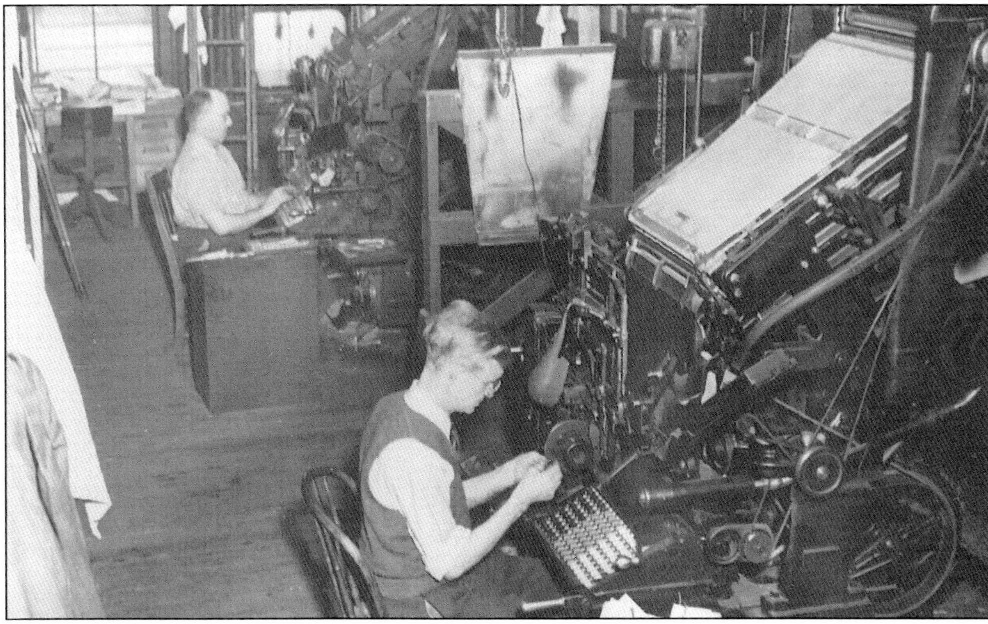

LINOTYPE OPERATORS, C. 1970. Charles Heller (left) and Steve Sabo set type for printing the *Independent-Leader* newspaper. The linotype machine, first used commercially in 1886, received its name from the unique operation of producing a complete line of type ready for printing. As the operator types a story, the machine places small brass molds of the letter typed in line and then fills them with molten lead forming one "line." (Nick Urban.)

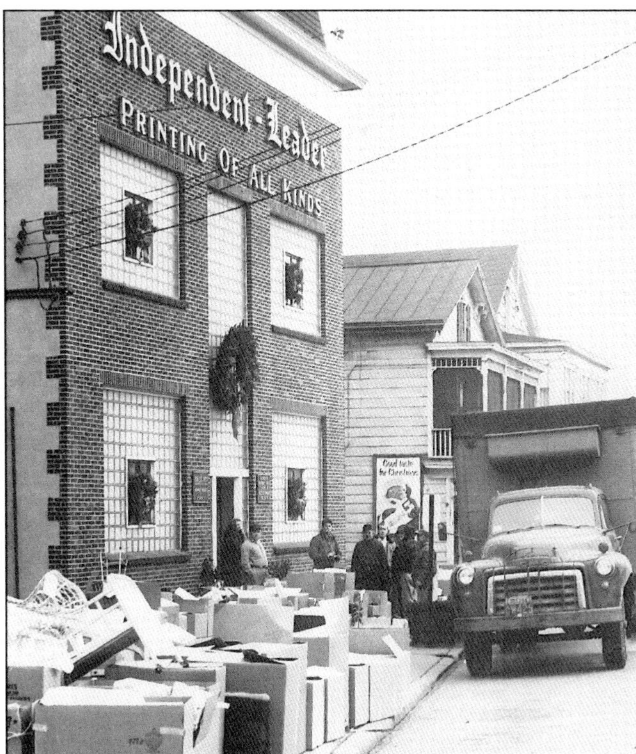

CHRISTMAS AT THE *INDEPENDENT-LEADER*, C. 1965. It has been reported that these boxes contain holiday gifts for needy local residents from a collection sponsored by the newspaper. Such good works were surely missed after the newspaper ceased publication on January 1, 1971. The building dates back to 1870 and, in addition to the *Independent-Leader*, has housed the Masonic Hall, post office, Peterson's Jewelry Store, and Ephraim Cutter, the township attorney in the early 1900s. It was torn down in the 1970s. (Nick Urban.)

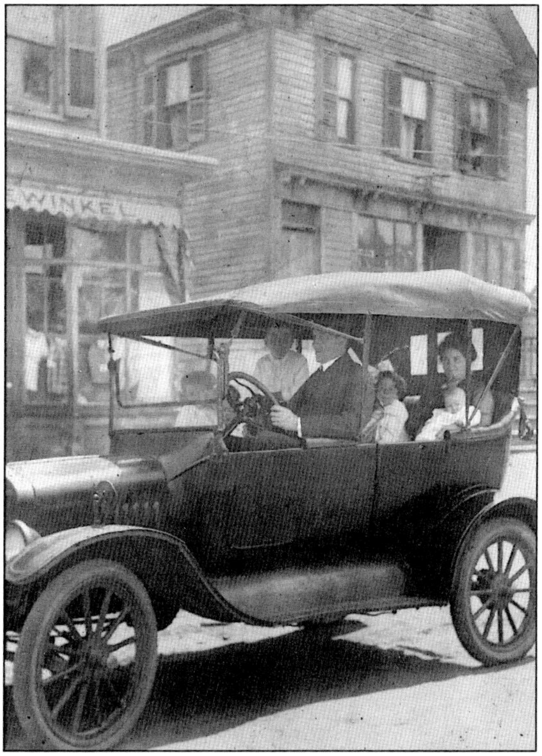

THE KREWINKELS, c. 1921. It looks as though Emma and Louis Krewinkel, who owned the Sunrise Bakery (on the left) at 53 New Street, and their children are ready for church or maybe a Sunday afternoon drive in their Model T Ford. Emma and Louis opened their bakery shortly after they were married in Woodbridge in 1909. Louis (1880–1955) came from Germany, and Emma (1882–1948) came from the Austro-Hungarian Empire (see next photo). (Diana Krewinkel.)

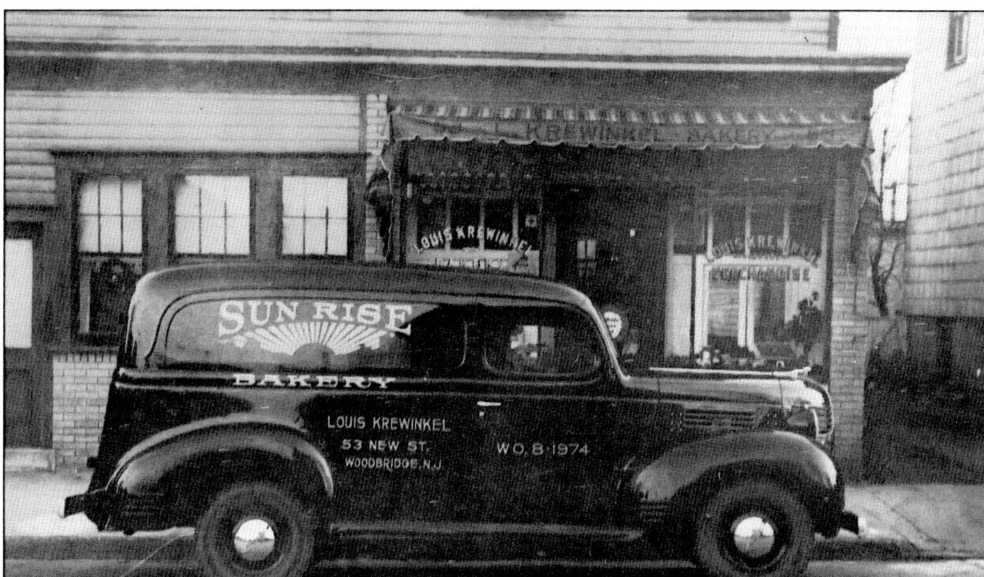

SUNRISE BAKERY, c. 1936. Before and after school the five Krewinkel children helped their father with his daily deliveries in a horse-drawn wagon and later in this truck. Louis, who served as a cavalry officer in the German Army during the Boer War (1899–1902), closed his bake shop in 1941. In 1964 his daughter, Margaret Krewinkel Jost, and her sister-in-law, Edna Oberlies Jost, included the recipe for Mr. Krewinkel's popular pumpkin pie in their Woodbridge cookbook. (Diana Krewinkel.)

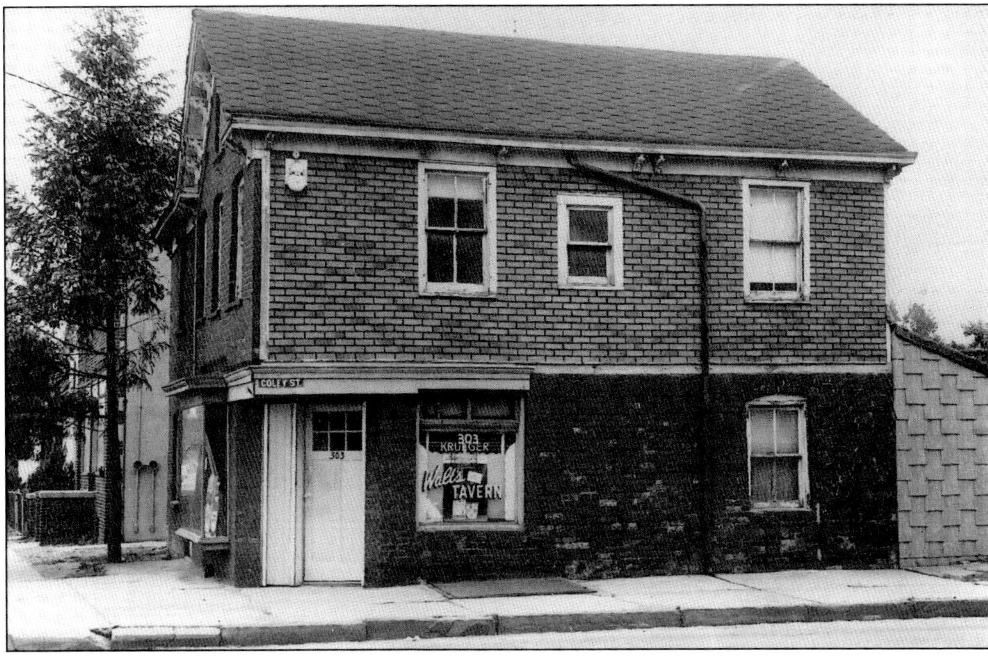

LOCAL TAVERN, C. 1960. Walt's Tavern at the corner of Coley and Fulton Streets was one of several small bars in this area of town. The bar, originally called Racz's Tavern, was opened in 1918 by Rose and Frank Racz. After several name changes it became Walt's Tavern when Frank and Rose's son-in-law, Walter Bertram, took over. He ran it until 1968 when it changed to Curly's Corral. Curly's closed in 1970, and the building was torn down in 1982 for safety reasons. (Bernie Anderson Sr.)

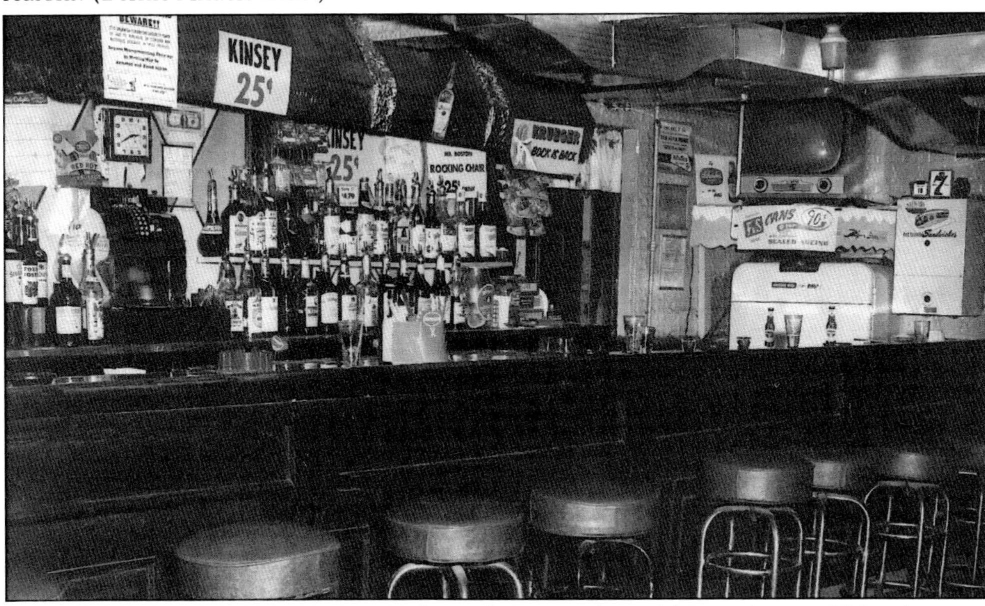

INSIDE WALT'S TAVERN, C. 1960. With its chrome and vinyl barstools, tiny TV, refrigerator with rounded, "modern" curves, first-earned dollar bill, and clearly visible clock used to shoo out the last late-night patron, this interior shot gives us a taste of the atmosphere of a small, neighborhood bar of the time. (Bernie Anderson Sr.)

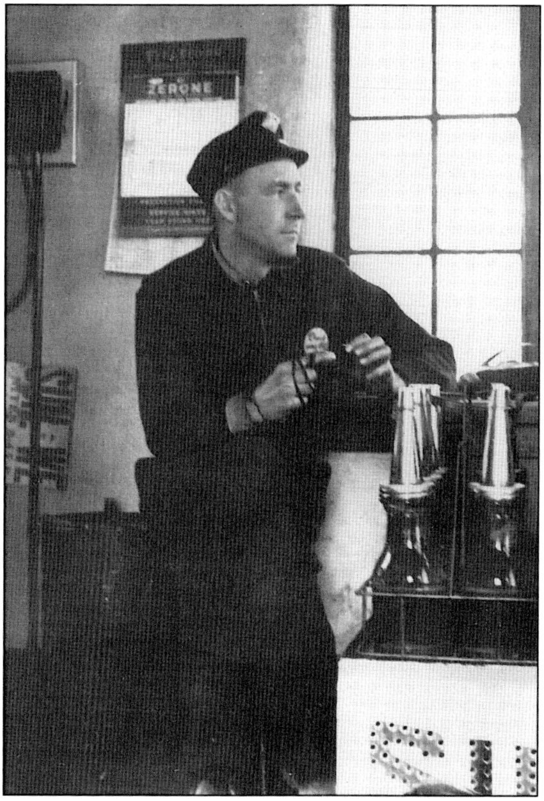

Frank Keating's Sunoco, c. 1935. *Left:* Frank Keating, brother of longtime Woodbridge Township Police Chief George E. Keating, watches for customers to pull into his Sunoco station on the corner of Amboy and Grove Avenues. His wall calendar spells out "Zerone," an anti-freeze to be mixed with water in a car radiator to prevent freeze-up. Frank's glass oil bottles were not tamperproof and were later phased out by the major oil companies. *Below:* The small, "cottage-style" station with side casement windows and tiled roof was typical of gas stations designed at the time. Frank later opened another gas station at the Amboy Avenue and Green Street intersection. (Kathy Jost Keating.)

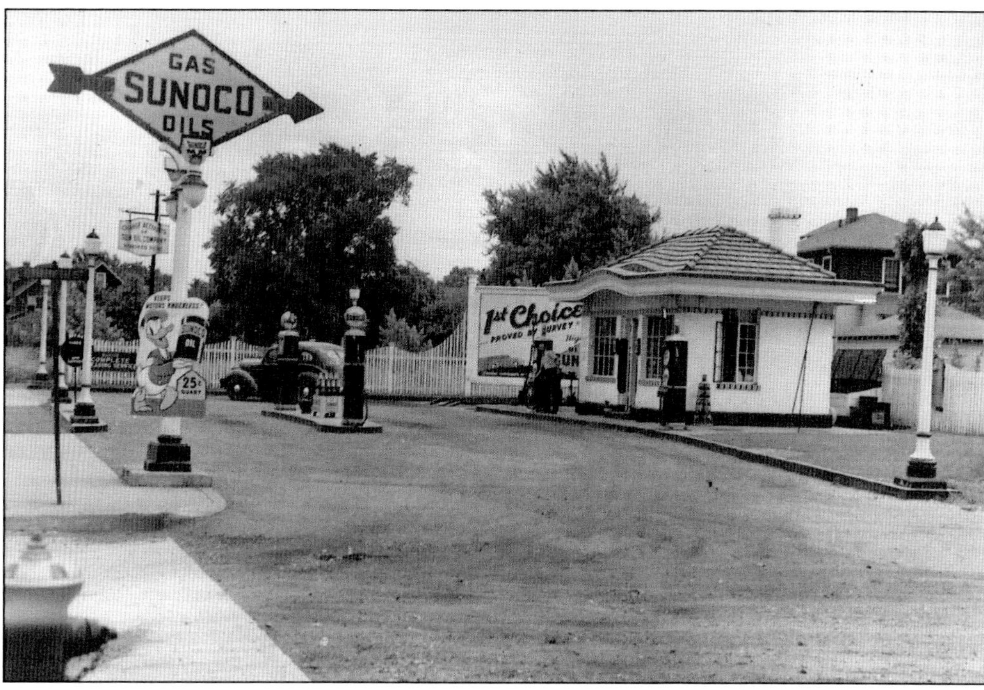

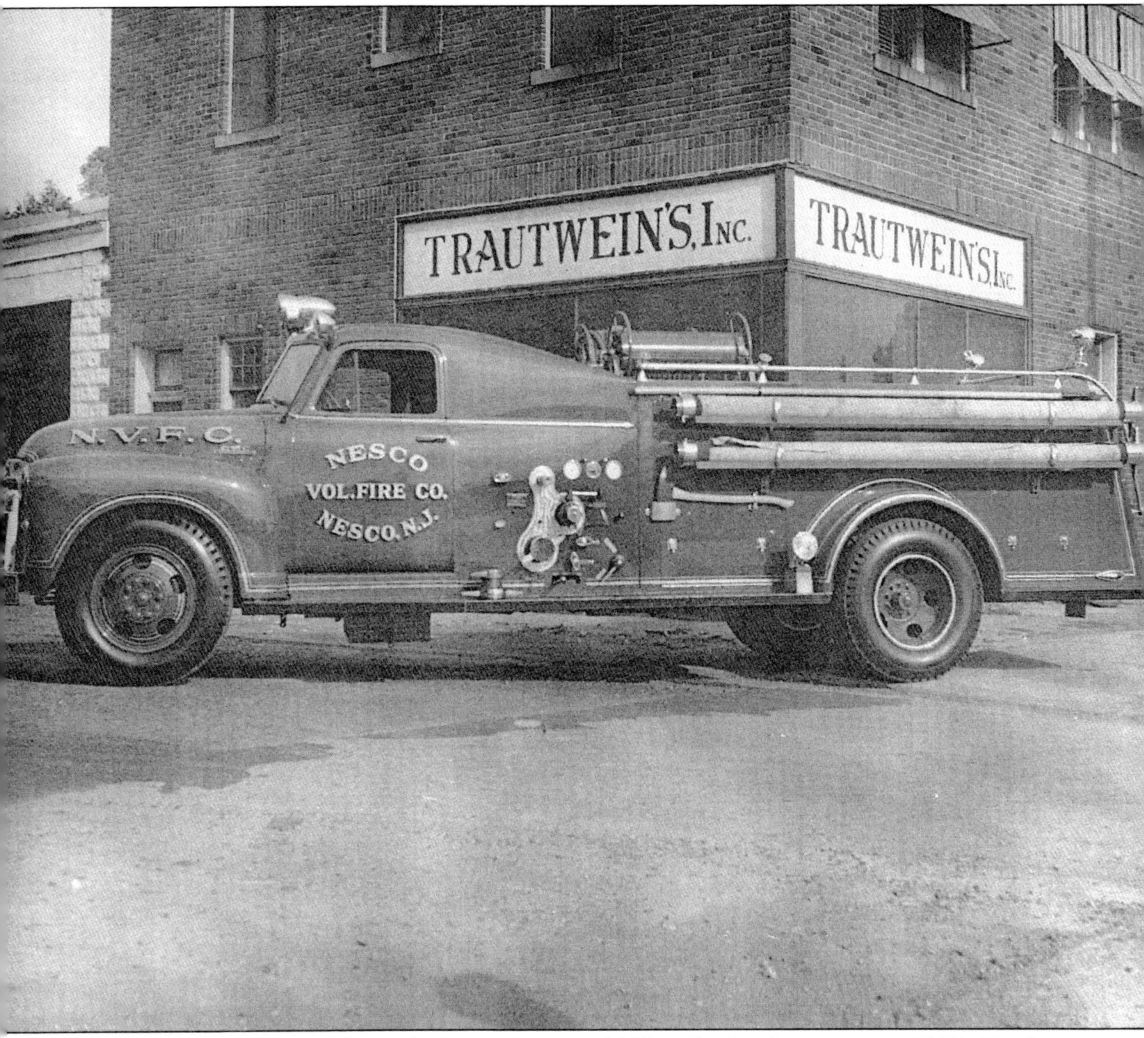

TRAUTWEIN'S, C. 1950. When asked to update an old Woodbridge fire engine in 1932, Charles Trautwein, a tool and die maker by trade, had sown the seeds of a new business. By 1939, his shop, located at the corner of High Street and Amboy Avenue, was ready to repair and custom build fire engines. Trautwein and his 18 employees built "Class A Rigs," engines that could pump at least 300 gallons of water a minute. One fire engine a month could be delivered to customers. His son Charles Jr. later joined his father in the business. After Charles Sr. died, John Crimmins, a Trautwein employee, bought the firm in 1987 and moved it to Farmingdale, NJ, where it still operates. The Trautwein building in Woodbridge now houses the Vatra beauty supply company. (For those interested, Nesco, NJ, is a small town in Atlantic County, south of the Wharton State Forest and close to the Atlantic City Expressway.) (William Harned.)

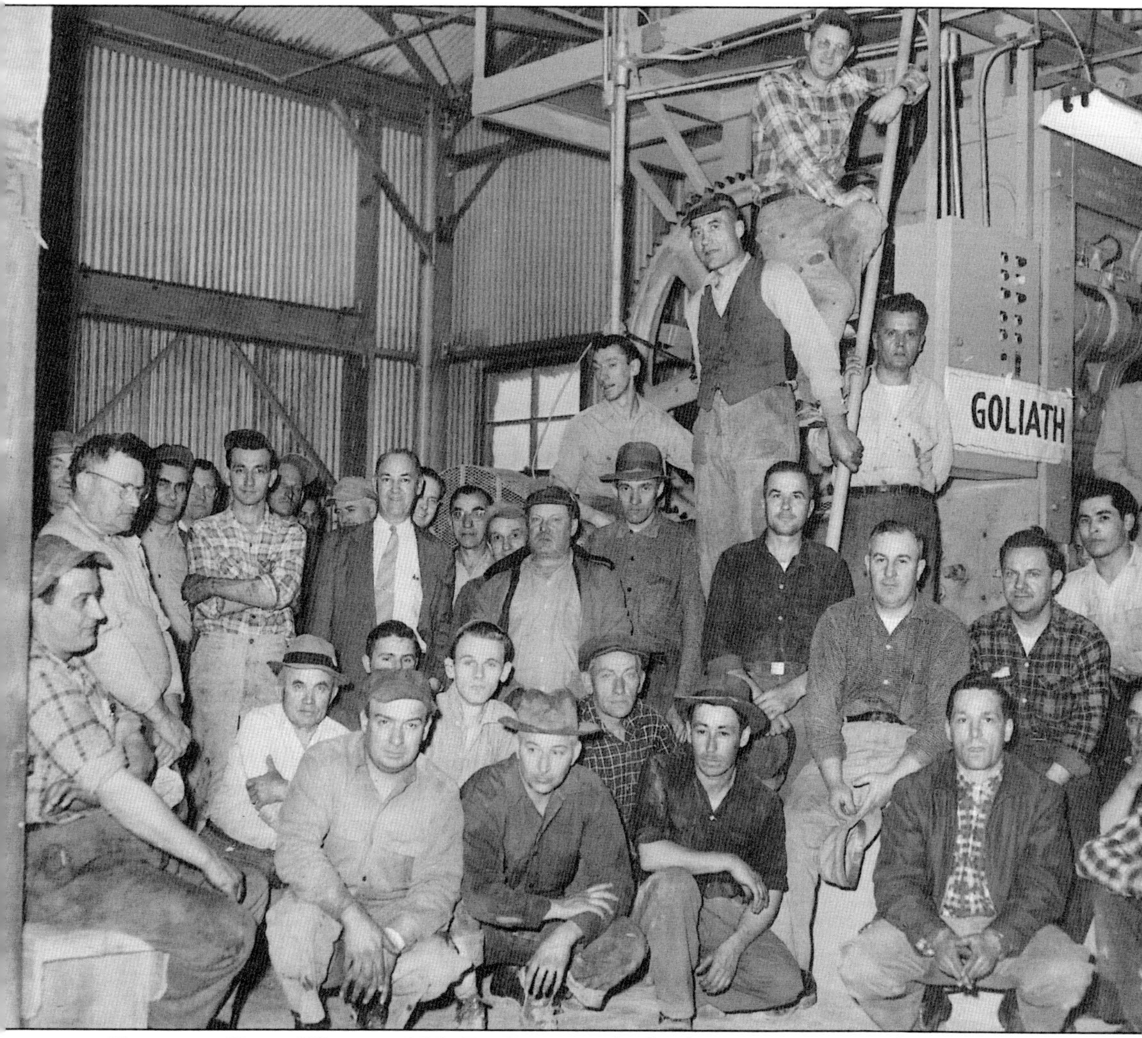

VALENTINE BRICK WORKS, 1955. Employees in the brick pressing section of the Valentine Fire Brick Company celebrate the arrival of a new machine, the "Goliath." From left to right, the workers are as follows: (front two rows) Paul Erdelyi (plaid shirt on bench), Paul Juhasz (white shirt), Frank Erdelyi (front), unidentified behind Frank, Maxie Soloman, Frank Nagy (dark shirt), unidentified worker (checked shirt), Angelo Jiminez, Steve Tomokovich (dark jacket), Joe Zelenak Jr. (hand on face), and Harry ? (plaid shirt); (second row, all standing) Bill Demler Sr., Frank Resko (wearing glasses), Joseph Puskas, unidentified, John Kissel (plaid shirt), Louis Boka, Ralph Cinacolla, Joseph Szebenyi, Walter Smith (jacket and tie), Bob Lutz, Joe Zelenak Sr., Wally Pierson, John Erli Sr. (open jacket), George Trout, Frank Petrick, Frank Dancsecs (holding hat), Frank Pinkiewicz (plaid shirt), and unidentified; (top five workers) Ernest Kijula, Mr. Shrimp (dark vest), John Balogh (plaid shirt), Paul Sabine, and Norman Strange (far right). (Andrew Csepcsar.)

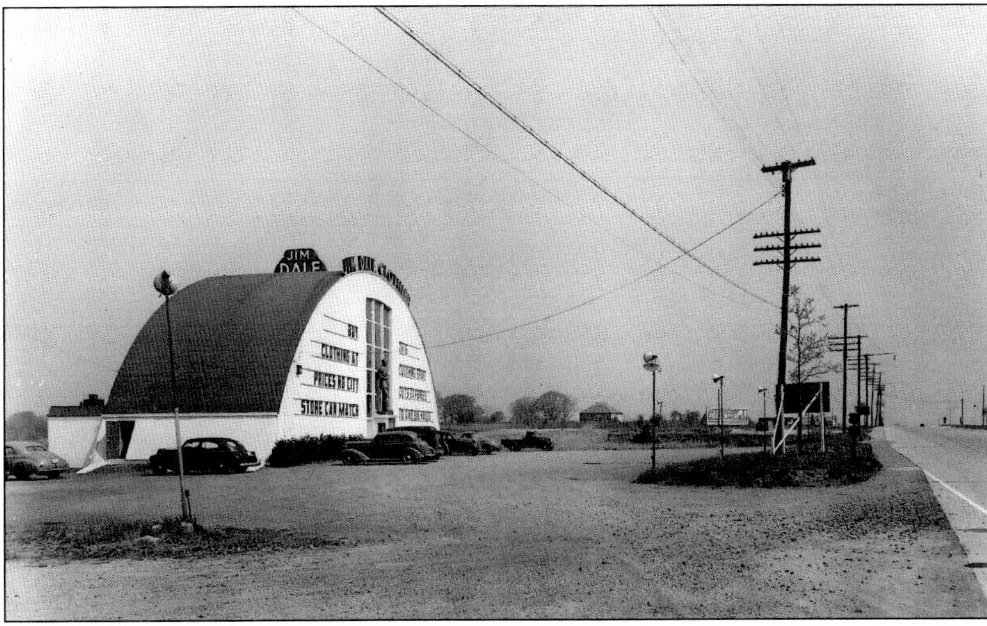

HIGHWAY CLOTHIER, C. 1949. The Jim Dale Clothing Store on Route 25 (now Route One) was an early highway discount store, nicknamed "the clothing store in a cornfield." Returning World War II veterans must have quickly recognized Jim Dale's unique architecture, designed in the style of the military's Quonset Hut barracks. (Bernie Anderson Sr.)

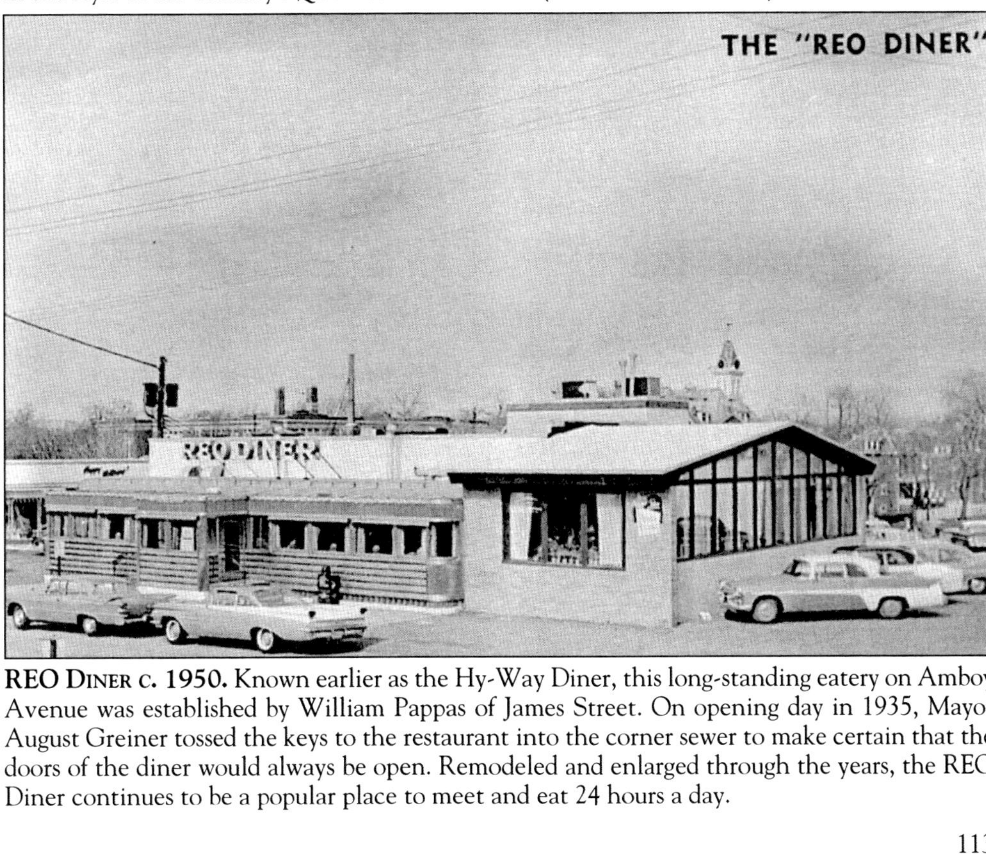

REO DINER C. 1950. Known earlier as the Hy-Way Diner, this long-standing eatery on Amboy Avenue was established by William Pappas of James Street. On opening day in 1935, Mayor August Greiner tossed the keys to the restaurant into the corner sewer to make certain that the doors of the diner would always be open. Remodeled and enlarged through the years, the REO Diner continues to be a popular place to meet and eat 24 hours a day.

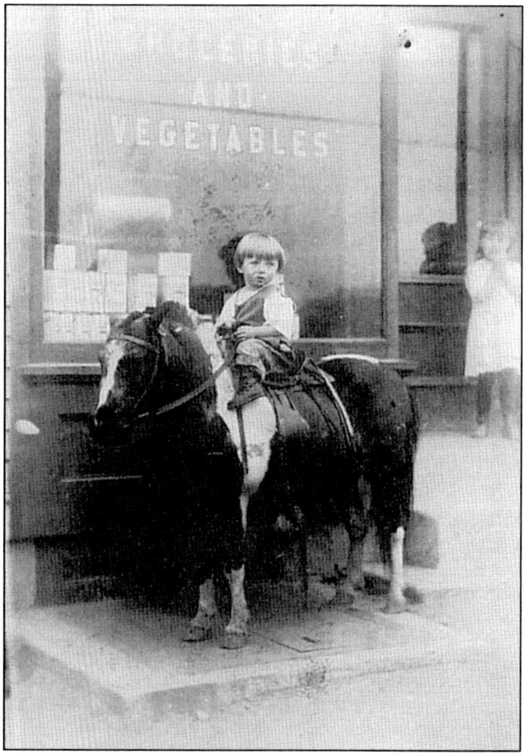

PONY RIDER, c. 1922. An apprehensive Paul Chovan was one of the lucky children to get a ride when the "pony ride man" came to town. Just think, a real pony, not one of those mechanical rides outside stores today. Behind him is Fords' Grocery at 488 New Brunswick Avenue, owned by Anna and Steve Nagy and operated by their daughter Emma and her husband, Paul, young Paul's parents. An unidentified little girl watches with interest. (See page 121.) (Ann and Paul Chovan.)

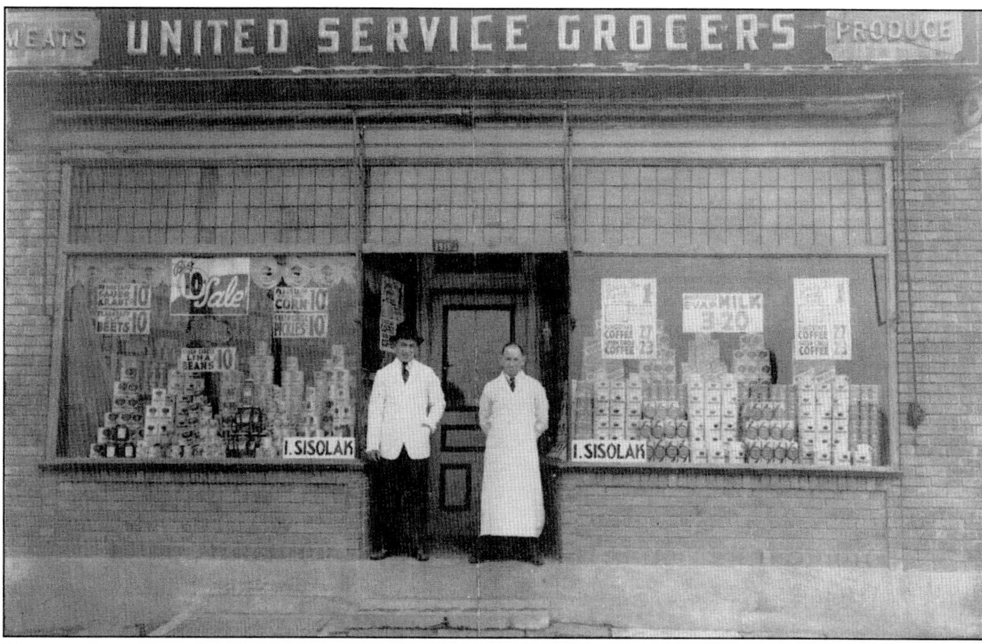

FATHER AND SON GROCERY, c. 1940. Sisolak's Grocery at 1516 Main Street in Fords, opposite School 14, was operated by I. Sisolak (right) and his son Paul. Their window prices tell us how far a dollar could be stretched in "those days." Fords was known earlier by the curious name of Sling Tail. The name changed to Fords' Corner and then simply to Fords, a name derived from the Ford family, who lived in the area. (Bernie Anderson Sr.)

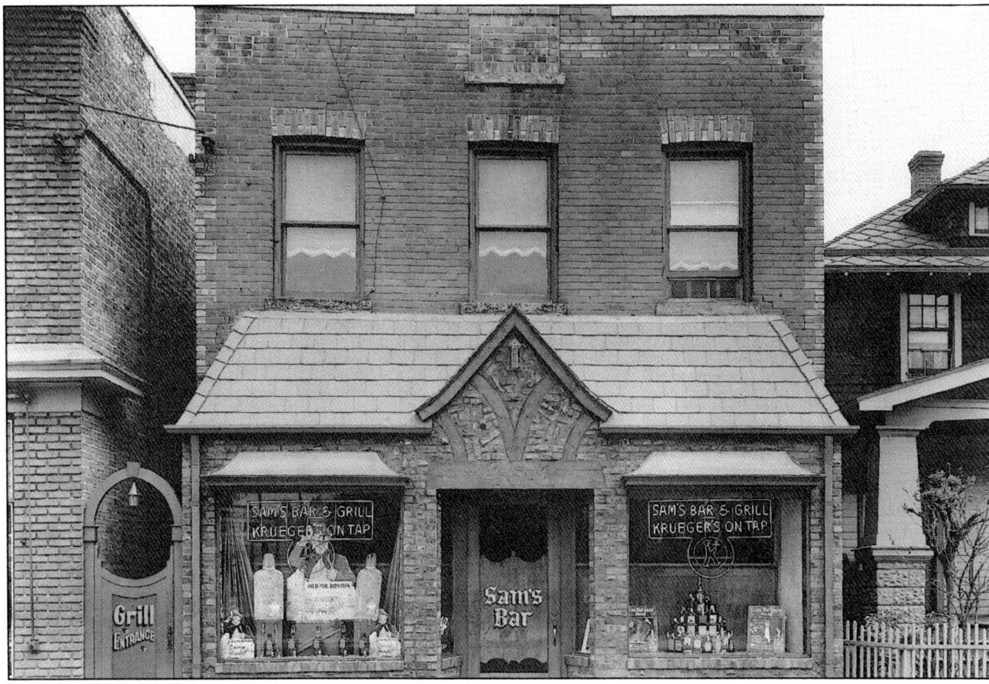

SAM'S BAR, C. 1950. This popular bar and grill at 464 New Brunswick Avenue in Fords was owned by Sam Hodes, who lived with his family on the second floor. Ladies stopping for a bite to eat could bypass the bar if they wished by using the inviting moongate-inspired Grill Entrance. The brick building on the left housed Balint's Hardware Store, which is now Thompson Sentry Hardware. (Bernie Anderson Sr.)

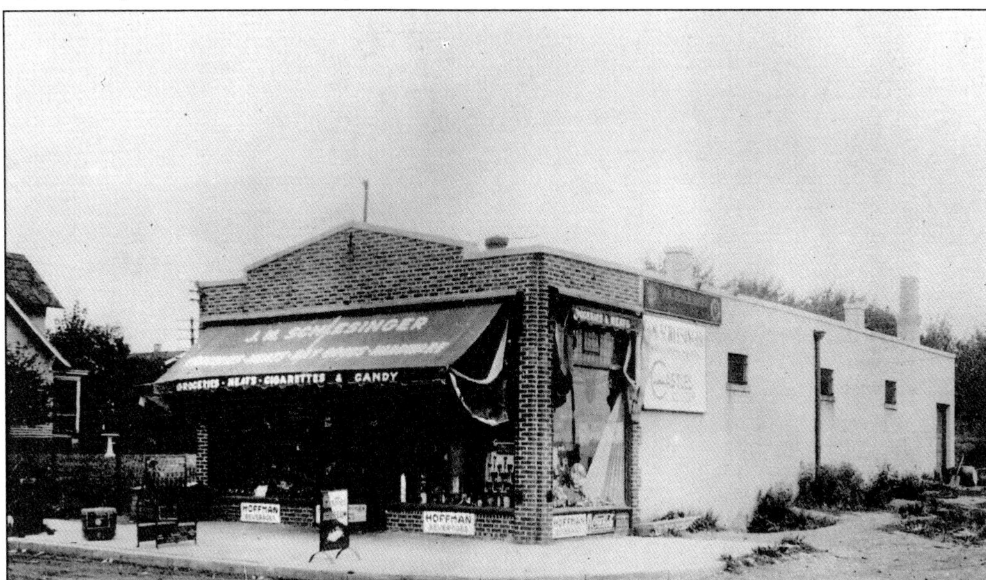

ONE-STOP SHOPPING IN AVENEL, C. 1950. It looks like J.M. Schlesinger's General Store at the corner of Avenel Street and Minna Avenue offered just about everything a shopper might be looking for, except maybe the proverbial kitchen sink! The store closed in 1976. At present a bridal accessories shop is located in the building.

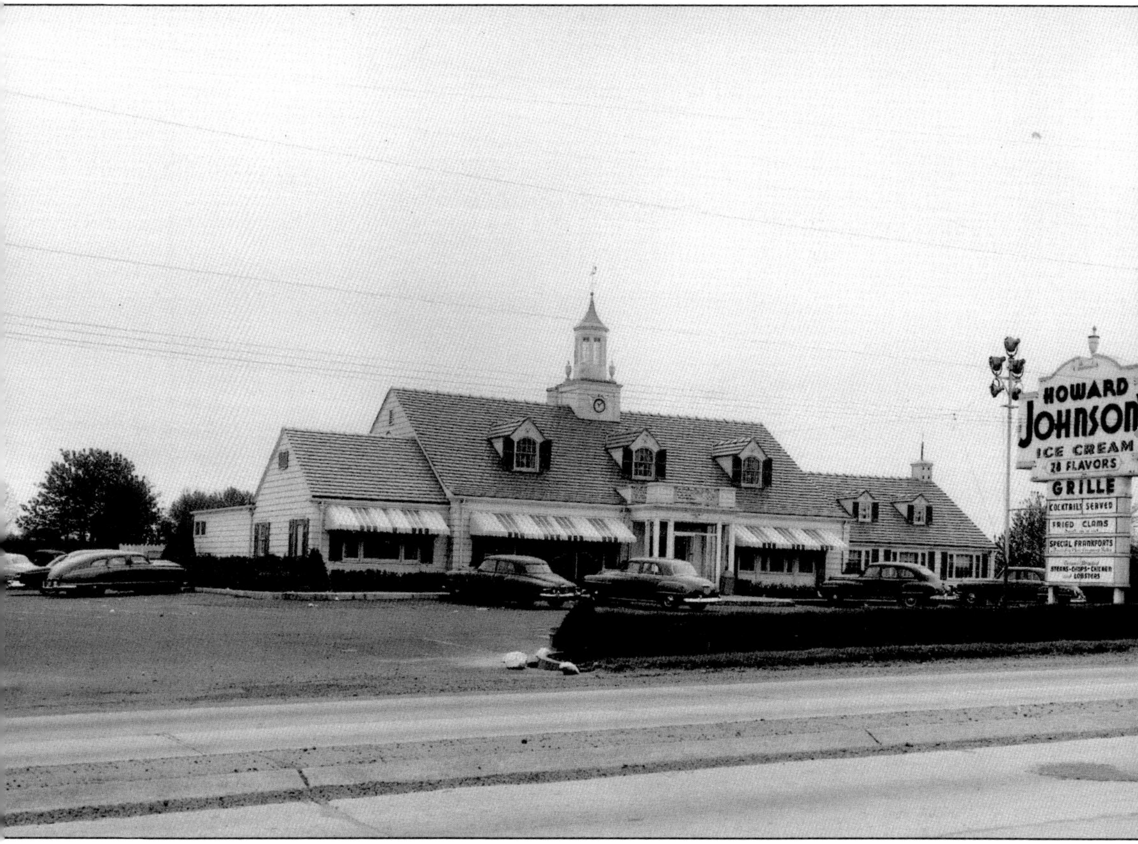

HOWARD JOHNSON'S, 1950. It's a good bet that almost everyone who lived in Woodbridge between 1938 and 1975 ate at Howard Johnson's Restaurant at one time or another. This time-honored, local establishment on Route One was famous for fried clams, a children's menu featuring Simple Simon, and, of course, "28 Flavors of Ice Cream." Stella and Peter Sideris opened the restaurant in 1938. A 1964 newspaper advertisement proclaimed Howard Johnson's as "The Ultimate in Gracious Wining and Dining Since 1938." After Howard Johnson's was destroyed by fire in 1976, the couple built a new restaurant, hotel, and banquet center, the Landmark Inn, on the same site. When Mr. Sideris died in 1978, his wife continued to manage the inn until 1998, when she sold the business. Through the years visitors included Senator Hubert H. Humphrey of Minnesota, the mayors of San Francisco and Athens, Greece, and two New Jersey Governors, Brendan Byrne and Richard J. Hughes. The inn has been demolished. An auto mall of car dealers now occupies the site, but Howard Johnson's remains a pleasant memory for many area residents. (Stella Sideris.)

Seven

Around the Township

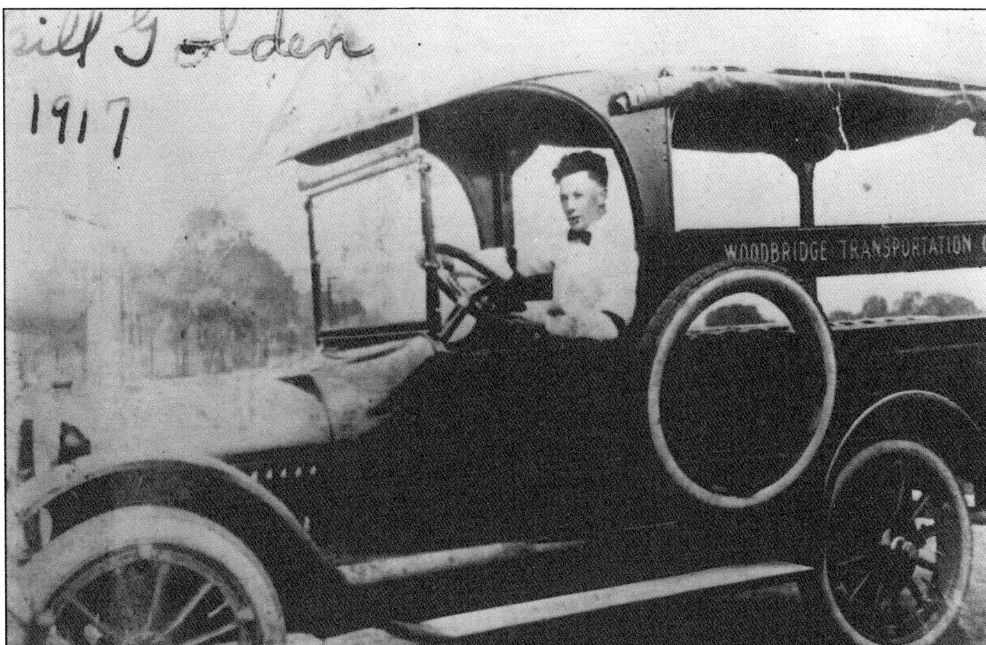

HAVE YOUR FARE READY! c. 1917. William Golden (at the wheel), together with Albert Thompson and Lawrence McLeod, owned and operated the first taxi service in Woodbridge. A taxicab was often called a jitney, which is a slang word for a five-cent piece, the usual taxi fare at the time. (Free Public Library of Woodbridge.)

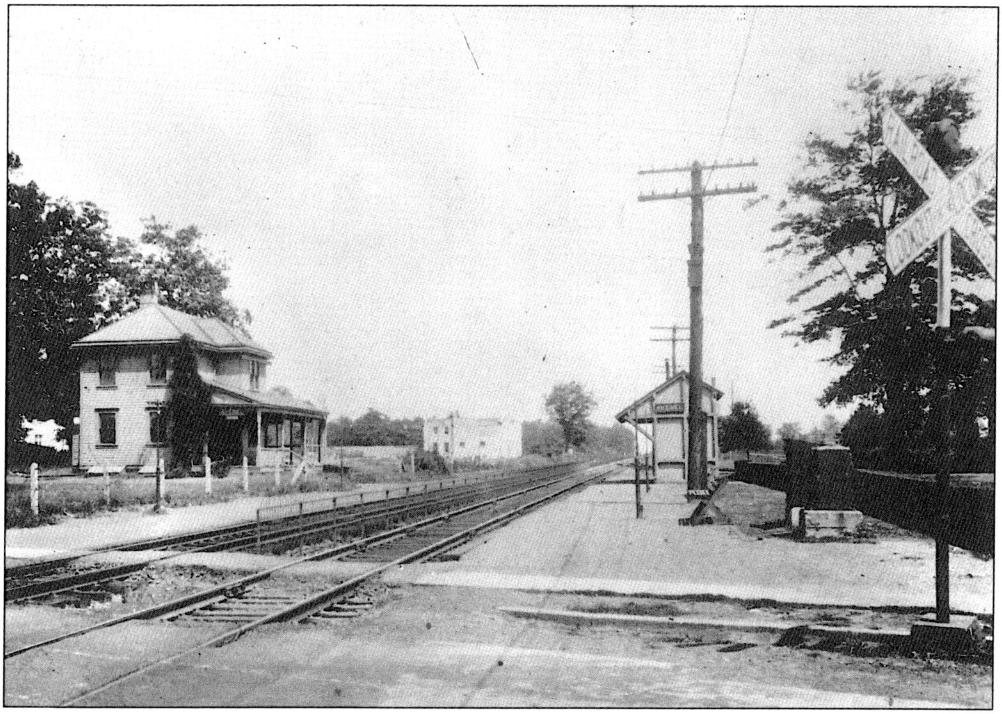

Along the Railroad, Avenel, c. 1938. The Avenel station on the PRR was a small, wooden building along the tracks until 1940, when the PRR grade crossings in the township were eliminated. Anyone entering the station found the waiting room on the left and the Avenel Post Office on the right.

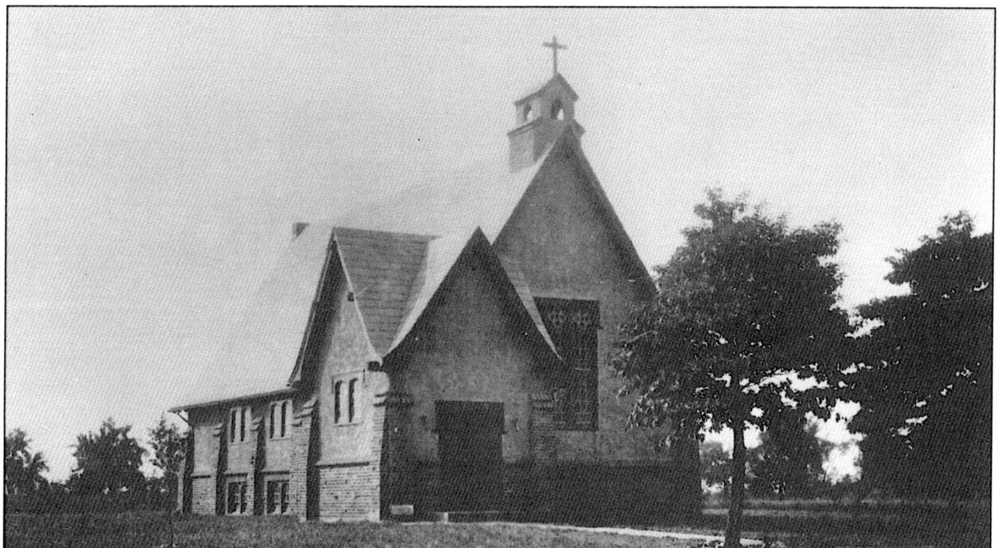

Avenel Presbyterian Church, c. 1950. Avenel Protestants first organized a Union Sunday School in 1871, which met at various locations until 1927, when they formally organized a Presbyterian church. In 1930 the original church building, shown here (now the Chapel), was dedicated. Since then, the Avenel Presbyterians have grown in numbers, built new buildings, and have adopted a "Sister Church" in the Dominican Republic.

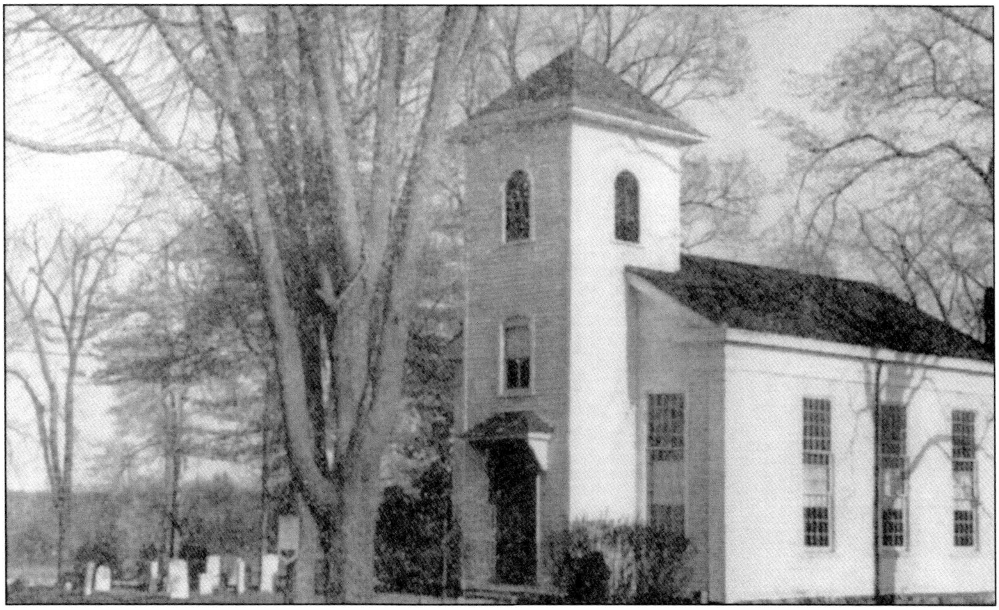

NEW DOVER CHURCH. The New Dover United Methodist Church is located about 1,000 feet over the Colonia border on New Dover Road in Edison, which at one time was part of Woodbridge. Methodist families from the Colonia area laid the cornerstone in 1849. Since then the church has continued to flourish. In the early days the New Dover area was called Dumplingtown because of the delicious dumplings made by the townsfolk.

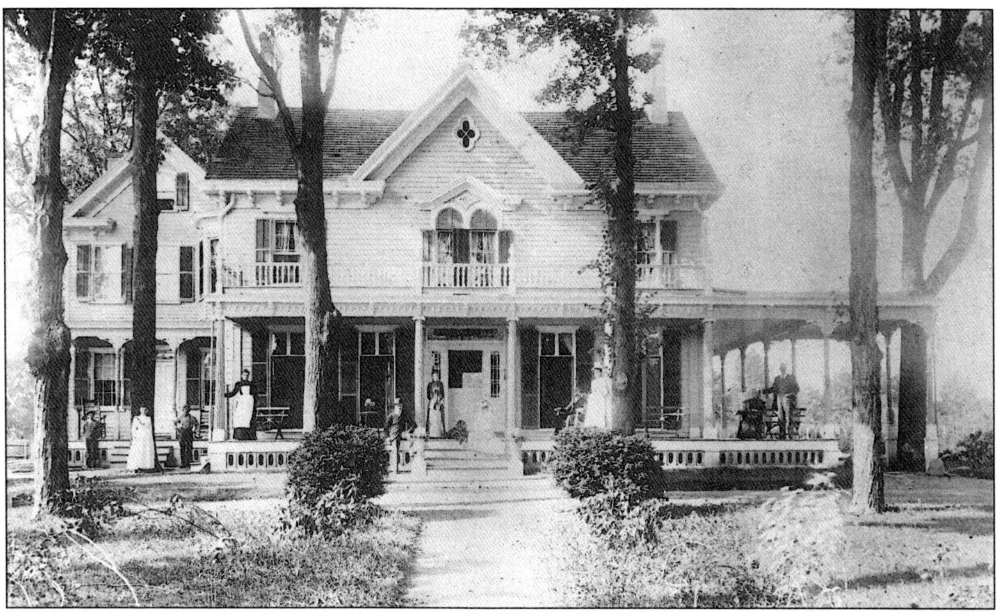

"THE TREES," c. 1900. In 1890 this Pre-Revolutionary homestead on New Dover Road in Colonia was bought by the Edward K. Cone family of New York City as part of a 60-acre farm called "The Trees." The Cones were actively involved in Colonia's development; in fact, Mrs. Cone is credited with changing the town's name from Houghtenville to Colonia. Today this house is owned by Bess Wiesenfeld, who purchased it in 1958 with her late husband, Dr. Benjamin Wiesenfeld. (Bess Wiesenfeld.)

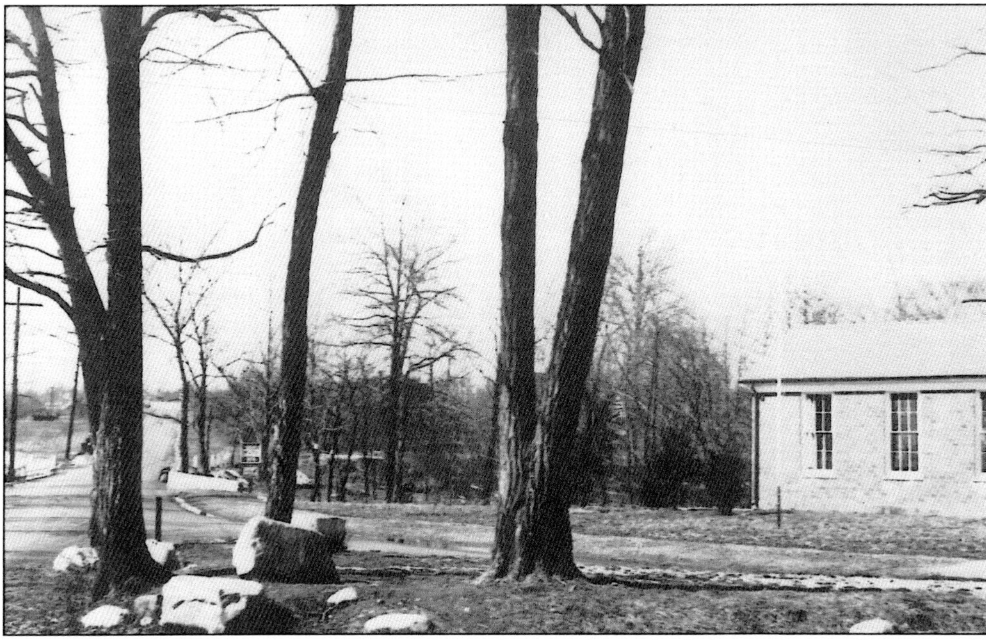

Colonia Library Corner, c. 1940. The Colonia Library (right) stands on Chain O'Hills Road near New Dover Road. Margaret Soulé, wife of orthopedic surgeon Dr. Robert Soulé, was the moving force behind the creation of the library. Before it was completed in 1939, Mrs. Soulé carried books to Colonia residents and acted as a traveling library. (Ray Schneider.)

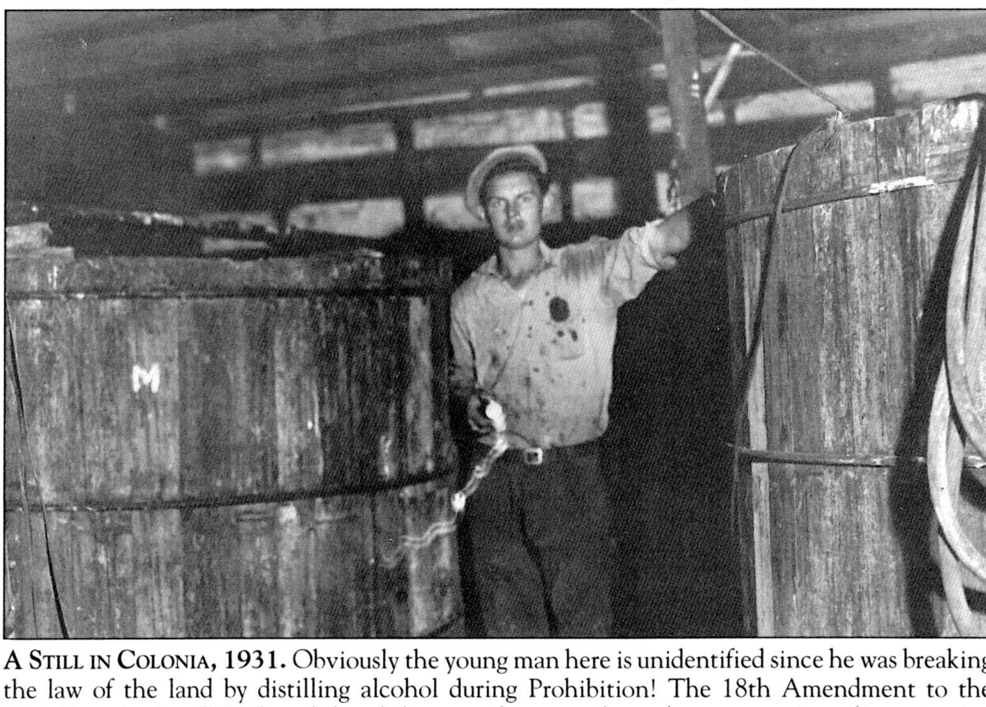

A Still in Colonia, 1931. Obviously the young man here is unidentified since he was breaking the law of the land by distilling alcohol during Prohibition! The 18th Amendment to the U.S. Constitution (1920) prohibited the manufacture, sale, and transportation of intoxicating beverages and was repealed by the 21st Amendment of 1933, leaving liquor laws up to the individual states.

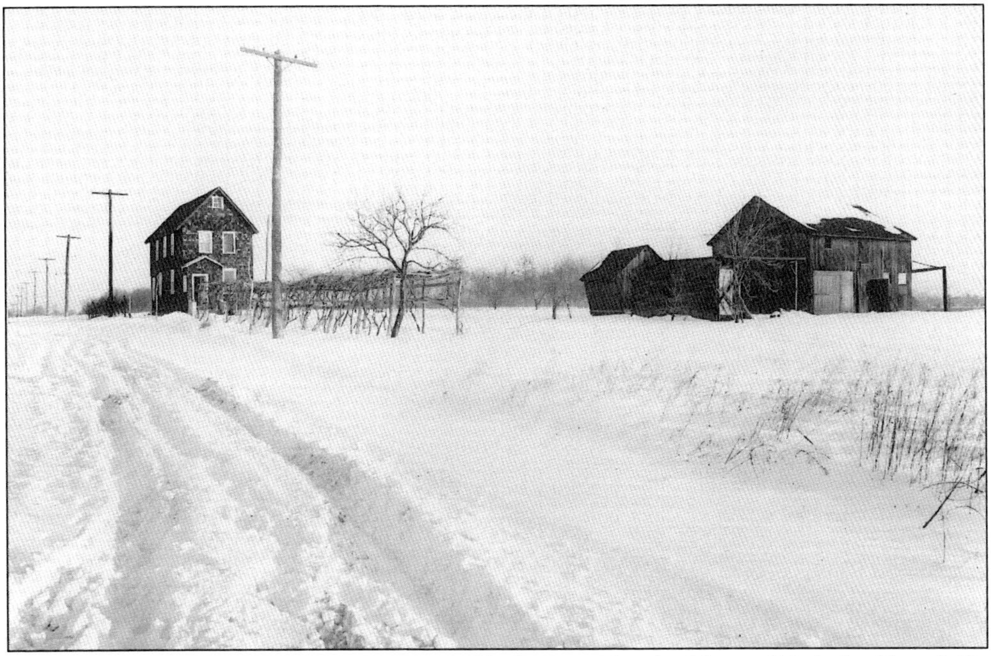

SNOWY DAY IN COLONIA, JANUARY 19, 1945. The home and outbuildings of Nicholas Chirichillo on Cleveland Avenue present a wintry, rural landscape. Rapid development following World War II changed much of Woodbridge Township.

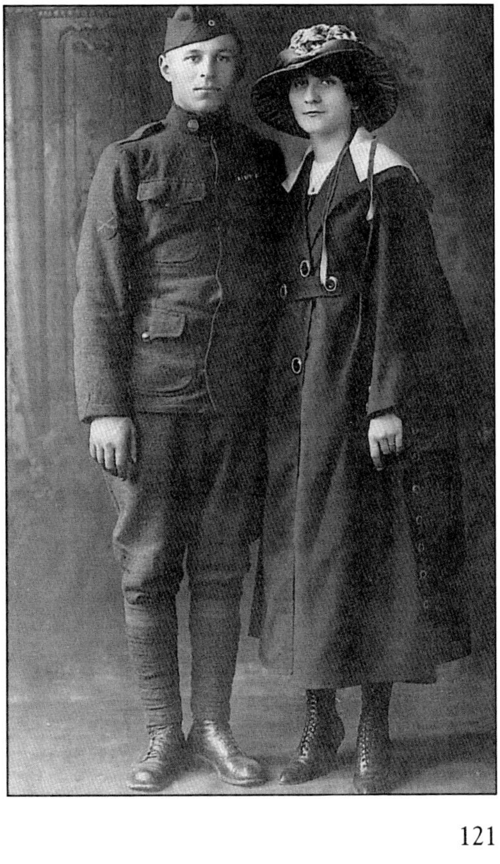

A SOLDIER MARRIES, 1913. Emma Nagy of New Brunswick Avenue, Fords, and Private 1st Class Paul Chovan were married at Camp Perry, OH. As a member of the Ohio National Guard, Paul saw service with Gen. John J. Pershing in Texas chasing Pancho Villa, and in World War I when the Ohio Guard was incorporated into the Army. The couple settled in Fords and raised two sons, Edward and Paul. (Ann and Paul Chovan.)

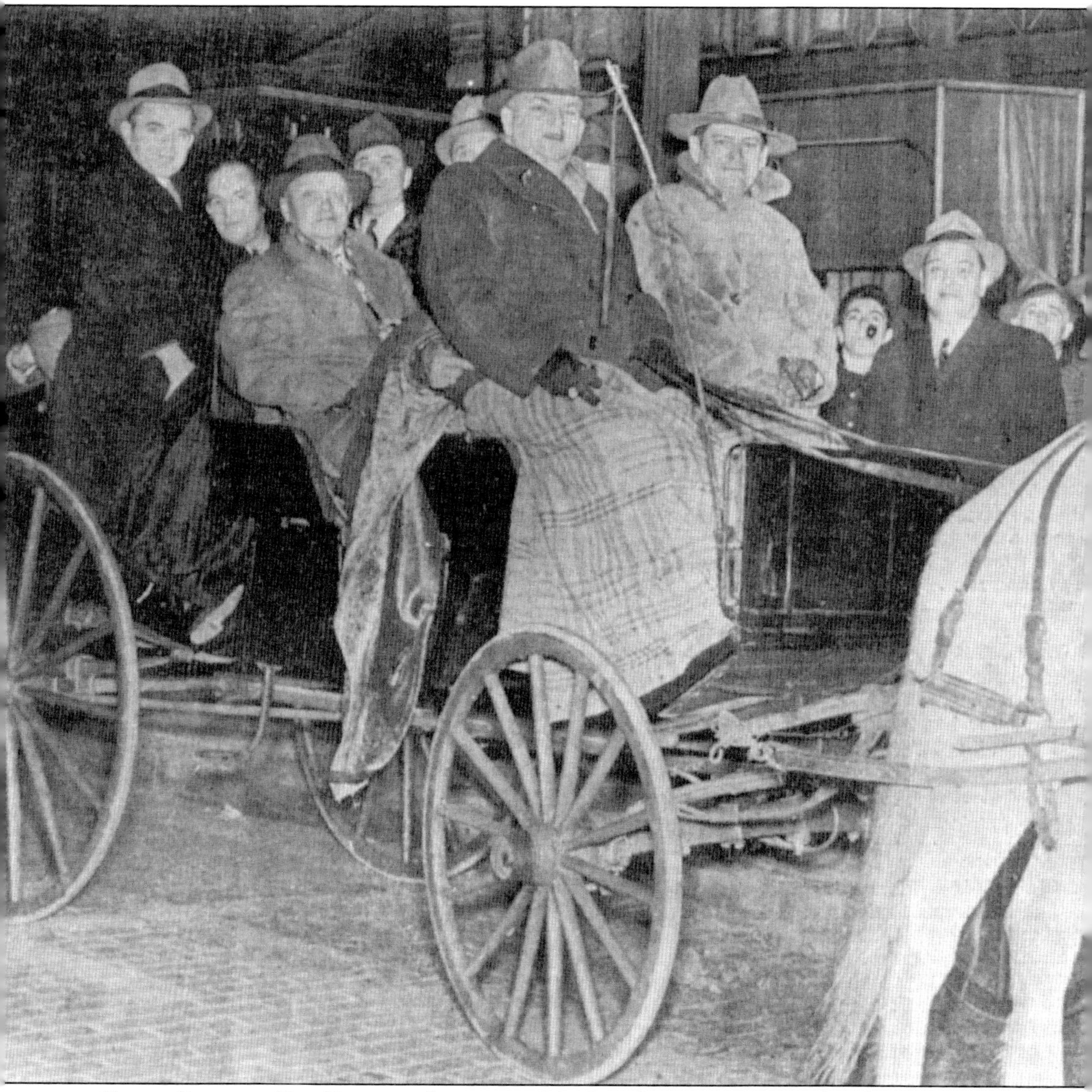

FORDS GASOLINE BAN BUSTERS, JANUARY 1943. Lund's Service Station bowling team, though sponsored by Anton Lund, who earned his living selling gasoline, decided to beat the pleasure driving ban imposed by the World War II gasoline shortage by traveling via horse and wagon from Fords to Perth Amboy. The group was greeted by shouts of "Get a Horse" as they drove up Madison Avenue to the Elks Building, where the team was participating in a special bowling match. The trip took about 30 minutes. From left to right the "gas ban busters" are Anton Horvath, Ken Van Horn, Anton Lund, John Heppinstill, Ed Seyler, county probation officer Ben Jensen (in the driver's seat), George Elko (behind Jensen), and team booster George Kovak (wearing cowboy hat). Bystanders are unidentified.

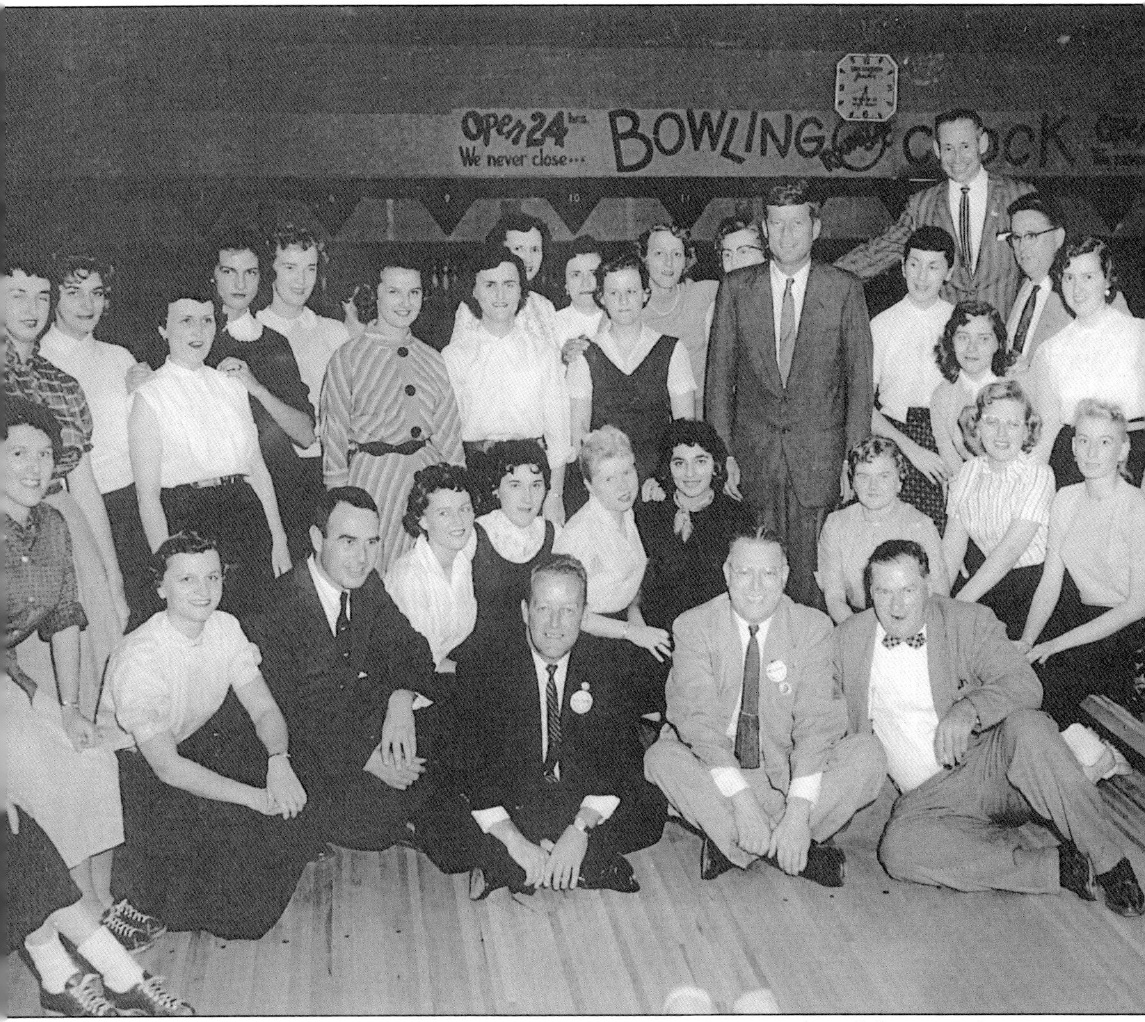

FAMOUS HOPELAWN VISITOR, OCTOBER 17, 1956. Enroute from a political dinner at Rutgers University in New Brunswick, U.S. Senator John F. Kennedy, who became President in 1960, stopped at the Majestic Lanes on Route Nine to visit a World War II Navy comrade, Moish Shihar (top right), part-owner of the bowling alley. Kennedy and Shihar were assigned to the same PT-boat squadron in the Pacific. On the morning that Kennedy's PT-boat 109 was sunk by a Japanese destroyer, Shihar was on patrol in another boat. Gathered around JFK are, from left to right as follows: (front row) Pauline Biernacki (white blouse), NJ Senator Harrison Williams, Carol Jugan Katona, Irene Bodo Khun, three unidentified men, Pat Geiling Marcinak, Pat Kosmyna, Dorothy Dudzinski, unidentified, and Barbara Wagner Dixon; (back row) Bernice Richard Herman (seated dark blouse, light skirt), Ellen ?, unidentified, Barbara Burns, Dolores Petrick Ziemba, Ann Hallahan Waltz, unidentified, Ruth McKenna, unidentified, Lillian Ernst, Barbara Bucholz, D. Kaczmarek, unidentified, JFK, and Connie Rebovich. Others are unidentified. (Peter and Roberta Bacskay and Robert White.)

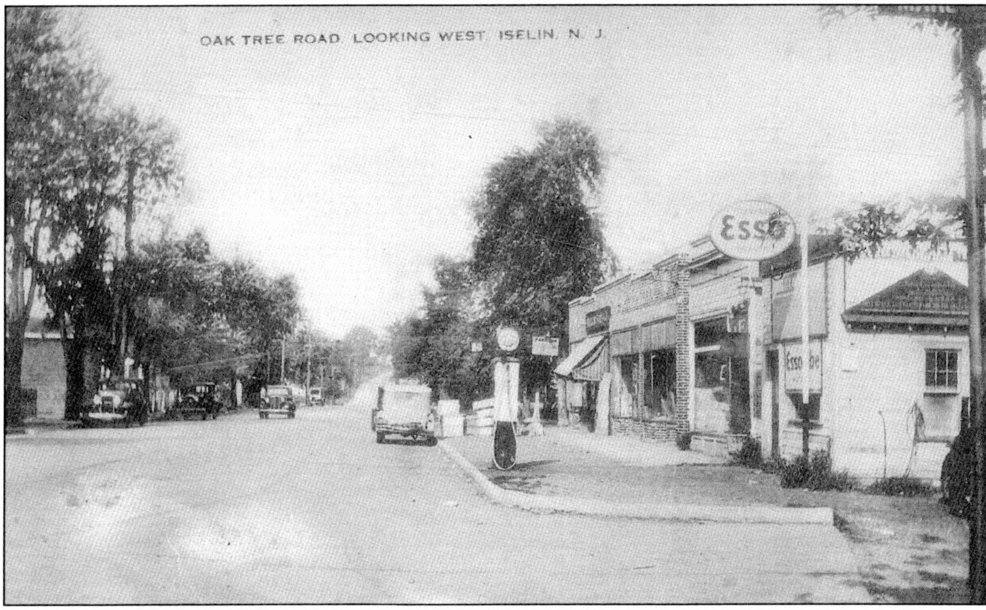

OAK TREE ROAD AT MARCONI AVENUE, LOOKING WEST, ISELIN, c. 1935. Iselin was originally Perrytown, perhaps named for local farmer John Perry. Around 1850 the name became Uniontown. In 1872 New York stockbroker Adrian G. Iselin bought Uniontown property for a girls' finishing school. At this time the PRR built a new station called Iselin, perhaps with a subsidy from the gentleman whose name remains with the town.

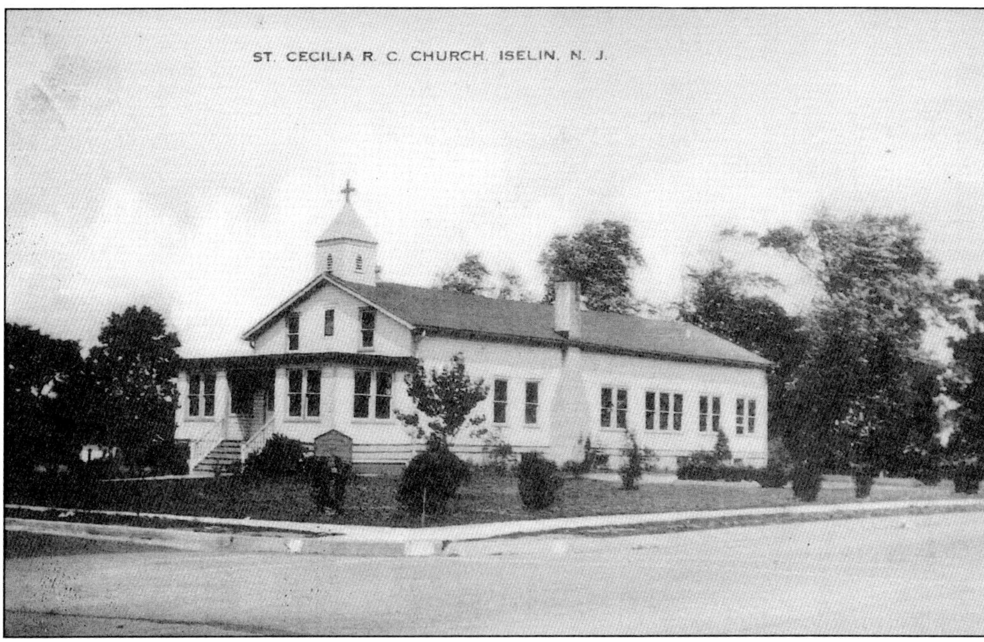

ISELIN CHURCH, c. 1950. St. Cecelia's Roman Catholic Church started in a bungalow on the Freeman estate in Colonia in 1913 and later moved to Iselin. St. Cecelia's first permanent church served earlier as the nurses' recreation hall for U.S. Army General Hospital No. 3 in Colonia. The building was moved in sections to Middlesex Avenue and Oak Tree Road in Iselin and became the house of worship for the parish until 1953.

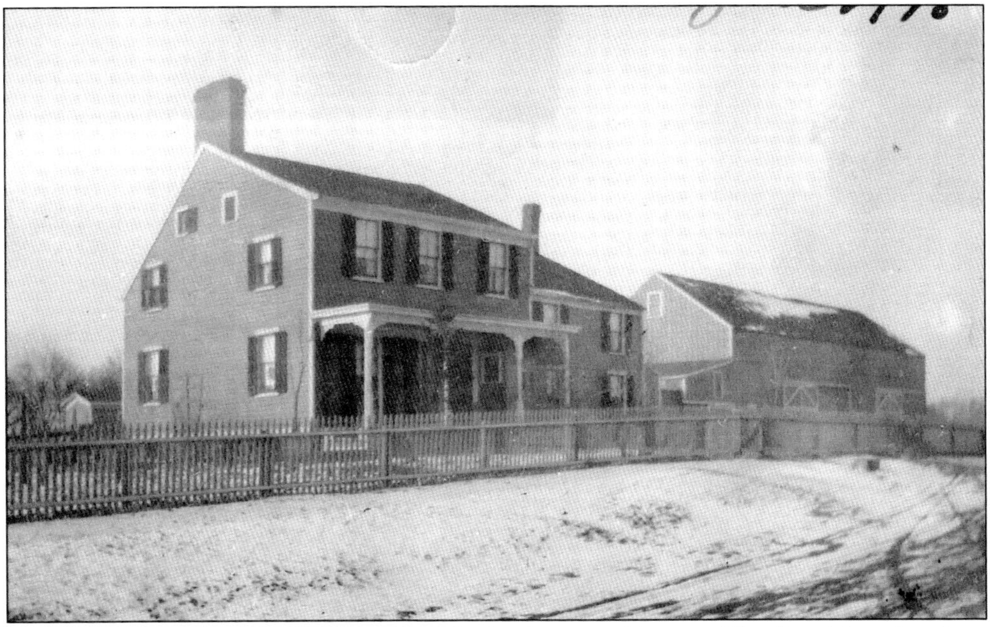

BLAIR FARM, C. 1915. This handsome, sturdy farmhouse and barn on Blair Road, Port Reading, were built in 1880. One of the early families to settle in the township, the Blairs now have descendants scattered throughout the country. The farmhouse has long since disappeared. (Free Public Library of Woodbridge.)

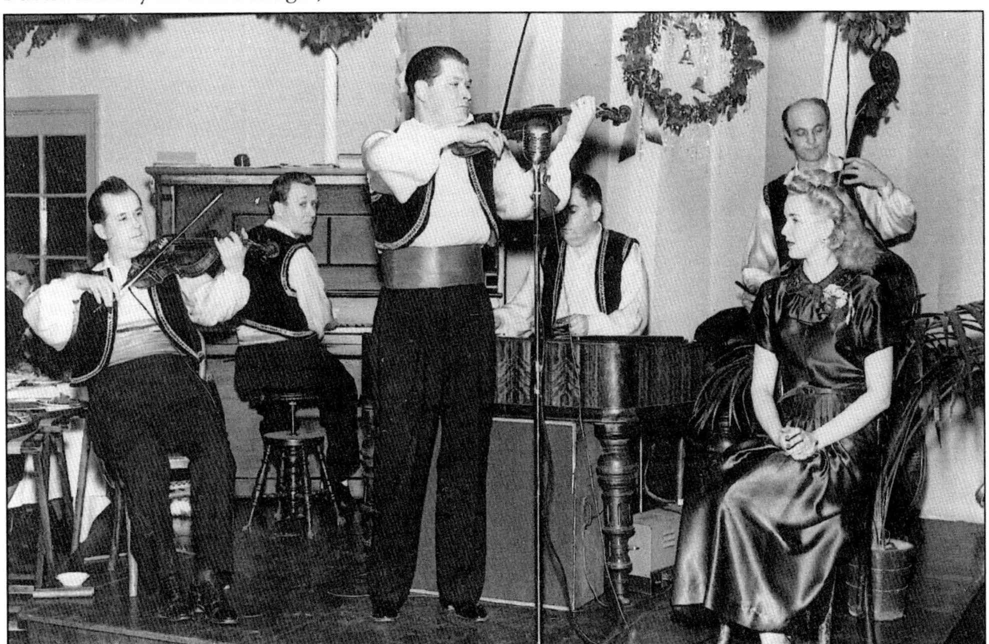

A LITTLE NIGHT MUSIC, 1953. The Gypsy Camp Night Club on the Woodbridge/Carteret border was a popular entertainment spot from the 1940s to the 1960s. The musicians, who also played at the Vienna Café in New Brunswick and at the 1939 NY World's Fair, are, from left to right, second violinist Louis Kedves, pianist Emery Hack, first violinist Kalman Kedves, cymbalist Paul Belso, bassist Alex Balog, and singer Ann Bennet. (Thomas Kedves Jr. and Sr.)

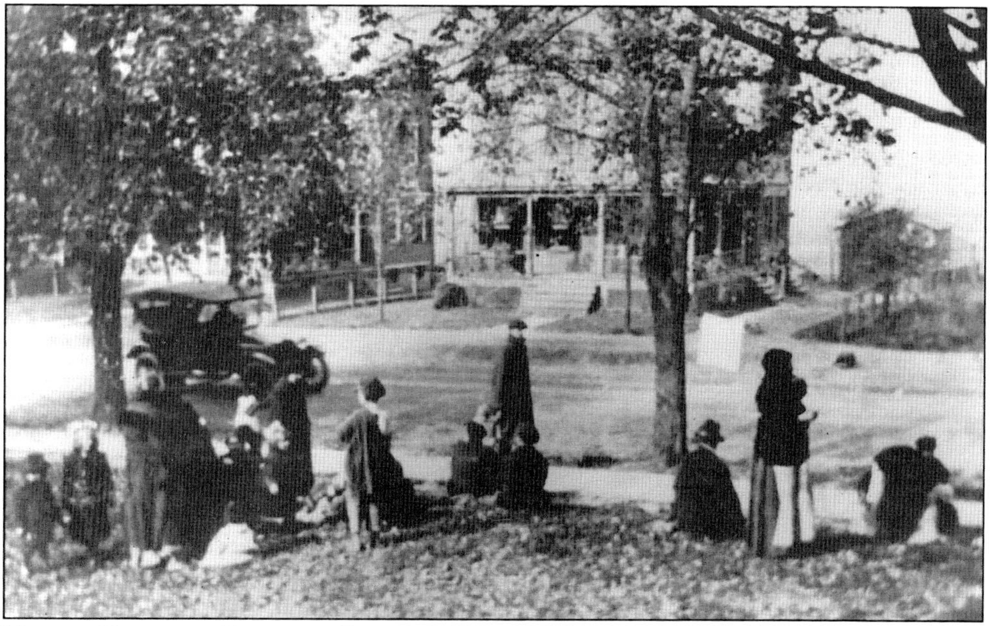

MORGAN EXPLOSION REFUGEES, OCTOBER 4, 1918. When a series of explosions erupted at the T.A. Gillespie Shell Loading Plant in the Morgan section of Sayreville, residents of the area fled to parts of Woodbridge. Some are seen here resting on lawns on West Avenue in Sewaren. The Woodbridge Home Defense League and the Red Cross participated in the rescue efforts. Sixty-four people were killed. (Free Public Library of Woodbridge.)

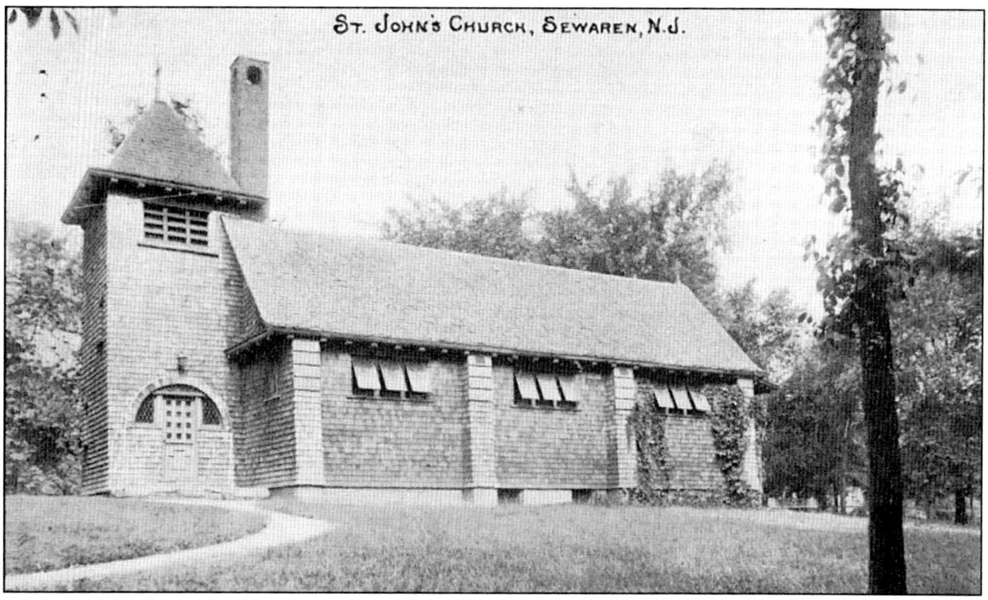

SEWAREN CHURCH, C. 1900. St. John's Episcopal Church, at the foot of Woodbridge Avenue and Cliff Road, celebrated its 100th anniversary in 1992. The church stemmed from a mission organized by Trinity Episcopal Church of Woodbridge and was built on land donated by John Taylor Johnston, Sewaren developer and Central RR of NJ president. The church has a working fireplace and a bell tower with an actual railroad bell from the Philadelphia and Reading Railroad.

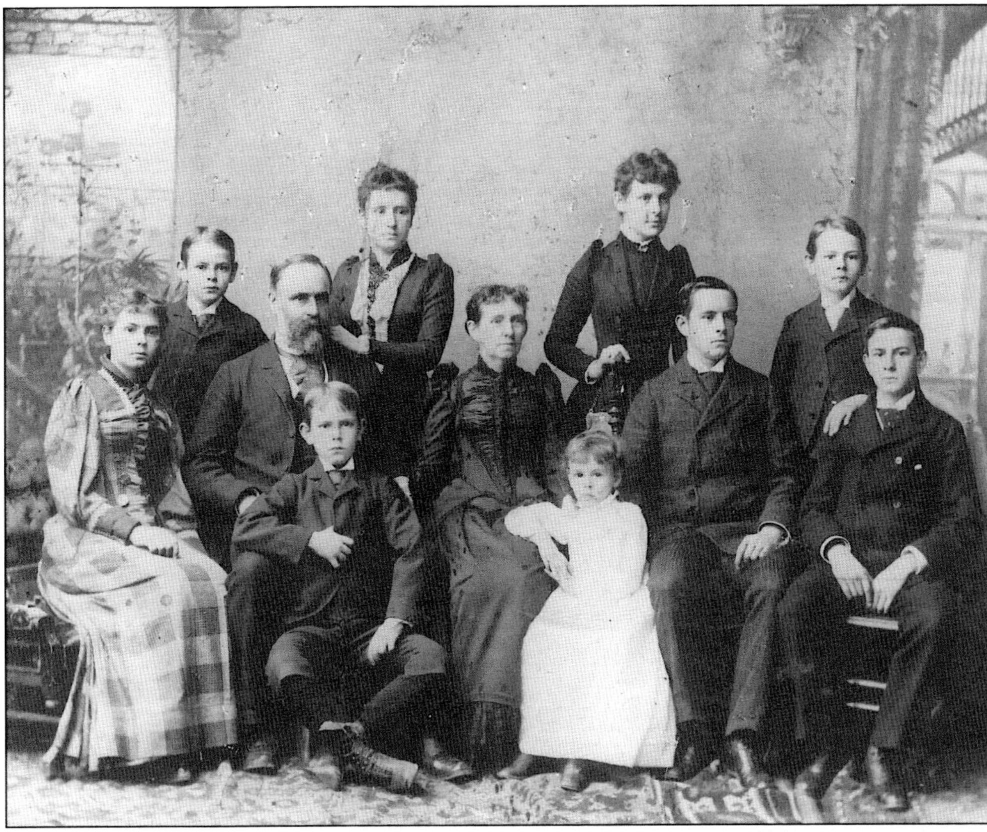

The Boyntons, 1890. Cassimir Whitman Boynton of Sewaren was a well-known manufacturer of hollow tile and firebrick and founder of Sewaren's Boynton Beach resort. From left to right, the Boyntons are as follows: (front row) Georgi (plaid drcss), Clancy, and Dorothea; (middle row) Mr. Boynton, his wife, Eunice Adelia Harriman Boynton, Gorham, and Whitman; (top row standing) Ernest, Helen, Louise, and Albert. (Catherine Clark Burns.)

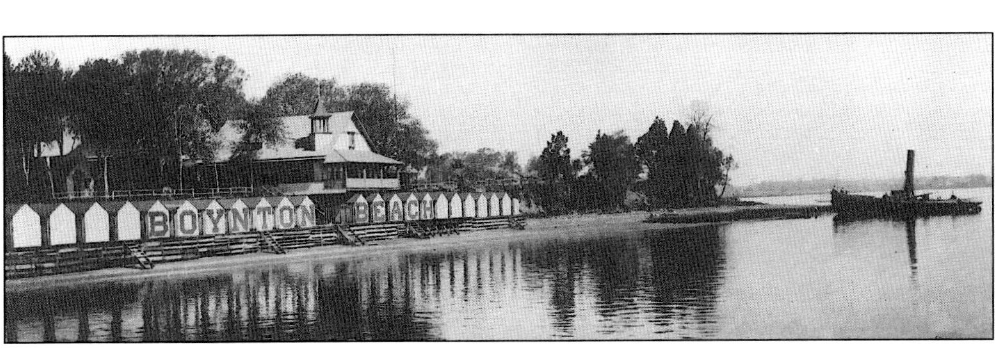

Boynton Beach, c. 1895. Bathhouses, proudly spelling out the name of Sewaren's popular resort, line the tranquil waters at the junction of Woodbrige Creek and the Arthur Kill. C.W. Boynton opened the Boynton Beach complex in 1877. It included a restaurant with New York City chefs, picnic groves, a dance pavilion, pony rides, amusements, and a fleet of 100 rowboats.

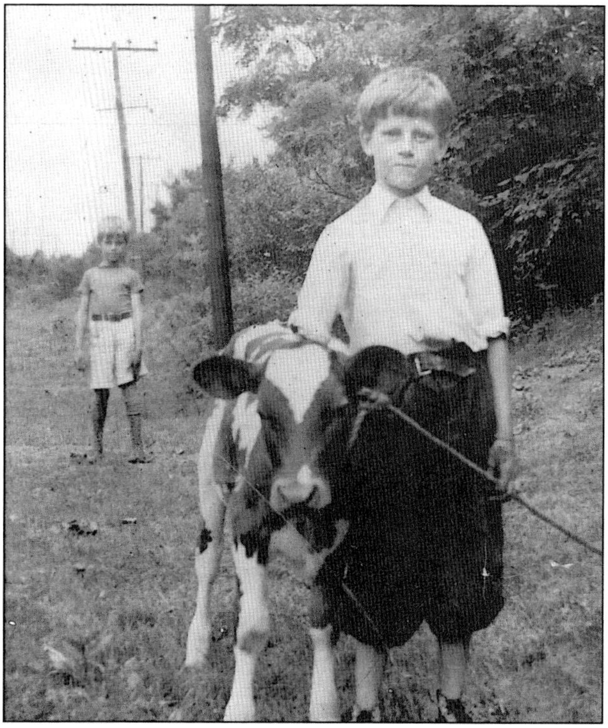

Down on the Farm, 1936. John Ambrose (right), his brother Frank, and their calf typify the rural character of many parts of Woodbridge Township during the years before World War II. After the war, open land gave way to housing developments, industrial complexes, strip malls, and the mammoth Woodbridge Center that took over the clay banks area of upper Main Street. (John Ambrose.)

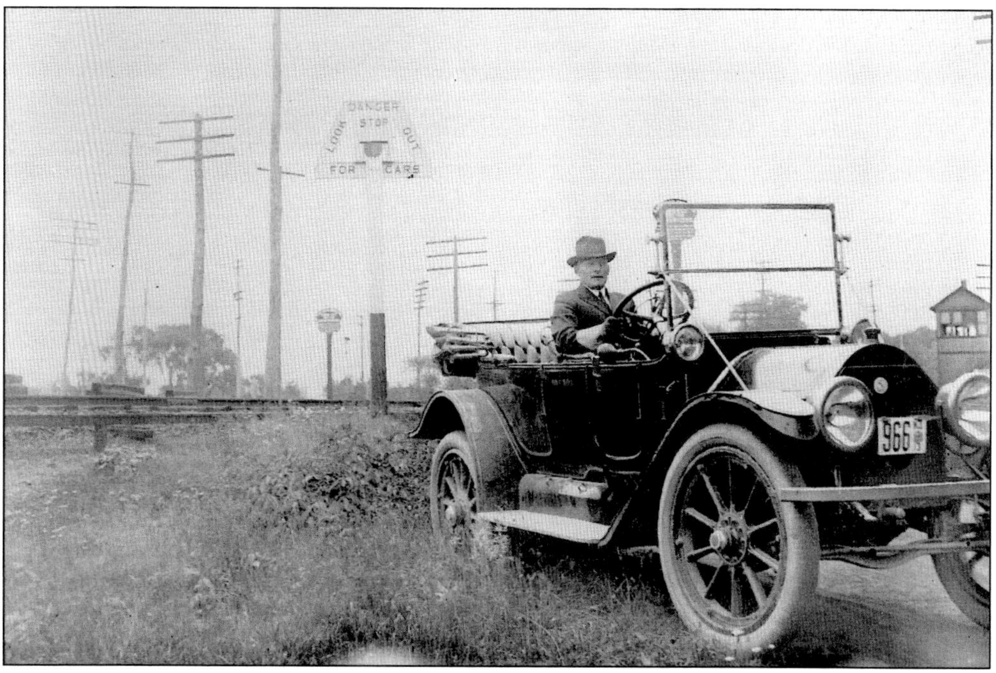

Sewaren Motorist, July 1913. Looking very much in control of his early touring car, Frank Chamberlin of Holton Street is traveling south on West Avenue and has apparently just crossed the railroad tracks of the NJ Central Railroad. One hopes that the engineers of oncoming trains always saw the warning sign in time to stop for automobiles. This crossing was later elevated. (Catherine Clark Burns.)